Architecture, Space and Memory of Resurrection in Northern Ireland

Northern Ireland has a complex urbanism with multilayered socio-spatial politics. In this environment, issues of communication, self-representation and expression of identity are central to the experience of urban space and architecture where the dichotomy of division and shared living are spatially exercised in everyday life. Unlike other studies in the area, this book focuses on the everyday experiences of local communities in both public and private spheres – issues of 'shareness' – challenging conventional approaches to divided cities. The book aims to layer its narratives of architectural and social developments as an urban experience in post-conflict settings over the past two decades.

Mohamed Gamal Abdelmonem is Chair in Architecture and the Founding Director of the Centre for Architecture, Urbanism and Global Heritage (AUGH) at Nottingham Trent University, UK. He is the lead of the University's Research Theme 'Global Heritage' and has led design studios and taught architecture history at Queen's University Belfast and the University of Sheffield, amongst others. A Fellow of the Royal Society of Arts, Professor Abdelmonem is the 2014 recipient of the Jeffrey Cook Award of the International Association for the Study of Traditional Environments (IASTE). His books include *Peripheries: Edge Conditions in Architecture* (Routledge, 2012) and *The Architecture of Home in Cairo: Social-Spatial Practice of the Hawari's Everyday Life* (Routledge, 2015). He advises several governments and international organisations on aspects of sustainable heritage preservation and urban planning and design and sits on several research advisory and editorial boards, as well as Research Councils UK peer-review panels.

Gehan Selim is a scholar and academic in Architecture at the University of Leeds, UK and a fellow of the Senator George Mitchell Institute for Global Peace, Security and Justice (2016–2017). Dr Selim's research covers interdisciplinary methods in Architecture, Urban Politics, and Sustainable Cultural Heritage, bridging between the social (people), the physical (buildings), and the urban (city). She has extensively written and published articles that examine the socio-spatial aspects of urban design and research fields in liberation politics and geographies of segregation in the Middle East and conflict zones (Egypt, Lebanon and Northern Ireland). Among her various research grants are those received by the Arts and Humanities Research Council (AHRC), Japan Foundation London, Newton Fund/Innovate UK and the Engineering and Physical Sciences Research Council (EPSRC). She is the author of *Unfinished Places: The Politics of (Re)making Cairo's Old Quarters* (Routledge, 2017).

Routledge Research in Architecture

The *Routledge Research in Architecture* series provides the reader with the latest scholarship in the field of architecture. The series publishes research from across the globe and covers areas as diverse as architectural history and theory, technology, digital architecture, structures, materials, details, design, monographs of architects, interior design, and much more. By making these studies available to the worldwide academic community, the series aims to promote quality architectural research.

Flexibility and Design
Learning from the School Construction Systems Development (SCSD) Project
Joshua D. Lee

Visual Spatial Enquiry
Diagrams and Metaphors for Architects and Spatial Thinkers
Edited by Robyn Creagh and Sarah McGann

Narratives of Architectural Education
From Student to Architecture
James Thompson

Migrant Housing
Architecture, Dwelling, Migration
Mirjana Lozanovksa

How Children Learn from Architecture and the Environment
Mark Dudek

Architecture, Space and Memory of Resurrection in Northern Ireland
Shareness in a Divided Nation
Mohamed Gamal Abdelmonem and Gehan Selim

For a full list of titles, please visit: www.routledge.com/Routledge-Research-in-Architecture/book-series/RRARCH

Architecture, Space and Memory of Resurrection in Northern Ireland

Shareness in a Divided Nation

Mohamed Gamal Abdelmonem and
Gehan Selim

Routledge
Taylor & Francis Group

LONDON AND NEW YORK

First published 2019
by Routledge
2 Park Square, Milton Park, Abingdon, Oxon OX14 4RN

and by Routledge
52 Vanderbilt Avenue, New York, NY 10017

Routledge is an imprint of the Taylor & Francis Group, an informa business

British Library Cataloguing-in-Publication Data
A catalogue record for this book is available from the British Library

Library of Congress Cataloging-in-Publication Data
Names: Abdelmonem, M. Gamal, author. | Selim, Gehan, author.
Title: Architecture, space and memory of resurrection in Northern Ireland: sharedness in a divided nation / Mohamed Gamal Abdelmonem and Gehan Selim.
Description: New York : Routledge, 2019. | Series: Routledge research in architecture | Includes bibliographical references and index.
Identifiers: LCCN 2018054372 | ISBN 9781138186934 (hardback)
Subjects: LCSH: Architecture and history—Northern Ireland. | Architecture and society—Northern Ireland. | Space (Architecture)—Northern Ireland. | Social conflict—Northern Ireland.
Classification: LCC NA2543.H55 A26 2019 | DDC 720.9416—dc23
LC record available at https://lccn.loc.gov/2018054372

ISBN: 978-1-138-18693-4 (hbk)
ISBN: 978-1-315-64351-9 (ebk)

Typeset in Sabon
by Apex CoVantage, LLC

Printed in the United Kingdom
by Henry Ling Limited

To architects, urban designers and planners working in
difficult conditions
To Nadeen & Hisham
To our students and colleagues at Queen's University
Belfast
To the wonderful and generous people of Northern
Ireland
Thank you

Contents

Figures

Tables

Acknowledgements

The authors are grateful for the help and support of many people who contributed in different ways to the work presented in this book. We wish to thank our colleagues, students, researchers, architects, officials, and community members for their patience with our curious desire to investigate and analyse several aspects of everyday living in Northern Ireland that, more often than not, have touched on sensitive issues peculiar to local culture and communities. The socio-spatial politics of Northern Ireland are unique, but so are the music, poetry, arts, and dance. To understand the former, you must engage with the latter. As neutral eyes, foreign to the landscape of division in Northern Ireland, our inquiry and critique were objective, looking from the outside of the condition of division into everyday lives and experiences of ordinary citizens and members of both communities alike.

Throughout this project, we did our best to be objective, free from antagonist politics, with a prime goal of interrogating the urban condition resulted from the centuries-long history of the dichotomy of division and attachment. To build our understanding and weave the narratives of this book we worked with many students and colleagues, mainly at Queen's University Belfast, to whom we are grateful for their work, energy, and enthusiasm. Their generous insights, reflections, and contributions, through discussions, research work, or dissertation meetings have helped us to engage more with the contentious, invisible, yet critical spatial and territorial politics of Northern Ireland. We are also grateful to the generous support of our current respective institutions and deans of schools who gave us the time and capacity to finish and complete this work. Special thanks are due to both Professor Muhammad Basheer, the Head of the School of Civil Engineering at the University of Leeds, and Dr Andrew Knight, the Dean of the School of Architecture, Design and Built Environment at Nottingham Trent University.

This work would have never been completed without the intellectual input, feedback, and discussions with colleagues and friends, including Frank Gaffikin, Brendan Murtagh, Stephen McKay, Ken Sterrett, Ruth Morrow, Michael McGarry, Karim Hadjri, Paul Larmour, Steve Larkin,

Cian Deegan, Tarla MacGabhann, Jane Larmour, and Patrick Wheeler, among many others. We also appreciate the contributions of our former students and current colleagues who shared our interests, ideas, insights, and reflections. Of particular mention are Clare Mulholland, Ryan McAtavey, Rachel McWhinney, Katherine Thompson, Ashlee Bell, Bassma Abou El Fadl, Helen Brunett, Stephen Crimmins, James Boyd, Andrew Abraham, Michael McKeown, and Finbar Bradley.

The number of our students who worked on research and design projects in Belfast, Londonderry, Armagh, and Portrush is quite extensive to be mentioned here by names, but their creativity, rigorous processes, and research have added critical layers of knowledge either directly or indirectly that our research needed. As we challenged our students to raise critical questions about the state of division in urban landscape, their responses and in-depth interrogations were impressive and have not only uncovered novel lines of inquiry in the post-conflict spatial division but also enabled them to act as agents of change through their individual careers. We wish to thank several architects and urban planners across Northern Ireland whose reflections, interviews or discussions were used in this book. Wherever relevant, we cited any views or quotes of interviewees or architects with a reference system (Interviewee, Date) or Interviewee (No of Interview, Date). Some interviews were undertaken by ourselves, and some were undertaken by our students or research assistants.

Due to the nature and content of this book, we had to rely on the assistance of specialists in seeking, reading and analysing archival and historical materials. We must thank the library staff at Queen's University Belfast and at National Museums Northern Ireland. In particular, special thanks are due to Stephen Weir, the picture library executive at the National Museums Northern Ireland, for his incredible help and assistance to research and find rare historic photographs of early 20th-century Belfast and Ulster villages' Linen Mills in Gilford and Sion Mills. We wish to thank Bassma Abou El Fadl, Paul Allen, and Henry Clark for kindly granting us the permissions to use their pictures. We would like to thank Routledge Editorial team for their patience and guidance throughout the editorial and production process of this volume, with particular mention to Aoife McGrath. We wish also to thank our friend David Moffat for his editorial critique and contributions in reviewing, proofreading, and editing the textual content of several chapters of this book. We wish to thank many journal editors and anonymous reviewers and referees whose feedback and comments to our published research or drafts were an integral part of the development of the theoretical framework and research presented in this volume. We acknowledge the generosity, kindness, and friendly culture of local communities and the public in Northern Ireland, where we made lifelong friends.

Author biographies

Mohamed Gamal Abdelmonem is Chair in Architecture and the Founding Director of the Centre for Architecture, Urbanism and Global Heritage (AUGH) at Nottingham Trent University. He is the lead of University's Research Theme 'Global Heritage' and has led design studios and taught architecture history at Queen's University Belfast and the University of Sheffield, amongst others. A Fellow of the Royal Society of Arts, Professor Abdelmonem is the 2014 recipient of the Jeffrey Cook Award of the International Association for the Study of Traditional Environments (IASTE). His books include *Peripheries: edge conditions in architecture* (Routledge, 2012) and *The architecture of home in Cairo: social-spatial practice of the Hawari's everyday life* (Routledge, 2015). Professor Abdelmonem advises several governments and international organisations on aspects of sustainable heritage preservation and urban planning and design. Professor Abdelmonem sits on several research advisory and editorial boards, as well as Research Councils UK peer-review panels.

Gehan Selim is a scholar and academic in Architecture at the University of Leeds and a fellow of the Senator George Mitchell Institute for Global Peace, Security and Justice (2016–2017). Dr Selim's research covers interdisciplinary methods in Architecture, Urban Politics, and Sustainable Cultural Heritage, bridging between the social (people), the physical (buildings), and the urban (city). She has extensively written and published articles that examine the socio-spatial aspects of urban design and research fields in liberation politics and geographies of segregation in the Middle East and conflict zones (Egypt, Lebanon, and Northern Ireland). Among her various research grants are those received by the Arts & Humanities Research Council (AHRC), Japan Foundation London, Newton Fund/Innovate UK, and the Engineering and Physical Sciences Research Council (EPSRC). She is the author of *Unfinished places: The politics of (re)making Cairo's old quarters* (Routledge, 2017).

Part I

The making of the Irish condition

1 Architecture and spatial memory in post-conflict urbanism

The here and now: Belfast's 'Berlin moment'

On the morning of 25 February 2016, bulldozers moved into Crumlin Road to take down a 30-year-old Peaceline wall that had been erected at the same time as the adjacent social housing estate. The removal of the wall was a community-led decision facilitated by the Housing Trust after years of relationship building and talks between various communities in North Belfast. The eight-foot-high wall had been built in the mid-1980s at one of the most contentious interface zones in the city. Prior to the demolition, however, paint bombs smashed windows of three houses it had been built to protect. The action confirmed that reconciliation after decades of unrest would not be a straightforward process and would have its anxious moments. It also revealed how the Peace Line walls were not just physical barriers but also spatial fingerprints of the past – non-desirable for local people yet essential to the propaganda of militant factions:

> The Berlin Wall had to come down for Berlin to be normalised. We have normalised Belfast without taking down the walls.
>
> Jonny Byrne as quoted in Peter Geoghegan's
> *Guardian* article (Geoghegan, 2015)

Hailed as Belfast's 'Berlin Moment', bold and brave (Black, 2016) and powerful and symbolic (McGuinness, 2016), the demolition on Crumlin Road was a progressive act looking toward the future and departing from that memory of the past. This was the first Peace Line wall in an interface zone to be demolished since the Good Friday Agreement of 1998, a first evidence of the desire to reverse 50 years of division and move towards a future of cohabitation and peaceful interaction. Following the unrealistic vow of Northern Ireland's power-sharing government to remove all Peace Line walls by 2023, it had taken 18 years to demolish just one. But, after all, this part of North Belfast had suffered one-third of the total 3,000 victims of the Troubles. Nevertheless, the next morning, the demolition was complete, the land was levelled, and 30 years of hostile history had been erased from the map. Looking at the resulting vacant space, we were anxious like many of the other onlookers and were warned not to stay there for long. An anxious moment it certainly was, but a celebratory Berlin moment for Belfast it was not. Whilst the Berlin Wall had been imposed by a central government to divide families and neighbourhoods, Belfast's Peace Line walls had been built at the request of local residents. And the walls had become the everyday norm for a population fearful of the past, obstructing its vision of the future.

Looking carefully into the meaning and timing of the demolition, further lessons could be learned. The demolition was a moment when a history of growing fear started to reverse its course and turn toward belief in a shared future. The removal of the wall was also one of several contemporaneous intercommunity collaborations reflecting initiatives for integrated parks, services, business centres, and other real estate developments. However, as the *Belfast Telegraph* put it, it is far harder to remove a barrier in the city than to build one:

> Defensive architecture, it turns out, is far easier to erect than tear down.
> (Geoghegan, 2015)

In the 1960s and 1970s, the construction of Belfast's defensive architecture represented a turning point in the history of community tensions in Northern Ireland. Communities had until then co-inhabited the city through periods of peace, tension, and conflict, but they had always maintained direct and constant contact with each other. Yet the decision to consolidate a pattern of segregation through concrete walls and timed gates asserted the permanence of the conflict, even as it mitigated its danger.

Defensive architecture's impact on the city and everyday lives of ordinary people was subsequently profound, and despite the initial sense of security, it had devastating physical, social, and psychological effects on local residents, creating isolated enclaves and at times putting communities under siege. Division of the urban fabric with walls was also not the only feature of this defensive architecture, which took multiple forms, shapes, and sizes. Temporary bonfire structures; gated access to public spaces and buildings like police stations, blank facades around public spaces, industrial estates located within residential areas; and inward-looking public buildings like the Metropolitan Arts Centre (MAC) were just examples of the other imprints of division that appeared on the city's map. Indeed, the implementation of defensive architecture and urban design during and after the Troubles altered the entire fabric of the city – its urban character, routes of movement, public infrastructure, and services. In short, it changed the city's identity, crisscrossing it with nearly 100 walls of different sizes, lengths, and heights and making it a self-declared model of divided urbanism. Yet, as Richard Kirkland (1996: p. 35) writes in his analysis of the dilemma of literature in a divided city, '[t]o write the city, to make it visible, is to stress its place in spatial territory yet also to perceive its contemporaneity through narrative within the process of a fragmented history'.

Referred to by locals as 'a big village', Belfast initially grew as a symbol of shared interest. Its origins were as 'a number of little village communities which come to have a separate, self-contained life of their own, through common interests, activities, and institutions of the people who live there' (Elliot, 2017: p. 64). However, this fabric of separate village units soon expanded towards the city centre, creating the political and economic hub. The well-recorded narratives of life before the Troubles confirm that shared living in peaceful and mixed communities was once the norm (Figure 1.1). One of these was Margaret Elliot's (2017) narration of her everyday life in the White City, a post–World War II social housing estate in Belfast built by the Housing Trust to accommodate families in need of suitable homes, which they could not otherwise afford. The White City was one of many similar projects designed at the time to support neutral, non-affiliated living environments. Its units were allocated according to objective criteria and evaluation according to a point system and an interview; ethnic or religious affiliation was never considered. It thus came to include residents from both

Figure 1.1 Belfast city centre, 1939, looking towards the city hall and the hills beyond.

Source: Courtesy of Belfast Telegraph © National Museums NI Collection Ulster Folk & Transport Museum, ref: BELUM.BT.674.

Catholic and Protestant communities, especially former servicemen of the British Army (30 percent; Ibid.).

Despite continuous tension, and flashes of violence in working-class neighbourhoods even before the Troubles, the historic norm in the region had never been one of polarised segregation. Thus, as much as the building of the first separation wall marked a turning point in the urban history of Northern Ireland, the first wall removal represented a credible gesture of reversal in the course of the conflict. It also signals the presence of a resurrection process – a rebirth of sorts, which is emerging at a decisive point in time when practices and processes of cross-community collaboration are beginning to recover the city from its divided and discriminative condition. However complex and long term this process may be, the emergence of new, shared visions, decisions, and collaborations obliges researchers, architects, and urban planners to revisit the theoretical discourse of post-conflict segregation in Northern Ireland and to consider the notion of '*shareness*' as a new force in practice. We have thus chosen a unique moment in Northern Ireland's urban history to look at the meanings, processes, and the impact of architecture and spatial memory not only on the city and its fabric but in people's everyday life as well.

This book presents an open-ended inquiry into the current condition of post-conflict architecture and urbanism in Northern Ireland at a crossroads moment. It aims to confront and challenge the theoretical stereotyping of post-conflict urbanism as a case of division and post-conflict reconciliation. It looks at the contemporary situation from the viewpoint of a shared struggle with the physical and spatial imprints of the past, rather than an engagement with the reality and demands of the present. Putting ordinary people's everyday life at the centre of our empirical investigation and critical analysis, we look at how people understand, engage with, or benefit from the city at large in Northern Ireland – its architecture, urban spaces, public parks, public squares, and residential areas. We also look at how history and industry have shaped both the cities and villages of Ulster. In the process, we anticipate responding to the following questions: To what extent have the Troubles and its continuous memory determined the predominance of defensive architecture and territorialised urban and civic spaces in Northern Ireland? How do people perceive their cities and urban life, and what determines their use of space and attitudes towards the public, shared, and integrated spaces of the city? And, what constitutes safe or unsafe architectural and urban spaces, buildings, and landscapes for ordinary people?

Why shareness in a divided context

In Ciaran Carson's poems, maps used to analyse zones, areas, and territories do not reflect the actual life of a city or its urban context. Rather, he advocates that the city should be seen and read through the moments that define the experience of its people in their everyday lives. In the middle of the Troubles, Carson was critical of the absence of discourse reflecting such understanding in a city otherwise defined on maps by barriers, barricades, and other spatial divisions such as the Peace Lines. In *Belfast Confetti* (1989) Carson stresses,

> No, don't trust maps, for they avoid the moment: ramps, barricades, diversions, Peace Lines.
>
> (Ibid.: p. 58)

> The map is pieced together bit by bit. I am this map which they examine, checking it for error, hesitation, accuracy: a map which is this moment, this interrogation, my replies.
>
> (Ibid.: p. 63)

Interestingly enough, this view was not embraced by one side only, and it remains a shared hurdle uniting both communities in a struggle to deal with the involuntary segregation imposed by the Troubles. It is thus through the implicit sublayers of segregation and division, and the unity of hardship, struggle, and unease they impose, that Belfast's daily life could be traced, mapped, and perhaps written.

Northern Ireland has been extensively researched, investigated, and written about in terms of its peace process, conflict transformation, and post–peace agreement reconciliation. Parliamentary committees, physical and social surveys, policy documents, and planning reports have all pointed to the ethnonational and political division as the underlying condition of Northern Ireland's modern urbanism. Likewise, a busy calendar of events, venues for expressing identity, and a rivalry of parades, protests, and elections have overshadowed a long history of shared urban development, spatial memory, and architecture. To control hostile altercations between rival communities during the Troubles, beginning in the 1960s, state planning policies implanted industrial estates, infrastructure, and bridges to create buffer zones and barriers, drawing spatial gaps in the city and sectioning it into isolated territories and voids between zones. Narratives of change from an integrated city to one of divided enclaves were also reinforced by security-driven policies that led to undesirable patterns of social engineering. The result today is a multilayered socio-spatial politics in which issues of communication, self-representation, and expression of identity are central to the experience of urban space and architecture and where a spatial dichotomy of division and shared living is a regular feature of everyday life.

As an alternative to taking this condition for granted, we aim here to interrogate instances of public and private intercommunity engagement in the city, as everyday life has continued to produce shared experiences of spaces, buildings, and urban myths over the past two decades. We thus seek to break from the political domain of division to highlight the reality of everyday encounter between local communities within cities and towns across Northern Ireland.

We do not therefore accept a condition of division as being the main diver of life in the region since the Troubles. Rather, considering both Contact Theory, through which individuals are seen as identifying themselves as a result of contact with others, and the Birmingham school of Cultural Identity, which perceives identity to be flexible, contextual, and determined by sociocultural factors, we question the state of division as a source of conflict, and we argue that identity was and remains a sociocultural construct that infers inner convictions of '*Self*' in relation to the '*Other*' In our perspective, as expressed in this book, conditions of division and conflict are always temporary, whereas shared living and mutual existence are permanent.

To clarify, by the very existence of the physical fabric of separation in Northern Irish cities, the dreadful past continues to influence actions in the present and determine future attitudes. In this sense, the built fabric becomes an object of remembrance that is paradoxical and contested, with different meanings and connotations. The notion of 'shareness', however, represents the antithesis of sociopolitical and ethnic division in the practice of everyday life. And we use it here to identify a condition of cognitive belief by an individual or group, in the equal rights of others (those different in racial, ethnic, religious, or cultural backgrounds) to coexist in public space. In this regard, we note that the term *share/shared*, which reflects the act or action of partaking jointly in activities with others, does not adequately translate the inner conviction of the rightness of such equal representation in public venues. In contrast, *shareness* communicates coherent social positions and defines the cognitive landscape of the urban experience in a given context. Throughout our research, interviews, and communications with members of various communities in Northern Ireland, we never encountered a situation in which community members denied the rights of others to live in the city or have access to the same services or public spaces they did. It is only through the private micro-urbanism of the community and its boundaries or through political representations of identity, involving such charged symbols as parades, flags, and bonfires, that threats of intrusion typically become matters of significant concern.

In this sense, our argument attempts to offer insights into counternarratives to the physical reality of division by examining the manner in which an urban landscape of shared living remains integral to the spatial practices of ordinary people. We look at spaces, buildings, and towns where both communities come together, and where the dichotomy between 'division' and 'co-existence' is best displayed. At times, political struggle and myth about the other are inherent in the way individuals use private space for protective acts or public space for defensive ones. Yet, at others, architecture and urban space seem to bring society to a condition of engagement, in which differences are overshadowed by temporal and spatial shared memory. Using the production of space as its central criterion of analysis, the book thus draws on the reality of socio-spatial spheres of engagement transcending space, time, and memory to investigate what makes the Irish condition and how it might serve as a metaphor for the future as a return to the past. In this sense, architecture and urban space are seen as potential agents of coexistence, liveability, and community regeneration. We, of course, look at both sides of the coin – at stories both of success and failure, including examples of urban spaces which, despite being designed for integration, have reinforced a sense of segregation and inequality. Yet we will also examine how architecture and urban planning have the potential to steer the social geography and spatial structure of Northern Ireland toward a more pluralistic condition while downplaying territorial gains and physical segregation.

Consideration of issues of modernity and community development, and of urban architecture and visions of the built fabric as a way to read the socio-spatial conditions of the city, are long overdue in Northern Ireland. Using a comprehensive investigation of socio-spatial practices, architecture, and urban design, we will attempt here to offer an alternative, ideologically and affiliation-free reading of the contemporary spatial condition. The absence of understanding of how people live, communicate, and relate to each other within their private spheres or public spaces leaves much to be uncovered in terms of the potential dimension and meaning of architecture as an agent of change. Indeed, the socio-spatial systems of living and the way these have developed historically and changed throughout the conflict years have yet to be investigated in any volume on the contemporary architecture and urbanism of Northern Irish cities. There is consequently a lack of awareness amongst architects and urban designers of the impact of social memory, spatial patterns, and cultural rituals on the success or failure of their new buildings, developments, or spaces.

Theoretical dispositions

In the post–Good Friday Agreement era, Northern Irish cities have witnessed a growth of spatial politics and an emergence of neoliberal urbanism that has not only reshaped their urban landscapes but also brought new architectural languages, urban management regimes, and new schemes for integration, interface zones, services, and urban containment. Large parts of the current landscape also provide a reminder of past experiences of segregation, division, and contestation, dominant for generations. Yet counternarratives involving the spatial practices of shareness have also developed through mutual living, shared interest, and communal need. To best illustrate such variance, the book utilises an interdisciplinary approach that accounts for sociological, anthropological, and spatial factors in the production and consumption of space by individuals and groups at different periods. How could a building or a public space instil either notions of exclusive identity or attitudes of shared living at different times? An investigation of everyday life experience through narratives of what was, has been, and will be and through interviews and spatial mapping can only build an interpretive bridge over this divide through credible analysis. The book thus approaches the Irish condition from a spatial and architectural standpoint, looking at buildings, spaces (public and private), towns, and various design approaches that have shaped the current built environment. However, it also addresses the impact of the sociopolitical landscape on the experience of the city and the way it may generate peripheries in the centre of the city, or dismantle and reassemble urban communities.

This book is based on extensive research between 2010 and 2017 spanning several projects and design studios. Its purpose is to uncover the notion of shareness as central to understanding architecture and urbanism of cities and towns in Northern Ireland. It expounds this concept through an investigation of the historical development both of formal architecture and urbanism and of spaces of everyday activity, interaction, and engagement. The experience of architecture and urbanism, the book argues, can never be separated from everyday engagement with social memory, politics, and intrinsic social–cultural encounters. However, there is no single way to analyse the complexity and interconnectedness of the components and elements of cities. Thus, a layering of narratives that renders visible their inherent dynamics appears to be the most effective approach. Hence, this study seeks to layer its narratives of architectural and social developments as an urban experience in post-conflict settings over the past two decades.

We have developed our argument in this book on the basis of 'the landscape of shareness', to establish a framework for understanding the architecture and urbanism of Northern Ireland as human settlements that have evolved to reflect a dichotomy of shareness and division, union and segregation, through time. The book thus investigates Northern Ireland as one spatial entity that developed historically as a society composed of different ethnicities, which at times were united and at others in collision with each other. It addresses and presents this path of history through two principal investigations. First, it examines the socio-spatial memory of the region, looking at the way its cities developed in the early 20th century. Second, it explains the spatial structure of the city through layers of historical narratives that take into account sociocultural memory, the makeup of ethnic communities, and the early years of Northern Ireland.

Contested space and social identity in Northern Ireland

Urban Northern Ireland is largely concentrated in a few cities. The largest and most contested ones are Belfast, the region's capital and long-term industrial hub, and Derry/Londonderry, the financial and business node on its north coast.

Belfast has a long history of division and violence that crosses several interlinked divisions – religious, ethnic, social, and political – that culminated in the outbreak of violence during the Troubles (Leonard and McKnight, 2011; Leonard, 2006; Coulter, 1999). The city grew progressively, beginning in the early 17th century, as a settler town largely populated by Protestants of Scottish and English origin. Segregation during the colonial period existed on a macro scale, with Catholics forming a majority outside the town's walls in 'rural' Ulster. A sharp change in the pattern of separation between Protestants and Catholics then appeared at the time of the Home Rule campaign, when, for the first time, it took the form of street riots. However, Belfast must be understood as not only segregated by religious identity, and there is much more to its historical separation than sectarianism.

The violence that erupted during the Troubles solidified those divisions and produced a period of great demographic change and migration. Informed by fears and threats, Protestants and Catholics who had formerly lived in mixed areas retreated to areas identified by religion, intensifying the state of polarisation. This population displacement was the largest experienced on the British Isles since World War II and one of the largest in modern post-war Europe (Shirlow, 2003). The new pattern of segregation was also not limited to residential areas but extended to educational institutions, recreational spaces, employment, and many other areas of life. And physical markers of that segregation started to appear during a period of rampant ethno-national riots, as a rise in paramilitary activity escalated conditions of ethnic, religious, and ideological struggle. Manifestations of this struggle existed in the form of bombings, shootings, and intimidation, with the result that the city became more divided than ever.

At the centre of this new condition of division/integration were the Peace Lines, introduced in the 1970s as temporary fences to relieve some of the pressure caused by the Troubles but eventually solidified as permanent barriers. These barriers were, and still are, problematic as they have actually heightened tensions and outbreaks of violence between Catholic and Protestant communities. Nevertheless, they emerged as the result of a bottom-up process, first installed by the communities themselves (Leonard and McKnight, 2011). Some argue that this urban architecture has reinforced the division between communities and strengthened the permanence of the problem (Gaffikin et al., 2010). Others question the usefulness of such boundaries generally in helping communities enhance social interaction and support identification (Carmona et al., 2003), while others argue that a good city is one with an uninterrupted fabric, not a broken one (Lynch, 1981, 1990).

In the years that followed the Troubles, the Peace Line walls have had two main purposes – as canvases and barriers. They have thus acted as local communicators of identity in segregated areas of the city, prevented opposing identities from interacting across them, and maintained local social hierarchies. In reality, however, the Peace Line walls (initially constituting 88 barriers separating 15 parts of the city) have largely separated working-class

Catholics from working-class Protestants so that these groups could live side by side, yet apart, in single-identity communities (Leonard and McKnight, 2011; Gaffikin et al., 2008). They are a complex of concrete walls, steel fences, and gates of different heights and lengths, some as short as a few metres and some located between backyard gardens. They have also increased in number due to concerns over safety as a result of small incidents following the cease-fire agreements, and today they designate buffer zones where the two residential communities come together. Neil Jarman (2005) associates such interface areas with extreme conditions of polarisation in low-income working-class neighbourhoods where there is a strong link between territory and ethno-political identity.

Whilst initially constructed during 1969 in response to violent outbreaks between the Catholic-dominated Falls and the Protestant-dominated Shankill communities, as a way to keep members of the other community out, the temporary barriers were later replaced by more permanent structures built at the request of local residents by the British Army and the Belfast housing authority (Ibid.). Leonard and McKnight (2011) further assert that these barriers are complemented by a range of local amenities and spaces so that individual shops, lampposts, and parks also serve as local community markers and territorial boundaries. In these interface areas, communities thus continue to live adjacent to one another, according to a system of parallel and duplicated services and facilities. And not surprisingly, the walls initially appeared at locations where distrust and suspicion were greatest as a result of attacks during the Troubles. They thus also reflect a historic geography of politically motivated attacks and murders, as one-third of all attacks took place within 250 metres of an interface area, and about 70 percent of deaths occurred within 500 metres of one (Shirlow, 2003; Leonard and McKnight, 2011).

Whilst these physical boundaries are not recorded on any map of the city, they are seen as evidence of 'visible authority' (McAtackney, 2011). This is why the removal of the eight-foot-high wall from the Crumlin Road in North Belfast on 25 February 2016 was such a signal event (Figure 1.2). The wall had been erected in the mid-1980s following completion of the nearby Ardoyne social family homes, which had been intended to give protection to residents living in this interface area during the Troubles. The removal act, unsurprisingly, took place at night, with no live media coverage. But the following day, Justice Minister David Ford acclaimed the substantial progress made by community representatives in Ardoyne, in partnership with the Housing Executive and statutory bodies such as the Police Service Northern Ireland (PSNI) and Department of Justice, 'in building community confidence to the point where they no longer wish to live behind such a barrier' (BBC, 2016). This achievement, despite being the first evidence of transformation at any of 21 recognised Peaceline wall locations, was seen as a crucial step to support regeneration projects and 'to change the physical environment and the lives of those people who live behind it' (Ibid.).

Figure 1.2 The removal of the 8-foot-high wall on the Crumlin Road in North Belfast.

However, to this day, Belfast's many other walls continue to provide a disturbing physical legacy and emphasise the deep divisions and differences that remain embedded in the city.

Northern Ireland's other principal city, Derry/Londonderry, on its north coast, provides a slightly different set of concerns and conditions to those in Belfast. Reflecting the circumstances of its founding at the beginning of the 17th century as a plantation colony at the direction of the London guilds, the city is well known in Irish Nationalist/Catholic culture as Derry and in Ulster Unionist/Protestant culture as Londonderry (Dawson, 2005). The city was also a scene of conflict long before the modern Troubles. Indeed, the slash in the phrase Derry/Londonderry reflects 'an important aspect of how landscapes gain their meanings, record aspects of history that may otherwise be forgotten' (Stewart and Strathern, 2002: p. 9). Political division in the city is explicitly spatialised through borders in the landscape – both material and symbolic – as the city is divided by the River Foyle and by man-made walls built between 1613 and 1618 to defend the lives and properties of Protestant settlers inside the city against local Irish Catholics who were mostly forbidden to live inside them.

Social and spatial segregation in Derry/Londonderry emerged long before the 1998 Good Friday Agreement and ceasefire. As the city developed, its Catholic communities were gradually excluded, a 'powerless majority hemmed into a ghetto outside the centre of their own city, currently known as the Bogside; but also as a powerless minority trapped by partition within a state-run by their enemies' (Farrell, 1980: p. 92). The Troubles in Derry/

Londonderry were marked by various atrocities perpetrated by Republican and Loyalist paramilitaries and by the British Army (Bryan, 2015). Violent conflict in the city also led to increasing levels of 'socio-spatial segregation and a reduction in inter-community socialising, education, work, and wider habituation' (Boland et al., 2016: p. 4). In, addition, it had a significant impact on the 'spatial imposition and contestation of state power, remembered in highly politicized cultures of public commemoration' (Dawson, 2005: p. 158). However, for Unionists, the city's famed survival of the Siege of Derry in 1688–89 had already transformed it into a mythical place, 'forever memorable as an impregnable bulwark of British Protestantism, of civil and religious liberty' (Ibid.: p. 158).

Other cities and towns in Northern Ireland align more or less with the spatial geographies of division characteristic of these two cities, although the physical barriers are less obvious. In cities like Armagh or Lisburn, the spatial division is largely based on the boundaries of neighbourhood, which become visible mainly on the eve of the annual 12 July parades when English flags dominate the facades of Protestant households. Otherwise, patterns of religious distribution across Northern Ireland defy any specific order and appear on maps as a mosaic of interlocking presence. However interesting that may appear on a national scale, it does not tell the story of any particular locality, where mutual coexistence is more typically configured according to subunits and interface zones that do not appear on maps.

Post-conflict condition: one concern, diverse perspectives

Since the peace process became a long-term proposition for Northern Ireland in 1998, intensive investigations have covered almost every aspect of its sociocultural and spatial conditions of conflict. Excited by the potential to help pioneer a model of peaceful transition towards institutionalised democracy, several funding agencies, including British, European, and American organisations, have attempted to research, understand, and contribute to the process. Much of their work has focused on aspects of politics, economics, social and cultural impact, as well as planning for reconciliation. Central to these studies has been an interest in understanding how deeply rooted divisions could be transformed through peaceful transition and how both communities could contribute to building a shared future. Many of these studies have been distinguished by the key words *post-conflict*, *segregation*, and *reconciliation*. Yet, however broad in scope these research endeavours have been, gaps remain unexplored. More important, narratives, questions, and arguments related to urban matters have been dominated by a disciplinary obsession with the sociocultural aspects of the division, leaving key questions related to the built environment unanswered.

According to Shirlow and Murtagh (2006), for example, divided cities are places within which policymakers and politicians project an image of normality despite the facts of social injustice, victimhood, and harm. Reliant on analyses of sociopolitical territoriality and ethnic sectarianism, they thus argue against the commonly held view that Belfast is emerging from conflict into a new era of tolerance and transformation. They instead assert that segregation, lived experience, and fear are key issues that undermine democratic accountability and that the politics of territoriality, as reinforced in the development of policy, decision-making, and community participation, provide a key defence mechanism for segregated communities. Such attitudes will inevitably lead to the reproduction of segregation, sectarianism, and further division in Belfast's landscape. Other important works that approach this issue include the monograph *Planning Derry: Planning and politics in Northern Ireland*, by Gerard McSheffrey (2000). This contextualises accounts of the politics of planning in the city of Derry within the state of division in Northern Ireland from before the Troubles in the late 1960s up to the post–peace agreement period. It also discusses planning institutions, structures, meetings, and decision-making, and it gives insights into the processes of house planning, land use, and the building of its connection bridge.

In their edited volume *Northern Ireland after the troubles: A society in transition*, Coulter and Murray (2008) capture the shifting realities of a society in transition from war to peace. A collection of essays by commentators from a range of academic and political perspectives, it examines cultural identities and practices essential to the formation and understanding of Northern Irish society. Taken together, the essays offer a comprehensive and critical account of a society in the throes of change. The volume, however, supports the view that the self-serving oversimplification and optimism of official discourse and media commentary need to be challenged. In a similar take on urban policy in a post-conflict context, Bollen's *On narrow ground: Urban policy and ethnic conflict in Jerusalem and Belfast* (2000) examines how nationalistic or ethnic conflict may penetrate the building of cities and explores whether urban policymaking may independently influence the shape and magnitude of that conflict. Using Jerusalem and Belfast as examples of urban polarisation, it studies the complex spatial and psychological qualities of urban issues within nationalistic conflict, using an integrative, analytic approach that combines the perspectives of political science, urban planning, geography, and social psychology.

The management and politics of conflict are further studied in a number of important works that examine the actions of urban and local authorities in divided societies to contain uprisings, riots, and other forms of civil unrest. In *The politics and pragmatism of urban containment: Belfast since 1940*, Murray (1991) explores the relationship between the intentions and outcomes of urban containment around Belfast, investigating institutional frameworks of governance, the operations of centralised planning by civil servants, and domestic state sectarian politics in shaping planning policies for both town and country. Set in the pre–Good Friday Agreement period, the book reports on problematic planning practices during the Troubles and offers important insights into 20th-century planning practices in Northern Ireland. From an economic point of view, Murtagh, in *The politics of territory: Policy and segregation in Northern Ireland* (2002), also studies the relationship between land-use planning and ethno-religious segregation. Using case studies to explore meanings attached to land in contested places, the book argues that planners have a significant role to play in managing land distribution, and he sets out ideas for fair and equal access to land as part of a transition in planning practices.

Several studies also look at different aspects of conflict, territories, parades, riots, and social attitudes in Northern Ireland, in general, and Belfast, in particular. For example, Blackman's *Planning Belfast* (1991), Buckley's *Memory Ireland: Insights into the contemporary Irish condition* (1985), and Kirkland's *Literature and culture in Northern Ireland since 1965* (1996) present studies of active practices during times of heightened conflict and instability. They offer unique perspectives on the way public art and intellectual discourse have been developed around stories of grievance, pain, and struggle and have thus become key to understanding the transition of the Irish landscape. On the other hand, many studies, such as Neil Jarman's *Changing places, moving boundaries* (2005); *Demography, development and disorder* (2004); and *From riots to rights* (with Bryan, 1998), look at the social tensions of everyday life in Northern Irish cities (but mainly Belfast), drawing in-depth pictures on how communities have struggled and dealt with issues of territory with regard to contentious activities such as parades.

Yarwood's *The Dublin-Belfast development corridor* (2006), Calley's *City of Derry* (2013), Abdelmonem's *Portrush: Architecture for the north Irish coast* (2013), Mackel's *Impact of the conflict on public space and architecture* (2011), Urban's *Community politics and the peace process in contemporary Northern Irish drama* (2011), and more recently, Elliott's *Hearthlands: A memoir of the White City housing estate in Belfast* (2017) further represent a collection of studies and essays from specific disciplinary, professional, artistic, or literary perspectives that provide a holistic view of how the contemporary urban condition in Northern Ireland has been shaped. Hocking's *The great reimagining* (2015) also offers a detailed ethnographic account of post-conflict visual transformation, and examines efforts to produce new civic images against a backdrop of ongoing political and social struggle and a contested urban landscapes. Through these endeavours, art, architecture, and literature are shown to provide vital tools for understanding the wider politics of a transforming the public sphere towards a more ethnic-neutral discourse.

The diverse perspectives of these studies have largely informed the design and interdisciplinary perspective of the view presented here of Northern Ireland's architecture, urbanism, and spatial politics. Our view is that the everyday urban experience is shaped and informed by multiple forces, as embodied in contrasting narratives and positions. In order to introduce a novel insight and in-depth understanding of the way architecture, urban space, and spatial memory have been shaped by the recent events of the conflict in Northern Ireland, we seek to dig deeper into the psyche of communities, their histories, practices, and spatial politics. Nevertheless, we have sought to retain a clearly objective position throughout our research, viewing its circumstances from an external vantage. This has been made further possible because, despite having lived and engaged with these issues for a number of years, we have maintained the independent observers position.

Makeup of the book

This book is divided into 11 chapters grouped into three parts based on thematic alignment. Each chapter deals with a particular aspect of architecture and urbanism in Northern Ireland over the past decade, based on research undertaken on issues of spatial memory, socio-spatial practice, and everyday engagement with the conditions of shared living.

In Part I: *The Making of the Irish Condition* we interrogate the historical and urban evolution of conflict, its roots, implications, and means of impact on the cities of Northern Ireland. Chapter 1, *Architecture and Spatial Memory in Post-Conflict Urbanism*, looks into the sociopolitical landscape of Northern Ireland following the Good Friday Agreement and its implications for spatial planning, urban design, and the architecture of public spaces, both in cities and in rural areas. The chapter highlights political, administrative, and governance structures and decision-making procedures, scrutinising the complexity of the spatial conditions of post-conflict division and the manner in which the notion of 'shareness' has been at the centre of changing patterns of living. Chapter 2, *The Condition of Change and Shareness in the Northern Irish City*, then offers a reading of the historic layers of ideological polarisation that make up the urban and rural built fabric in Northern Ireland. In particular, it examines the urban layers of Belfast as an industrial city and economic powerhouse, including its iconic early 20th-century buildings, spaces, and political structures. Aspects of the city's character and perceptions of it as the capital of the North will also be presented through an archival survey of newspaper articles, novels, and popular cultural events from the interwar period from 1922 to 1939.

In Chapter 3, *Spatial Memory and the Shaping of Public Space in Belfast*, we then address current challenges to the transformation of Belfast's public spaces into inclusive and plural venues for cross-community interaction. The chapter discusses how spaces in divided cities may be carved up into perceived ownerships and territorialised areas, increasing tension between spatial, as well as psychological, territories, the control of which can lead to intercommunity disputes. It also interrogates neoliberal urban policies and architecture, with a focus on rejuvenating the city into four shared quarters with designated cultural and economic agendas. And the chapter explains how, instead of offering new spaces of engagement, new developments and buildings have further alienated local communities and deepened patterns of division, adding a socio-economic component to ethno-political conflict by further marginalising lower-class individuals.

In Part II: *Architecture and Spatial Memory in Rural and Urban Environments* we move on to examine different histories in the evolution of architecture and urbanism as defined by the modern history of conflict in Northern Ireland. The book here first examines various architectural and urban design practices according to which the cities of Belfast, Derry, and Armagh developed different forms and characteristics across different periods of history. This first involves examining the history of urban space and architectural intervention in Northern Ireland and the manner in which certain towns and villages evolved as industrial hubs containing linen mills and the homes of important capitalist families. This analysis then paves the way for an exploration of contemporary design interventions in these cities, including an analysis of defensive architecture in Belfast and Derry, the potential for architecture to act as an agent of change, and an analysis of the design of urban parks in Belfast.

As part of this section, Chapter 4, *The Architecture of the Linen Mills and the Social History of Rural Ulster*, provides an in-depth study of the linen industry and its role in shaping the rural and urban architecture of Ulster. Looking at social, industrial, and family history, supported by local memory, it interrogates the development and evolution of certain rural settlements around linen mills, documenting times of prosperity and growth, and a resultant architectural elegance, followed by the eventual decline of the built fabric. The chapter envisions these ups and downs in Ulster's rural landscape through a study of small towns such as Gilford and Soin Mills. Chapter 5, *Defensive Architecture and the Shaping of the Urban Experience*, then looks at the design principles and public interaction underlying the construction of defensive architecture in the public spaces of Belfast, particularly the ways that a reduction in the permeability of building facades has decreased pedestrian activity in adjacent public spaces. Based on a fear of intrusion, vandalism, and/or destruction following a series of bombings during the Troubles, the lower-floor facades of these buildings have increasingly been designed to be disengaged from the pedestrian experience. Recently, however, some designs have sought to reverse this trend by offering to re-engage with public spaces, but behavioural patterns have yet to escape an inherited sense of fear as a result of political events and rival politics.

Chapter 6, *Community Architecture and the Question of Spatial Agency*, looks at architecture as a potential agent of change in Northern Ireland, emphasising the challenge to architects concerned with issues of social equity and sustainability. It critically envisages the role of architects within community-regeneration projects in Belfast, interrogates how notions of social and professional agency could refine elements of socially informed design, and offers analytical examples of the work of two local architects. Chapter 7, *Spatial Voids and the Integration of Urban Parks* in divided Belfast, then analyses community strategies of self-defence and control of shared space and the use of physical and spatial settings to enable the constitution of social boundaries, borders, and territories. It looks specifically at integrated urban parks designed to ease division through an open transitional landscape that may, contrary to their intent, actually further segregation. The chapter provides a comprehensive analysis of space organisation, facilities layout, and the resultant 'social voids'. And it identifies space, time, and distance as effective tools with which to engage in negotiations of privacy, manifest power, and the interplay of dominance and self-confidence. It reports that a strong community culture tends to reproduce new boundaries and territories within the shared landscape.

Finally, in Part III, *Understanding Spatial Practice* and Planning in Divided Cities, the book turns to the sociopolitical implications of conflict in Northern Ireland for the built environment, urban spaces, and urban spatial practices. As part of a discussion of the way planning practices have facilitated division in contemporary Northern Ireland we examine here how, as a result of the Good Friday Agreement, gated communities have now evolved and developed into isolated enclaves and city spaces, in general, are being reshaped to capitalise on or counter processes of reconciliation. We thus ask, 'Which spatial objects and spaces facilitate integration, and which facilitate remembrance of the ills of the violent past?'

In this section, Chapter 8, *Landscape of Difference: Encounters of Contact, Segregation and Urban Justice in Derry/Londonderry*, deals with landscapes of division in Northern Ireland's second-largest city. It examines 'everyday' life in segregated communities and discusses socio-spatial relations between people and their built environment through everyday urban encounters of difference. And it interrogates the way that living in divided enclaves leads to perceptions of social inequality and imbalanced use of space. Chapter 9, *Intertextual Spaces: Young People's Memories of Segregation in Derry*, then studies young people's relationship to territory in Northern Ireland and the way this group formulates its own strategies of contact and segregation coloured by heavily 'mythologised' memories of the Troubles. The chapter also questions whether the growing cultural and ethnic diversification of societies in Northern Ireland may lead to transformative social relations of integration and belonging beyond groups defined by ethnic identity. However, many young people today experience territoriality as a form of 'cultural capital' handed to them from preceding generations in a way that eventually generates closed groups, distanced from 'other' communities, which in turn affects their mobility, employability, and social contacts.

This is followed by Chapter 10, *Images of Social Memory and the Construction of Division in Belfast's Contested Spaces,* which investigates diversified memories of division in Northern Ireland, as these were impacted by the political conflict known as the Troubles. Societal division in Belfast, for example, is manifested in its built fabric and territories largely divided between a Unionist east and a Nationalist west. The aim of this chapter is to explore how current approaches in planning contested spaces have changed over time, leading to success in many cases. Finally, Chapter 11, ***Derry/Londonderry's Siege Monument and the New Segregated Urbanism*** looks at how transformations of Derry's medieval walls during the 20th century have shaped an urbanism of segregated settlements within a city of religious confrontation. Military blockades, Peace Lines, and watchtowers have thus led to a disintegration of public space within the walls and created areas of 'no-man's land' around the peripheries of the Siege Monument. The chapter examines the pivotal moments of physical transformation in urban planning around the city walls, including the shifting of residential settlements in the Bogside/Fountain areas and the movement of Protestant settlements towards the 'Waterside' of the city. The chapter includes an analysis of historical maps of the city from the 1600s, when the first medieval walls were constructed, through the 1948 housing crisis, the 1968 urban area plan/beginning of the Troubles, and up to the present day.

2 The condition of change and shareness in the Northern Irish city

Contextual dispositions: conflict in a shared society

The majority of contemporary societies are structured around one or more aspects of division. Whether these are social, cultural, ethnic, or religious in nature, they create implicit sublayers by which different communities define themselves in contrast to others. This condition creates a shared sense of unity and purpose, which contrasts to the distinctiveness of individual neighbourhoods. Such divisions have varying degrees of visibility across socio-economic boundaries of affordability in cities like London, with its varied neighbourhoods and lifestyles, or via ethnonational physical boundaries, as in Belfast or Derry/Londonderry. Yet, whilst these conditions evince many typologies across the globe, it is rare to find an example in which the communities on one side of such divisions seem to know, understand, and share so many of the values as those on the other, as is the case in the cities of Northern Ireland.

It would be naive to underestimate the considerable difference in cultural practices that divide Northern Ireland's Nationalist and Loyalist communities. Yet what is unique in this case is that both communities maintain a discrete sense of identity and belonging to the land and a distinctive culture that is different from that of mainland England or the Republic of Ireland to the south. In fact, cultural practices in such areas as food, music, and performing arts tend to unify these two communities rather than divide them. Our intent in this book, however, is to detect and trace spatial practices that reflect how embedded and embodied histories of conflict and contestation have arisen in this landscape. Yet these aspects of unity and division between communities must be seen through the objective lens of shared history, culture, and place. And this is precisely why practices of shareness in everyday life may be the most appropriate response to the apparently opposite condition of a divided society. Building on aspects of Contact Theory, we argue that enduring coexistence eventually builds shared heritage, understanding, and engagement with similar contextual, social, and cultural constraints and that these, by nature, infuse the population with similarities, coherence, and familiarity. Thus, if we stripped out ideological loyalties and political affiliation, we could see how Northern Ireland, in fact, represents a coherent society with much in common, despite its self-declared polarised identities.

In making these observations, and in our analysis of both the rural and urban landscapes of Northern Ireland, however, we are the beneficiaries of an external, foreign perspective, which has allowed us to look objectively at the evidence and offer a novel reading of the contemporary scene. Being free from the pressure of rival identities and associated loyalties has allowed us to take a critical and analytical view of how both communities engage with their spaces, buildings, and cities as part of everyday life. As architects, we are also interested in helping to liberate the cities, public spaces, and rural landscapes of Northern Ireland from the shadow of the Troubles, a violent period that not many alive today witnessed yet whose consequences they continue to struggle with.

In a divided society, children and young people must come to understand and experience the divisions their particular society prioritises if they are to reach a point where they can practise and control behavioural patterns towards its shared spaces (Leonard and McKnight, 2011). To a certain extent, engaging with community spaces in the contemporary city requires a process of training, practice, and defence, which is communicated from one generation to another through inherited systems of action. Knowledge of the past thus shapes the way present activities and behavioural patterns are measured and appropriated. Assuming control in such urban spaces, hence, implies an understanding of human practices of domination and defence – of gaining territories and protecting rights – apart from the ideals embodied in legislation granting equal access and right to the public domain. This process is as apparent in such 'peaceful' contexts as London, New York, and Cairo as it is in such 'contested' ones as Nicosia or Belfast. One only needs to observe how areas of pavement in modern cities may be occupied and used by coffee shops, beggars, or tradespeople to understand the operation of territorial conflict and games of domination.

In politically charged and segregated societies such as Belfast or Beirut, however, control of shared space is a daily political and social exercise, through which each community emphasises its power and protects its position in a process of negotiation. For example, 86 percent of surveyed inhabitants of the two main communities in Belfast stated that they would not walk through an area dominated by the other group, while 79 percent would not even travel through it by car at night (Shirlow, 2003). However, such social conflict is not always viewed in a negative light.

Whilst conflict may create frequent altercations and a volatile environment, it also reshapes the expression of power within society, giving more authority and control in a city to smaller units in relation to a relatively weak and ineffective central administration. In such conditions, individuals must revert to engaging with their neighbours to sort out their concerns and ensure their security, rather than seeking assistance from the structure of the state as represented, for example, by a city council. In a study of similar urban conditions of conflict in Jerusalem (Misselwitz and Reiniets, 2009) thus describe conflict as a positive force helping to produce the valuable ties typical of a modern, democratic society, and providing these ties with the strength they need. In this perspective, modern society is too large a construct to work without being divided into groups and communities, which are then strengthened by means of conflict with one another, creating cohesive subgroups (Ibid.). The state, in this view, is mainly responsible for bringing these groups together in a shared and democratic public sphere, where they all have equal rights.

Layers of inherited history of hostility and conflict

Northern Irish cities have had ingredients of division embedded in their urban and spatial fabric from their very beginnings. Belfast, for example, emerged according to a complex political and religious topography, as a patchwork of disjointed communities whose animosity toward one another is not a contemporary or even a recent phenomenon (Bollens, 1999a). Maps from as early as 1685 show the beginnings of such segregated communities, although it wasn't until 1969 that the relationship between them took a drastic turn for the worse following the rapid expansion of the Catholic community in the industrial city centre (Boal and Douglas, 1982). Nevertheless, several centuries of fear, contested territories, and aggressive and violent rule did establish a comprehensive sense of grievance within the psyche and social heritage of both communities. This inevitably led to conflict, the most recent episode of which, the Troubles, left at least 3,600 people dead and more than 30,000 injured – as a result, however, of complex histories and inherited cultures far deeper than a religious binary (Leonard, 2006).

Indeed, it has not been religious affiliation or loyalty, per se, despite its visible presence as a source of conflict, that has determined the longevity of division in Northern Ireland. It is rather how religious affiliation has been used to create unequal patterns of privilege within society. Unequal conditions of access to wealth, work, education, areas of residence, political representation, infrastructure, and services have all infused the relations between communities with animosity and created a collective sense of resistance among those who claim to have been excluded. Thus, in Belfast, although antagonisms are typically expressed as a religious division, there are many underlying causes of sectarianism (Coulter, 1999). Whatever its origins, however, the expression of social division takes the form of residential segregation, with any open space surrounding or within an area becoming the exclusive territory of its community, access to which is prohibited to others. Physical segregation, in this sense, has also been shaped by the presence of more recent boundaries: Peaceline walls, interfaces, and buffer zones creating 'no go' areas for both communities. According to Neil Jarman (2005), this is 'a product of a process of contest over domination of a social space, and this contest contains the fear, threat or actual use of physical forms of violence'.

Within these conditions of division, the development of integration within Belfast's communities has been further inhibited by embedded values and cultural differences that differentiate the way people think and act towards each other. Over the last 40 years, social issues and physical location can be identified as one of the main sources for feelings of tension and fear (Calame and Charlesworth, 2009). Distinct demonstrations of character and emotion influence 'control' on a daily basis within any shared open space to emphasise the existence of majority/minority relationships. As a response to such expressions of intimidation, the weak minority typically withdraws while the powerful majority controls and expands its presence as a demonstration of power imbalance. But a central question addressed by this book is, in a post-conflict city such as Belfast, what makes certain communities more successful at gaining power and control over shared public space than others, and why does this relationship change from one space to another?

This chapter looks into the socio-political landscape of contemporary Northern Ireland following the Good Friday Agreement, and it examines its implications for spatial planning, urban design, and the architecture of public spaces. It highlights political, administrative, and governance structures and decision-making procedures, and it reflects on the complexity of the spatial manifestation of conditions of post-conflict division and the manner in which the notion of 'shareness' has been at the centre of changing patterns of living. The chapter also offers a reading of the historic layers of ideological polarisation that make up the urban and rural built fabric in Ireland, tracing the urban layers of Belfast as an industrial city and economic powerhouse of the North, including its iconic early 20th-century buildings, spaces, and political institutions.

A history of rival identities: the protagonist formation of Northern Ireland

> *The Troubles which broke out in the late 1960s had roots going back many decades, for Northern Ireland never resembled a place at peace with itself. In what are today assumed to be quiet and uneventful periods, even a cursory glance at the records of the time reveals a most unsettled society. A stream of incidents, large and small, testified to deep and dangerous fault lines in the society.*
>
> – McKittrick and McVea (2002: p. 1)

Both during episodes of violence and reconciliation, everyday life in the cities of Northern Ireland has always been one of spatial and demographic division. It is nevertheless easy to forget this also means the region has a history of shared coexistence that spans five centuries. This is not to suggest that the condition of society has ever approached those of a cohesive, non-sectarian utopia. The case has rather been much the opposite. To crystallise understanding of this condition one must start with the moment that brought the conflict into starkest relief and that shaped contemporary perceptions of the Irish condition: 30 January 1972 in Derry City, or what is better known as 'Bloody Sunday'. It was on this day that a handful of British Army soldiers transformed Irish history and that ordinary, unarmed protesters against government policy were shot dead by forces who had been prepared and trained to react in the face of expected violence (English, 2003). The shock continued for days, resulting in unprecedented violence and waves of local migration that changed the demography of the city. Responsibility for the day's events would eventually be determined to lie beyond the soldiers and junior officers on site, extending to the generals and politicians who controlled them. But the violent conflict precipitated would continue until the Good Friday Agreement of 10 April 1998. In hindsight, it was Bloody Sunday that was the defining moment when urban communities which had previously coexisted with one another were split apart, not only in Londonderry but also in Belfast and other, smaller cities.

To understand the roots of violent conflict in Northern Ireland, a brief review of its history is essential. Northern Ireland has struggled with its identity since it was founded as a by-product of the violent revolution that led to the independence of the Irish Republic in the south from British rule. The fundamental problem is that its political structure is British while its culture is Irish. Its settlements and landscape thus express a rivalry between two powers: the British Crown and European, Republican Ireland. Yet despite its formation in the early 20th century, its real search for an identity stretches back to the 16th and 17th centuries. It is thus important to recognise that communal divisions in Northern Ireland did not begin with the riots there in 1968. We thus offer a brief account of its society from its earliest formation.

After St Patrick brought Christianity to Ireland in the first half of the 5th century, the island played a pivotal role in supporting the Christian faith across Europe, especially during its medieval Dark Ages. Ireland's importance and attachment to Great Britain, however, emerged after the Norman invasion of the island in 1169, when it was recognised as important to the stability of the English kings. To legitimise this control, a Lord Deputy was appointed as the King of England's representative, supported by a Council and a Parliament that was authorised to raise taxes. A key aspect of this new political condition was an offer of land in the province of Ulster in the north-east in 1609 by King James I (1603–1625) to any who would claim his patronage. This proved to be a successful strategy for building loyalty and countering future rebellions, and it was critical in the decades and centuries that followed, as Britain became largely Protestant and Ireland remained faithfully Catholic. New waves of migration from Britain also followed, consisting of Protestant settlers who were required to build communities, defensive works, schools, and parish churches (Smith, 2005). Early waves came not only from Scotland, but settlers also later came from the rest of England, assisted by investments by the City of London Guilds – which were used, for example, to develop County Londonderry as a financial and industrial hub.

Aggressive settlement tactics and the forceful eviction of the native Irish population ended up fuelling the first rebellion against British rule, known as the 1641 Uprising. As many as 2,000 settlers were killed at this time, followed by an even larger number of native Irish, who were killed in retaliatory attacks. Tit-for-tat attacks continued through the following decade, with the English army leading several major assaults against the rebellious Irish as part of the bloody 17th-century English Civil War. The religious nature of this contest further became central to the Irish condition when the Catholic King James II was deposed and attempted to form a pro-Catholic army in Ireland to regain his crown from his nephew and son-in-law, the Protestant King William (the former Dutch prince William of Orange). After James II's defeat at the Battle of the Boyne north of Dublin on 12 July 1690, religion forever became central to politics and nationalist discourse on both sides of the Irish Sea. The Parliament in Westminster passed legislation prohibiting any monarch from being Catholic or married to a Catholic. And in Ulster, Protestants even today mark the anniversary of the battle with parades and huge bonfires to commemorate the victory that established their right to the land.

In the years that followed, in an effort to consolidate and spread the Protestant faith, a British loyalist elite and major landowners deployed discriminatory legislation that denied basic rights to Catholics in Ireland. For the better part of a century, these laws prohibited Catholics from buying, selling, inheriting, renting, or owning land – or from having jobs, receiving an education, or benefiting from civil rights. Yet such aggressive tactics, intended to enforce a new state religion, did not make a major difference; neither did major evictions. The result instead was fierce resistance that continued throughout the 18th and 19th centuries, causing a severe drain on the British Crown. This political movement and resultant acts of civil disobedience also came to be infused by Irish nationalism, which emerged as a new threat to the Crown. And this led to the Home Rule crisis of the 1880s and 1890s, out of which was born a revolutionary resistance movement led by the Irish Republican Army (IRA).

With the support of some Protestant politicians and the Liberal Prime Minister William Gladstone, Home Rule for Ireland became a matter of contest in Parliament in the latter half of the 19th century, but it was defeated by votes in 1886 and 1893. However, as a result of land reforms in 1879, Catholic farmers once again became eligible to purchase land and register to vote, changing the composition of the Irish Parliament. The involvement of the Catholic Church in support of Home Rule, however, alienated the

Ulster Protestants, who had strong business ties to London, and this became a particular issue in Belfast, which was a major British port at the time. Thereafter, unionism also emerged as a counterbalance to the role of the Catholic Church – as well as to the political philosophy of Home Rule – by advocating that Ireland should remain part of the British Empire.

The declaration of Northern Ireland as a separate state followed the passage of the Government of Ireland Act in 1920, which created two separate parliaments, one for the north and one for the south. The seven Protestant-majority counties of the north have since been governed by this parliament as part of Great Britain. The south, by contrast, led by the radical Sinn Fein party, never recognised the legitimacy of British rule. The Irish revolution thus continued until the Anglo-Irish Treaty of December 1921, after which the 26 southern counties declared their independence as a free state. The line of division between the new Irish Republic and Northern Ireland thus came to reflect religious affiliation and demographic dominance. And whilst the south has operated since as an independent state with a clear identity, the north has struggled to accommodate its slowly changing demographics and separate ethnonational communities (Figure 2.1), a condition which

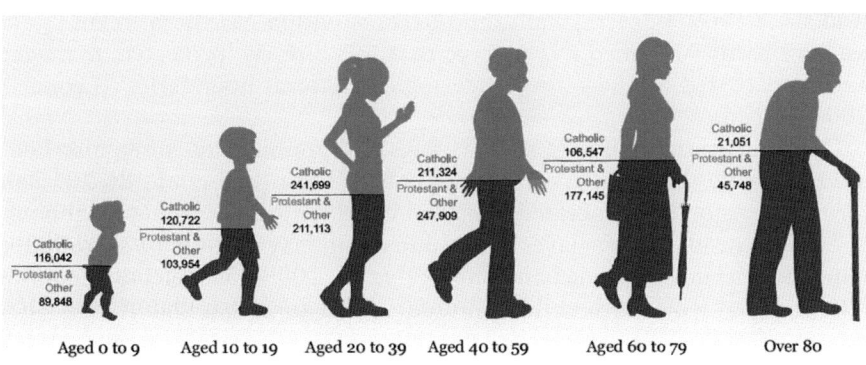

Religious background: a comparison between 2001 and 2011					
	Census 2001		Census 2011		
Religion (or religion brought up in)	Number	%	Number	%	Change (%)
Protestant and other Christian	895,377	53.1	875,717	48.4	−2.2
Catholic	737,412	43.8	817,385	45.1	10.8
Other religions	6,569	0.4	16,592	0.9	152.6
None	45,909	2.7	101,169	5.6	120.4

Figure 2.1 Ethnic demographic changes in the Northern Ireland population across age groups.

Source: After NI Peace Monitory Report #3, 2014.

resulted in sporadic rioting during the course of the 20th century and, of course, the Troubles.

Space, memory, and territorial segregation

Northern Ireland thus has an extended history of profound conflict along a number of dividing lines. This has led to the rise of the 'fractal city' and 'frontier urbanism', materialised through the construction of differences that signify the 'other' (Soja, 2000). Social segregation and the ongoing legacy of religious clashes have also led to the formation, institutionalisation, and consolidation of two distinctive and opposing cultural traditions: Protestant and Catholic. These traditions exhibit forms of exclusive social organisation that first emerged during the 17th century and which led to nearly constant violence until comparatively recently (Cunningham and Gregory, 2014). Segregated structures of urban and public space played an important part in reproducing this overall pattern and became a fundamental feature of the city (Murtagh, 2001; Boal, 2002). Since the creation of a separate state of Northern Ireland in 1921, its very existence and legitimacy, as discussed earlier, has been the outcome of a careful demarcation of what could be described as a territory of power, mostly ensuring a Protestant political majority (Shirlow et al., 2012; Graham and Nash, 2006: p. 6). And since 1969, borders, walls, and barriers within Northern Ireland's cities have further fortified a landscape that was already 'protected, managed and perpetuated by the gerrymandering of electoral boundaries' (Leonard, 2006: p. 225).

Other territorial markers, such as flags and murals, have often also been used to define the contours of spatial contestation (Bell et al., 2010). This form of division has generated marginal interface areas, turning neighbourhoods into residential enclaves where one group may represent a surrounded minority within a larger urban context (Nagle, 2009). Madeleine Leonard's (2006) social work with children in segregated zones has shown how they thus express deviating conceptions of place and territory. Typically, a sense of place not only articulates the physical features of a built environment but is defined as a social space tied to family and friendship relations. By contrast, the children studied by Leonard defined territory in relation to Protestant and Catholic identity, and as space imbued with memories of inequality and injustice (Ibid.). Demographic variation in such areas, as Neil Jarman (2003) notes, has been translated into hardened territorial claims to ensure that boundaries between communities remain in place and that territory does not slip into the hands of the 'other'. These territories, in turn, become spatial milieus for practising power and claiming authority, as each group manages its condition of insecurity by fortressing physical boundaries that gradually became part of its identities.

The implications of such territorial markers and the spatialisation of conflict place a particularly devastating burden on the daily lives of young generations through accounts of the past. Youngsters today are largely the sons and daughters of the 1994-ceasefire generation who lived through and witnessed traumatic violence and bereavement (Kilkelly et al., 2004; Gilligan, 2006). In the 1990s, when their parents were children, discussions on the 'peace process', community difference, sectarian violence, and shared spaces were active and at times heated, but they mostly drew on young people's own lived experience and the experience of their families and communities (McGrellis, 2010). These communities' transition to peace has been slow and not without political or social challenges (McAlister et al., 2013). Nevertheless, the peace process did begin a progressive turn in young people's lives and a crossing of lines of division (McGrellis, 2010).

A clear shift in the political landscape towards a more conciliatory tone has contributed to young people's narratives of community, affiliation, identity, and perceived opportunity – specifically, as these reflect either optimism and confidence or enduring fear and suspicion (Ibid.). It has also endorsed practical opportunities for physical mobility into the territory of the other to support stronger social bonds and new relationships (Caballero et al., 2008). Young people from either side, while suffering from distrust of and prejudice towards the other community (the same attitudes that have burdened their parents for decades), are thus more open and outspoken on their future in a conflict-free society. Indeed, there is a growing belief in shared living conditions and challenges as part of coexistence in a contemporary post-conflict society. While young people today continue to engage in verbal confrontations and occasional violence in the street in efforts to define territories, they have also tried to make larger sense of their personal encounters and experiences, especially as these relate to engaging with and occupying public space (Pickering et al., 2012: p. 945).

In a way, young people's dependent or independent status is still fragile, and their experience of association with territory is often challenging and problematic compared to adults. Growing up in segregated enclaves that perpetuate myths about the 'other side' provokes natural fear and anxiety while establishing a sense of spatial and physical division that cannot be dismissed in their everyday life (Leonard and McKnight, 2011). Yet they have no memories of violence themselves and must instead rely on history books and the accounts of family members to reflect on the inherited conflict. The undeniable fact, however, is that despite these circumstances of attenuation, young people are still growing up in a divided society, where beliefs about 'us' and 'them' endure in the forms of engagement with architecture and urban space.

Spatial imprints of conflict on public space

Many Irish towns were built around open space for utilitarian purposes rather than recreational ones (Butlin, 1977). Indeed, the earliest reference to 'recreational' public space was to a small enclosure, for village games, off

Belfast's Waring Street in the mid-17th century (Scott, 2000). The origins of such public spaces in Belfast can be traced to early 19th-century fairs and festivals at sites such as the Cavehill, with the subsequent establishment of pleasure and botanical gardens coming as part of a response to emerging problems of urbanisation (Scott, 2000). Yet despite a huge investment in public spaces in Belfast, cross-community interaction in these places remained difficult due to the ongoing feud between Republican and Loyalist communities.

A contested space can be defined, according to Hepburn (2004), as a location shared by two or more segregated groups, where no side accepts the dominance of the other. It is usually partitioned to exclude weak or opposing minorities or as a dense mechanism to emphasise group identity (Calame and Charlesworth, 2009). Researchers argue that such conditions of inaccessibility may further deprive communities of drive and ambition for education and employment, which further alters communal behaviour and attitudes towards the use of exterior/cross-community space. In this regard, Hickey (1984) believes that religion is the main factor behind the continuous presence of violence and hostility in the public spaces of Northern Ireland. However, Coulter (1999), points out that religious categories such as Protestant and Catholic are only indicators of identity and social character, and that the legacy of colonialism has been the main divider of Belfast. This view was also highlighted in Michael McDonald's *Children of Wrath* (1986), which called on the government and policymakers to formulate policies of short- and long-term socio-economic change rather than planning for forced integration, which would lead only to further conflicts of interest and mutual territorial defence.

Based on a public discussion in 1996, Smyth concluded that segregation creates a problem of mutual accusation, with each community holding the other responsible for ongoing violence and unrest (Jarman, 1999). Among the opinions he recorded on the issue were the following: (a) that segregation causes civil unrest and heightens problems of sectarianism; (b) that children don't have the same freedom in segregated areas, as parents are wary of customary fighting at boundaries; (c) that considerable support for a united community exists within Belfast based on the belief that segregation plays a major role in intensifying problems and keeping communities apart; and (d) that outsiders within segregated areas are the ones who see it as sectarian (Smyth, 1996).

In fact, throughout our fieldwork and research in Northern Ireland, and particularly away from hot spots of violence, we found a high incidence of desire for a more integrated and sustainable community through processes of social change, but there was also widespread belief that this could only take place when people began to feel more comfortable with each other, encouraged through education and the shared pursuit of crucial demands for employment and an improved economy. Smyth (1996) similarly asserts that integration is more likely to occur when communities share values, morals, and work ethics. In addition, Shirlow (1997) states that it is becoming apparent that both communities are beginning to take steps in this direction, sharing similar values, lifestyles, and economic goals and that such social and cultural change should be highlighted.

During the Troubles in the decades of the 1970s and 1980s, Belfast witnessed a huge decline in the population of its inner city, as residents moved to suburban areas. This migration was the greatest local movement of population in Europe since the Second World War and that it has been explained as the result of a desire to seek refuge from increasing levels of political violence within the city centre. However, it is important to note that the movement of the population at this time was not restricted to people leaving the city centre. Population movement also took place in various residential communities surrounding the city centre as a result of intensifying conflict among working-class groups, too. Overall, people either moved voluntarily or were forced out of certain areas at this time to seek security and protection in neighbourhoods of their own ethno-religious community. And threats to the continued mixing of communities became evident by menacing symbols of political defiance, especially murals painted onto the gable ends of houses.

Sterrett et al. (2011: p. 110) argue that the highest levels of violence (and an estimated 80 percent of all politically motivated murders between 1969 and 1999) were concentrated in North and West Belfast. Such elevated levels of conflict provoked a unanimous governmental response not only to reduce the number of 'troublesome households' in close proximity to the city centre but also to increase the level of physical separation between this centre and its North and West communities, as we can see today in Cupar Street Peaceline wall (Figure 2.2). This was seen as one factor that influenced the commissioning and construction of Belfast's Westlink Motorway and Inner Ring Road infrastructure, which appears today as a thick line drawn directly through the city and around its commercial centre and whose aim was to isolate the political violence to within the aforementioned neighbourhoods. Security in the centre of Belfast was then reinforced with the erection of a 'Ring of Steel' in 1971, designed to diminish the potential for bombings and/or rioting in the commercial core of the city. The enforcement of this security zone also led to the removal of cars from many urban spaces within the city centre through the installation of concrete-filled oil drums connected by scaffolding poles. These drastic security measures have since also led to the pedestrianisation of many public squares and streets within the city centre, with the crude concrete-filled drums having now been replaced with bollards, benches,

Figure 2.2 Cupar Street Peaceline wall.
Source: Courtesy of Bassma Abu Al-Fadl.

and/or planting – now seen, ironically, as elements of enlightened urban design.

More recently, following the Good Friday Agreement, the government has also attempted to counter the image of a city at war through building projects and other injections of capital into the city centre to boost its dwindling retail economy. This initiative involved the deployment of '*significant urban development grants for new developments and the refurbishment of existing buildings*' (Sterrett et al., 2011: p. 102) Such attempts at regeneration also included the heavily subsidised construction of a new shopping and office complex known as Castlecourt Shopping Centre, whose architecture was more of a political statement than an aesthetic one (Figure 2.3). An initial design in the late 1980s by the Building Design Partnership, in the form of a pastiche with a neo-Victorian facade, was flatly rejected. Instead, the city demanded a building that would communicate a message of modernity, safety, and resilience. Thus, the final design utilised vast curtain-wall facades as an implicit vote of confidence in the future safety and security

Figure 2.3 Castlecourt Shopping complex facade, Royal Avenue.
Source: BDP Ostick & Williams Architects.

of the city. Writing about the design of the Castlecourt Shopping Complex,
McEldowney et al. (2001: p. 107) note,

> The aesthetic, it was argued needed to communicate a confidence in the
> future, it needed to be bold and progressive and it needed to signify that
> Belfast had a role to play in the international modern world.

Such a bold move took place on the site of the demolished Grand Central
Hotel – formerly Ireland's finest such structure and an ornate work of Victorian architecture directly connected to Belfast's social history (Figure 2.4).
However, it also changed the formerly strong pedestrian character of
Royal Avenue, the major artery within the commercial core, through the
construction of a megastructure that effectively cut off all pedestrian links
with surrounding communities. Clad with stretches of tinted-plate glass, it
thus could also be interpreted as a security measure, providing an image of
openness and safety but offering little evidence of such confidence on the

ground. However, the architecture and urban design of this complex is just one example of a post-conflict Condition in which fear of the violent past continues to shape the urban experience and the design of buildings and public spaces.

Theoretical framework

Spaces for encounter: contact with the other

Recent debates related to diversity, inter-ethnic encounter, and spatial and social integration have raised questions about the ability of 'spaces of inter-action' to alter relationships between social groups whose isolation from one another is driven mostly by political and social conditions (Askins, 2008; Amin, 2002; Laurier and Philo, 2006). Gordon Allport's (1954) Contact Hypothesis originally theorised that constructive interactive relationships among distinctive groups might minimise prejudice and increase meaning-ful engagement across conditions of supposed otherness. Kwan (2000) thus argues that the development of mature bonds with 'others' is not sufficient to produce emotional empathy beyond a strictly reasoned approach; never-theless, expressing indirect interpersonal contact may increase constructive attitudes between groups. It is common, then, for individuals to have mixed feelings for those they see as being other to themselves and that this may result in qualitatively different forms of encounter.

Another way of conceiving of this is that while indirect interpersonal con-tact may increase constructive attitudes between groups, such contact on its own is not enough to generate respect or reduce conflict (Valentine, 2002; Valentine and McDonald, 2004). This proposition is supported by research on the practices of ethnicity, which raise questions of reliability related to recording, monitoring, and analysing instances of mutual contact. Although such encounters may help address problems of political violence, post-conflict communities are still largely unable to improve inter-ethnic relations and promote the kind of shared identity needed to overcome attitudes of sectari-anism and racism. Self-defined ethnic groups, for example, tend to maintain high levels of intergroup isolation regardless of their geographic proximity (Schnell and Yoav, 2001), a finding that provides further evidence of the destructive effect of territoriality in conditions where fear prevents young people, in particular, from travelling outside zones of comfort.

Scholars have explained how alternative 'contact zones' may provide less hardened territories of interaction, in instances where 'cultures clash and grapple with each other' (Pratt, 1992: p.7). Thus, young people may engage with each other on streets, in community and youth centres, schools and church halls, on boats, or in the mountains. But these neutral localities are governed by questioning relationships among individuals and groups, and they offer a setting for challenging dominant opinions, thus opening new possibilities and opportunities for integration (Ibid.). Simple contact between groups, on its own, is not sufficient to produce diverse communities and mutual respect for the other; indeed, it can 'entrench group animosities and identities' (Ibid.: p. 971). In some cases, then, recognised contact areas may allow for tolerant behaviour, but they may equally reproduce segregation in various forms (Matejskova and Leitner, 2011; Sennett, 2005; Abdelmonem and McWhinney, 2015). Along this line, Alan Bairner and Peter Shirlow (2003) argue that the sectarianising of place in Northern Ireland has had a massive impact on the use of leisure facilities. And they explain that fear of the other, whether based on personal experience or on imaginary scenarios, has been the key factor deterring citizens from making use of such places. Similarly, migrants construct their own contact zones that are both embodied and metaphorical, leading to the establishment of interconnections with others based on the representation of simple, bounded geographies. In fact, contact zones 'are not natural servants of multicultural engagement', considering how such spaces may be 'territorialized by particular groups, and therefore steeped in surveillance, or [. . .] spaces of transit with very little contact between strangers' (Amin, 2002: p. 967).

In examining the experience of minorities in multi-ethnic Europe, Amin (2013) argues that the politics of intolerance is symptomatic of a breakdown in social cohesion and that attitudes may benefit from the correction offered by community and contact. He focuses on the figure of the stranger, which taps into a deep-rooted vernacular of phenotypical prejudice and intolerance. Marco Antonsich (2010) has likewise examined ways to avoid falling into the trap of 'socially de-contextualized individualism', claiming that the possibility of constructive contact is profoundly linked to a positive sense of belonging and identity. And he argues that the quality of belonging required to 'construct, justify, or resist forms of socio-spatial inclusion/ exclusion' must be analysed from various perspectives such as personal emotions, place attachment, and the sense of being 'at home' (Ibid.: p. 644).

Drawing on Henri Lefebvre's (1996) idea of the right to the city as 'the right of all its inhabitants to shape urban life and to benefit from it', Amin (2013: p. 1941) advocates a politics of the commons that makes space for, and makes a public ritual of, cohabitation – 'a welfarist bio-politics and other collective interventions that might strengthen civilities of indifference to difference'. Such arguments connecting the question of rights to debate over conditions of encounter in urban space may be particularly pertinent with regard to the encounters between ethnically divided groups in contact zones. Such encounters necessarily raise questions of rights and the ability or inability to occupy common ground 'that allows multiplicity as a gathering of equals, a meeting ground and shared turf' (Ibid.: p. 1941). There is no doubt that denying certain groups the privilege of celebrating basic entitlements robs them of the same rights and means as others to participate and contribute to urban life.

In their report *Public Space for Shared Belfast*, Gaffikin et al. (2009: p. 8) highlight two narratives that have provided as a basis for such attitudes of exclusion in Belfast, and that offer contrasting views of the city: 'a narrative of "nostalgia" on the Protestant Unionist side and a narrative of "utopia" on the Catholic/Nationalist one'. The authors suggest that these views may only now be slowly moderating towards a shared vision but that this only materialises through continuous and safe contact in shared public spaces, which helps transform 'antipathy into empathy, if not enmity, into amity'. They report that amongst four possible strategies for transformation, that of 'positive interaction, reciprocity and mutual enrichment' seemed the most popular amongst local residents (Ibid.). Such contact between members of both communities is encouraged through a variety of shared spaces, public services, and educational institutions. Families from both communities have thus begun to make friends among members of other groups at integrated school events, or by working together in the city.

The transformation of the contested to the shared, whilst not the smoothest of processes in Northern Ireland, has also made significant progress toward dismantling what have been called 'mental walls', ideological dispositions that normally prohibit contact with others in the first place. Breaking through those barriers and systematically dismantling the precondition of an enclosed and insular way of life is thus a first step towards reconciliation (Ibid.). After all, several modern, residential communities, whose residents were of mixed religion, did exist in the pre-Troubles era, including the White City estate in Belfast, designed and built by the Housing Association in 1949 (Elliott, 2017).

Segregation and spatial division in post-conflict Irish cities

Research on segregation in divided cities was reinvigorated in the 1980s following the publication of *Ethnic Segregation in Cities*, by Peach et al. (1981). Segregation, as they describe it, produces a state of socio-spatial exclusion, polarisation, and isolation between groups, and as such, it has been associated with a number of opposing cultures that have brought different societies into ethnic and racial conflict (Anderson, 2008; Sibley, 1995). Other recent work critically investigating lived spaces of encounter chronicles the reinforcement of such conditions of conflict (Boal, 2002; Hepburn, 2004; Hirst, 2005; Weizman, 2007). Likewise, Paddison and McCann (2014) have investigated contemporary conflicts and contradictions inherent to cities undergoing neoliberal restructuring, in an attempt to grapple with questions of diversity, equity, and justice. And Sophie Watson (2013) has conducted ethnographic studies on how performances differ between the public and private realms, noting that in the absence of tension, negotiation may help redraw the boundaries between them. This does not negate the existence of communities where integration has collapsed completely or where desegregation has made noticeable progress, but the core of the matter is its spatial component. In a sense, images that overrepresent the concentration of certain groups frame the discourse of social domination (Kempen and Ozueren, 1998: p. 1632), while politicians voice concern over the fate of other groups that must struggle against conditions of social fragmentation. Yet such groups may equally become victims of urban planning agendas that trap them into fortified enclaves to ensure their safety or reduce crime (Weizman, 2007).

On the practical level, social psychologists have also gathered evidence on the mental and emotional benefits of desegregation, as it has been shown to reduce levels of anxiety, produce a positive mix of emotions, and increase tendencies to establish inclusive identities in which 'they' become 'we' (Pettigrew and Tropp, 2006). In the early 1960s, Jane Jacobs celebrated diversity and complexity in the city, arguing that streets allowed strangers to 'dwell in peace together' (Jacobs, 1962: p. 72). Sennett (1977), following in her tracks, then discussed the role of low-level conflict in potentially shaping new hybrid cultures and ways of living together with difference. Others have tried to push the socio-spatial logic beyond Jacobs's conceptions of informal practices and guided behaviour (Sandercock, 1998), but it is unknown how this might realistically be achieved (Bridge and Watson, 2002). Yet, while contemporary cities are now celebrating a cosmopolitan turn toward diverse engagement and cultural contact, another vision that may ultimately be more relevant to analyses of segregation emphasises a world of 'distanced interaction' tied to increasing flows of information (Giddens, 1991). One example, as Sennett (2005: p. 47) suggests, is the impact of flexible work, especially as this may affect the future of social relations in the city.

Such a 'flexible order' increases the salience of distant relations and encourages people to withdraw from public interaction (Slevin, 2000). As a form of urban diversity, it has thus been criticised for neglecting the values of the 'other', resulting in inequality and a lack of social justice (Schiller and Irving, 2014). Such a condition may even become a source of intolerance that intensifies discrimination (Forbes, 2004). Feminist scholars, for example, claim that gender or ethnic difference leads to space-time constraints that affect activity–travel patterns from a time–geographic perspective (Kwan, 2000). This view has been supported by research on time and location constraints, especially as related to the everyday experience of different subgroups in terms of visiting worksites, attending to household needs, or participating in social activities. From such studies, it has also been shown that underprivileged groups suffer most when faced with socio-spatial barriers in their daily encounters (Kwan, 2009).

From another point of view, living in isolated enclaves in divided and post-conflict cities has been extensively studied in the fields of cultural geography, planning, and social policy over the past decades, particularly with regard to aspects of social hierarchy, urban fear, and cultural identity (Morrissey and Gaffikin, 2006; Harvey, 2000). Such studies have examined enclaves in terms of the structure of societies, the blurring of social and economic boundaries and invocations of manufactured identity and collective memory. But the shared focus of studies of urban enclaves and insular communities in these fields involves the central idea that space is socially constructed and that the way it is physically organised informs social patterns, relations, and interactions (Lefebvre, 1974; Gregory and Urry, 1985). Special emphasis is typically placed here on the complex connections among space, identity, and collective memory. These are what gives space meaning as place. From these perspectives, a city is not reducible to a series of well-organised spatial and physical forms. Rather, the power of its implicit history contributes significantly to shaping its identity for its residents. According to Henri Lefebvre (1974), the built environment thus both shapes, and is shaped by, narratives, stories, debates, and discourses, which, in turn, are made legible as references in the making of society (Lefebvre, 1974).

In this regard, Morrissey and Gaffikin (2006) have distinguished two forms of 'contested space': spaces where the contest relates to issues of pluralism and involves disputes over power and status between rival groups and spaces demarcated by sovereignty where disputes about equity and access are interlinked with ethnic-nationalist challenges to the legitimacy of the state itself. The latter largely defines the nature of territorial disputes in post-conflict urban environments like Belfast, Jerusalem, or Beirut, where access to land defines legitimacy, authority, and control. Rival groups in those cities thus use claims of repression and inequity as part of transitional political strategies, in pursuit of the greater objective of a restored homeland. Here, the claim to land and its defence may be linked to the right to existence and national identity. These concerns often have sacred meaning, and they typically confront assumptions about the unity and solidarity of the nation state based on the realities of deep disparity. Hence, Parekh (2000: p. 341) has argued that to progress toward a more peaceful and equitable condition, such divided societies must attempt to instil a sense of common belonging that is not tied to ethnic or cultural roots but, rather, to a shared commitment to continued coexistence and wellbeing.

In this context, the predominance of a discourse of spatial division in Northern Ireland reflects a deeply rooted concern for the very nature of existence and survival. In its cities, various working-class neighbourhoods, segregated by lofty concrete walls, exist as physical embodiments of fear, threat, and conflict, on both sides of which living spaces are controlled and monitored and lack facilities that might permit ordinary levels of consumption or leisure. Within the minds of inhabitants, perceptions may flow beyond the politicisation of land embodied by these lines of separation. Yet the harsh reality of segregation is that it has serious ramifications for how public life is shared and used, raising crucial questions about how human activity and communal contact may provide something other than a catalyst for future conflict. With this purpose in mind, we have chosen to engage with the Contact Hypothesis literature with scholarship that has investigated integration in the public realm and its role in mediating differences.

Memories of resurrection

To many students of Northern Ireland's history, literature, or urban culture, the events of the second half of the 20th century, especially the Troubles and its associated violence, remain the point around which all modern narratives revolve and which dwarf events before and after (Howe, 2011). The painful echo of these 30 years of conflict appear as sounds of grief in every household and inform the collective perception, knowledge, and awareness of all of Irish history. Graham Dawson's *Making Peace with the Past* provides one such record of the trauma and memory of Bloody Sunday and a subsequent journey of recovery from the Troubles. But it is just one of a rapidly building wave of work on the memory and commemoration of the violence of the Troubles and its many victims (Ibid.). To a foreign eye, even if it is possible to escape the culture of commemoration engraved in every community and family, it is hard to escape their imprint in public space through walls, fences, memorials, murals, and bonfires. Likewise, the performance of solidarity with the past is exploited continuously by politicians in their election campaigns.

A plethora of literature in Northern Ireland also focuses on practices of commemoration. This is because the role of memory has a much more substantial place in collective identity and psyche here than elsewhere. Indeed, a sense of loss serves as a never-ending narrative on both sides, which has become a part of each community's identity and history. What is involved is never one or more incident of violence; each such event rather denotes a history of struggle that spans centuries and that continues to inform all steps towards reconciliation. As history reveals, each moment is only a brief segment of a long story of contestation. But what is often overlooked is what Contact Theory emphasises as the necessity of coexistence with the other. Sharing struggle, anxiety, and a history of pain has, to some extent, shaped understandings of the past by both communities, just as it continues to inform how they go about everyday life. It is this mirroring of identities, according to which one cannot be identified in isolation from the other, that fascinates us and chiefly informs this book – just as it also underpins the endurance of the memory of resurrection in the Irish landscape.

Not surprising as a reflection of this condition is the predominance of Irish poetry and performing arts as the encapsulation of hard realities. Many Irish poets have excelled particularly at creative expressions of collective memory and historical storytelling, as in Edna Longley's 'The Rising, the Somme and Irish Memory' (1991) and the later work of Jane Leonard and Nuala Johnson. As did Seamus Heaney, Ciaran Carson likewise uses his critical eye to present a continuous yet refreshing pattern of engagement with the city, its people, and memories. All this work pays particular attention to the 'spaces of memory': war memorials, cemeteries, and battlefields.

By contrast, some critics have complained about the commercialisation and commodification of this painful past, and in particular, some historians of modern Ireland have been critical of the manner in which particular historical episodes have been packaged for public and commercial consumption as part of the heritage industry (Dunn, 1998, 2004). The pattern of commodification in art is thus followed by other forms of commodification, such as tourism. Within this economy at present in Belfast, the main attractions include the Black Cap tours to Peace Line walls and other sites of the Troubles. No doubt, the management of history has become a major Irish industry, which could have long-term deleterious effects on more critical practices (Howe, 2011).

Yet, Kirk Simpson (2013: p. 3) also makes an eloquent and thoughtful case for 'the construction of a universal, morally normative paradigm for dealing with the past in Northern Ireland'. Unfortunately, his appeals against artificial and obstructive disciplinary barriers, distorting politicisations of the past, and the instrumentalisation of history in the service of short-term policy objectives are unexceptionable. He is perhaps also too reliant on the power of reason and goodwill to overcome these tendencies rather than recognising the need for more practical strategies that engage with real life. More powerful in this regard is Susan McKay's (2008) *Bear in Mind These Dead*. This work is far less analytical than Simpson's because McKay devoted herself to hearing the individual voices of the bereaved and the maimed, those whose pain will not ease so long as they live and those who have rebuilt their lives, those who seek to forgive or reconcile, and those who cannot do either. This is (apart perhaps from the elegies written by some Northern Irish poets that detail every fatal casualty of the conflict) the finest and most moving work of remembrance Northern Ireland has yet produced. Framed by a conceptual and historiographical discussion of notions of cultural memory, tradition, remembrance, and trauma, it provides a powerful investigation of both memory and commemoration as related to the Troubles.

3 Spatial memory and the shaping of public space in Belfast

Introduction

The contemporary city produces a spectrum of physical, social, and virtual spaces that ascribe individuals to shared interest groups and positions within social debates (Arendt, 1958). Whether these spaces are a materialistic production of capitalist ideologies or act as instruments of coercion and violence related to issues of inequality in ethnonational conflict, they stand as vital platforms of engagement where individuals and communities negotiate the merits of their membership within society (O'Dowd and Komarova, 2013). According to Henri Lefebvre, it is through negotiation over space that individuals carve out their right to the city, and therefore, such structures constitute the urban condition of the city. In cities whose structure is chiefly contested according to ethnonational divides, planners and politicians may attempt to confront the status quo through spatial reform, the restructuring of territories, and place regeneration (Murtagh, 2011). For the divided city to escape its wounded fate and overcome its problems, they argue that the image and identity of its spaces must be redefined into liberal and modern forums of the 'new' to create a contrast with the 'old' (Smith, 2002). However superficial these efforts may be, cities with divisions tend to invest heavily in them, according to Adele Lee (2013), in an effort to 'normalise' or 'neutralise' problems of social truncation and political polarisation.

It is in this context that officials and planners have developed the concept of 'shared space' as a way to move beyond 'ethnic norms' and promote alternative venues of integration with different social and spatial outcomes (Jordan, 2011). The vision, by definition, implies an effort to inscribe space with certain social prerequisites and modes of interaction that will help heal inherited wounds of sectarianism (Calame and Charlesworth, 2009). As anticipated forums of sociopolitical engagement, such spaces within the urban context are intended to render memories and histories of the past forgettable by realising a new vision of responsibility towards a shared future (Komarova, 2011). Nevertheless, new shared spaces in cities may also fall victim to struggles over issues of class, race, gender, and religious disunion. Indeed, some shared-space strategies may produce their own woeful long-term consequences by transforming ethnopolitical divisions into socio-economic ones. This may especially be the case when, to neutralise national/ethnic identities, planners introduce themed quarters of a cultural, economic, or touristic nature, which, despite being open to different groups, contribute to neoliberal, socially exclusive agendas fundamentally at odds with the notion of 'shareness' (O'Dowd and Komarova, 2013; Jordan, 2011).

The conception of sharing in Northern Ireland is thus based on the logic of struggle over rights and territorial claims, which it tries to refute by using its extreme opposite – the spatial embodiment of neutrality in public space (Yacobi, 2009). Sharing space, however, does not necessarily entail the construction of a unified, neutral culture. In fact, positive engagement necessitates opportunities for self-expression, negotiation, and the contestation of identities in nonviolent ways (Amin, 2002). Thus, whilst the strategy of introducing cultural or themed quarters as new business districts in post-conflict cities may eliminate the physical expression of sectarian division, it reproduces a neoliberal ideology of gated castles: even though these areas are not fenced off, they remain mostly inaccessible to ordinary citizens due to the high cost of being there. Such capital-driven restructuring may be advocated as a way to attract new investment to urban real estate as a challenge to spatial-sectarian inefficiencies, reducing the relevance of ethnic structures (Murtagh, 2011). However, it could likewise be argued that these areas simply develop an alien identity that is mostly irrelevant to the everyday lives of ordinary citizens. Local people, in most cases, do not visit these places except on specific occasions or seasonal events, such as cultural nights and family holidays. According to Murtagh (2011), some urban areas have thus experienced resegregation during comprehensive efforts of desegregation, as new, socially segmented spaces come to overlie older, stubborn patterns of racial segregation.

Any real test of the notion of shared space, however, would involve the construction of public-service buildings in interface zones – precisely those areas where strategies of shared space in Northern Ireland have been deliberately delayed. And here the more salient evidence is that, while areas of themed identity have flourished away from already-contested areas in Northern Ireland, the number and the size of residential areas bounded by Peace Lines or other separation barriers have actually increased since the Good Friday Agreement in 1998. One cannot help but ask, therefore, whether programmes of 'shared space' have ever been promoted as a means of conciliation or whether they have been used primarily to facilitate an agenda of neoliberal urban transformation. Meanwhile, research has also confirmed that policies and strategies of 'shareness', as an ideological campaign, have largely been missing from these efforts and have thus not been able to contribute much to changing the attitudes of the ordinary citizens.

This chapter, therefore, discusses instances of new 'designed space' as sites of a coerced agency of conciliation, beyond which lie the older frontlines of everyday interaction and newer ones that reinforce an emerging economic elitism. It argues that the notion of 'shareness' needs instead to be developed as a persuasive choice in the realm of everyday need, rather than being imposed from the top down according to strategies that take for granted imagined socio-spatial success. As such, the chapter presents a theoretically grounded discourse on the effective use of shared space in divided cities, which it applies to the realities of everyday life in Belfast's contested border areas.

Shareness and division in the public space

Most urban theorists argue that modern cities are by nature sites of division. Grounded in social fragmentation and polarisation, as part of larger patterns of structural complexity, the experience of division may, in fact, be a precondition of urban life. This is part of every city's challenge and what shapes its identity and condition of modernity (Leonard and McKnight, 2011). However, for cities explicitly defined as 'divided', the challenges of modernity may exacerbate physical and social polarisation, as evident in patterns of everyday social exchange between different groups in Jerusalem, Nicosia, Tripoli, Belfast, and Beirut (Calame and Charlesworth, 2009). In these cities, segregation is visible in multiple aspects of daily life, such as housing, education, the workplace, and cultural and social practices. Segregation is also not simply a physical phenomenon but is also cognitively constructed so that it occurs simultaneously at every level of interaction through the pervasive use of the phrase 'the other side', causing communities to live 'parallel lives that often do not seem to touch at any point, let alone overlap and promote any meaningful interchanges' (Leonard and McKnight, 2011; Figure 3.1).

Figure 3.1 A gate through the Peaceline wall between the Springfield Road and the Shankill Road in Belfast.

Relationships between segregation and inequality are likewise intertwined. Madanipour (2010) thus argues that the spatial manifestation of social polarisation is evident in physical inequalities of urban space, where preferential accessibility or prohibition of access may be its most obvious forms. Its spatial expression may also be evident in forms of insular community that come to dominate the city's spatial structure (Goldie and Brid, 2010). In such insular forms, myths about the 'other side' proliferate, provoking imaginings of fear and reducing the desire for intercommunity engagement (Ibid.). Such myths may, in turn, be transformed into inherited systems of living, as younger generations reproduce spatial behaviour patterns similar to those they have been taught (Leonard and McKnight, 2011). Thus, elements of segregation and socio-spatial exclusion pass from one generation to the next, continuously reproducing the sectarian past (Schnell and Yoav, 2001).

How do attitudes of division and shareness interact with memory to influence everyday practice? Myths reproduce ideologies in narrative form (Lincoln, 1999). They are products of popular culture that communicate coherent social positions, norms, or even fears. And when they attach to buildings and structures, they may become powerful tools of the collective memory (Abdelmonem and Selim, 2012). By their very existence in the physical fabric, then, buildings from a horrible past may continue to signify that past and determine future attitudes because they inform daily habits, institutions, and ways of life. Architecture in this sense may provide one of the most durable elements in the fabric of remembrance, even if its role may become paradoxical and contested when it engages with collective memory (Bevan, 2006).

In post-conflict cities, buildings and spaces fulfil a substantial role in the landscape of urban experience. Thus, in Belfast, by their very existence, Peace Lines and gates between communities serve as potent signifiers of past divisions. In theory, if their significance could be recast to emphasise the need to forget old times, they could potentially be transformed to embody hope for a better future. But this would require disassociating them from the memory of past bad times, leaving behind only their physical manifestations. And the mysterious condition by which buildings and spaces embody certain memories cannot magically be altered to represent a new condition without the continuous, sustainable performance of new acts, rituals, and normative social behaviours (Connerton, 1989).

Conditions of division likewise connote the idea of protection and security. Being divided emphasises the social strength of one's own unit, which must always be braced in readiness for sudden attack – whether physical, cultural, or political. Each side in such a division becomes a powerful agency of communication and negotiation between the individual and society. This agency of division has, surprisingly, been understudied in cities in conflict, where much attention has rather been given to spatial and social features and outcomes. In this sense, an insular encampment that reproduces myths about its other is, in fact, a by-product of its own self-consciousness need for protection. Thus, even when a condition of conflict ceases to exist, the agency of division will continue to reproduce it. This explains why protests easily emerge in defence of trivial gains and isolated incidents.

This raises the question of why, in cities in conflict, the notion of shareness is so problematic, despite being the cognitive norm in the public structure of more ordinary urban areas. Because urban living is based on shared services and resources, however, practices of division may emerge in any city as a consequence of events, incidents, or experiences that assert inequality on ethnic, religious, political, social, economic, or racial grounds. This has been the case recently, for example, as a consequence of neoliberalism. According to Setha Low (1997: p. 53),

> [t]he increasing inequality of neighbourhood resources and services, the escalating price of decent housing, the ever-widening income gap between rich and poor, and the dismantling of the legislated safety net leaving families homeless, has resulted in the buttressing of social and physical barriers that separate people and communities by race, class, and gender.

Constructed around fear of a 'privileged other' and a sense of vulnerability and insecurity in the face of an unfair system, the agency of the locality may thus assert its grip on the powerful social institution of the community. In such conditions, however, it may be precisely the state's failure to fulfil its moral obligations towards vulnerable individuals that opens opportunities for other societal forces to move in and fill a 'power void'. Whatever the case, Larbi Sadiki (2013) asserts such conditions may ultimately translate into societal opportunities, potentialities, and capacities that empower micro-units in the face of the macro-politics of city management.

Spatial divisions in urban landscapes are thus infused mainly by lack of confidence in political processes and administrative structures, which are seen as fostering unequal access to resources, protection, or opportunities. This, in turn, forces groups of like individuals to cluster into enclaves for support and protection, when such concerns would normally be a government's responsibility. According to Fainstein (1994: p. 1), as quoted in Low (1997),

> [t]his built environment forms contours which structure social relations, causing commonalities of gender, sexual orientation, race, ethnicity, and class to assume spatial identities. Social groups, in turn, imprint themselves physically on the urban structure through the formation of communities, competition for territory, and segregation – in other words, through clustering, the erection of boundaries, and establishing distance.

It is thus a natural consequence of inequality for groups to seek to overcome their sense of insecurity by fortressing behind clearly defined physical boundaries that become part of their identities, the demolition of which becomes a non-tolerated offence.

In the presence of such conditions in cities in conflict, calls for a plural society, in which each individual has an equal right to urban space without the mediating agency of community groups, pose a serious threat to the social structures that provide more local assurances of solidarity and support. The structure of division thus stands ingrained in the very existence of each community, seen by many as a matter of survival rather than choice. But how is it that in a city of long standing, only a few decades of conflict and suspicion can so easily overwhelm more recognised practices prioritising the interests of collective society and responding to the needs of diverse majority/minority interests? Why should the practice of division be more persuasive than the notion of shareness, despite the short history of the former compared to the latter? To answer this question requires exploring the epistemological connotations of both terms within the construction of contemporary society in an attempt to clarify some contingent consequences of the condition of conflict.

One reading of the city is that it is a hub of infrastructures onto which urban living is layered by means of buildings, spaces, and domains of sociopolitical and economic interaction. The credibility of such a spatial system stems from its accessibility and openness to the needs of different groups. City spaces are thus hierarchical and structured according to political importance, from formal governmental and administrative spaces that celebrate and confirm democratic institutions to the most private residential quarters, where the state withdraws and integration within the locality thrives. And while the former may rely on collective confidence, the latter works based on mutual interest between neighbours developed through everyday interaction. When this system is operating smoothly, the concept and practice of shareness may go unnoticed as the everyday norm of public life in city-owned spaces. As a practice, it may indeed endure for centuries, through decades of political struggle and scarcity of resources. City life thus essentially involves the precondition of giving up part of what one might otherwise seek to claim as one's own, accepting equal access by others to the space of the city. However, the condition of the post-conflict city provides an alternative scenario in which the accountability of urban institutions, and subsequently access to urban space, is in doubt and must be continuously scrutinised. Such doubts, in turn, feed the agency of units of locality, which then negotiate with the state on behalf of residents, assuming an overtly political role under the pretext of providing for the collective security of the group and thus establishing a parallel hierarchy of institutions.

Such institutions of division typically develop spatial enclaves whose physical boundaries assert their authority. Similar to sovereign countries, they require such boundaries to define lines of authority. As physical proof of this divided political condition, nothing could be clearer than the walls dividing urban neighbourhoods in Northern Ireland, Cyprus, or Israel/Palestine. Yet all these situations are nurtured by a sense of vulnerability related to propagated fears of the other. In post-conflict cities, parallel institutions of division may develop quickly but require a long and sustained effort to dismantle. Thus, as long as practices of conflict remain in Belfast, the call for more pluralist attitudes and equal rights will be of little, if any, relevance for individuals who have grown up in conditions of institutionalised division. And neutralisation of these microstructures and their spatial consequences can only come from restored confidence in the collective management of the city as an institution of equality.

Division, space, and intergenerational memory

Conflict stemming from ethnic, national, or religious polarisation is a common feature of the contemporary city. Indeed, ethnonational division is what makes certain cities unique and interesting to urban theorists. In such conditions, citizens 'co-exist in a situation where neither group is willing to concede supremacy to the other' (Anderson, 2013). More critical to our investigation here, however, may be the manner in which psychological barriers develop out of this divide to inform individual perceptions of space and disrupt individual spatial readings of the city, provoking coping strategies as a reflex to anticipated danger. Individual mental maps based on personal experience and community knowledge may thus reproduce negative readings of public space (Jarman and Bell, 2009). Anderson (2004) suggests that people accustomed to navigating segregated spaces on a daily basis may thus actually contribute to conditions of conflict and ultimately reproduce its dynamics. Likewise, the presence of physical, visual, and psychological barriers asserts an urban condition of continued insularity that hinders the possibility of accidental communication or positive intercommunity engagement (Goldie and Brid, 2010).

Here, it is worth looking at the influence of space and buildings on the behaviour of individuals in divided and contested territories. Theorists and sociologists like Maurice Halbwach stress that individuals' memory is indelibly inscribed in space and that spatial memory has the strange potential to conjure up a dense web of images and events related to particular localities, especially when these are near a person's home (Yaari, 2008). Material-culture studies also show how personal memories may be transferred to solid objects in the process of creating symbols or capturing narratives so that the durability of these objects may preserve these memories in perpetuity (Forty, 2000). By contrast, memories of placed-based events or incidents require the creation of specific narratives that give meaning to space (Rosenfeld, 2000). Societies and groups may then retain and reinforce these memories through the continuing, sustainable performance of acts, rituals, and normative social behaviours that re-enact elements of the story (Tonkiss, 2005). The very presence of a wall, fence, or barrier building dividing one community from another thus serves both to contain and preserve the memory of past events and re-enact the shared meaning of being protected from it.

In a previous study, we questioned the temporal reality of memory – whether it belongs to history or engages with the everyday practice of living in the present. As we then asked, 'Is it about the desire for remembering or about the fact of forgetting?' (Abdelmonem and Selim, 2012). In social terms, spaces may not perhaps be the principal agents for collective memories, but they are significant for privileged or feared memories, especially those that would otherwise disappear from people's minds. Such memories also tend to continue to inform people's behaviour and practice in the present. Prejudice towards the other may thus arise from the education of a younger generation in the same physical setting that experienced a horrible past. Collective memory here is formed of layered events that correspond to specific places, times, and people (Connerton, 1989). In this way the past may guide how present activities and living conditions are measured and appropriated, especially when accompanied by social performances like parades deliberately intended to keep these memories alive (Abdelmonem and Selim, 2012). Such combinations of space and narrative are particularly good at expressing complex histories of pride and grievance at a popular, everyday, intergenerational level. Moreover, while every age and generation has a distinctive sense of the past, people in conditions of conflict, particularly in interface zones, view their history through the everyday imperative to remember lost loved ones. These are among the factors that privilege a continuing emphasis on conflict over the sense of 'shareness' needed for social coexistence in the present and future.

Spatial strategies of shareness in public space

The division of Northern Ireland into insular communities has been shown to have significant economic as well as social impacts. For example, the cost of segregating community services and facilities was estimated to be £1.5 billion per annum during 2004–2005 (Deloitte, 2007). In 2011 the Belfast City Council noted that 'the need to design, promote and manage increased shared spaces in the city of Belfast has emerged as an overarching priority for the city'. This statement cannot be understood without understanding the complexity of current spatial categorisations. From a typological point of view, the city's spaces may be divided between territorialised, neutral, shared, or cosmopolitan/corporate (Gaffikin et al., 2008). But government reports and policies further lack agreement as to what 'shared space' constitutes (Komarova, 2010). In fact, the condition of Belfast as a post-conflict city is also theoretically debatable, as this would require confirmation that there has been an end to conditions of conflict, which has yet to be practically achieved (O'Dowd and Komarova, 2013).

The rejuvenated vision of public space in Northern Ireland seems to bypass the complex reality of this ongoing state of affairs, recognising only the precondition of diversity and the desire for new democratic spaces that are open and non-hostile: 'a place where different forms of cultural heritage can be expressed in an environment that is safe, welcoming, good quality and accessible for all members of society' (Belfast City Council, 2011). Such new space is seen as free from territorial and sectarian claims; it is impartial, free from barriers, and accommodative of difference (Jones and Boujenko, 2011). McKeown et al. (2012) categorise three actual types of shared space in the divided context in Northern Ireland: first are 'naturally shared environments', everyday melting pots; second are 'policy driven shared environments', created as deliberately shared spaces, such as integrated schools; and third are 'field interventions', which are generally short-term projects, for example, cross-community programmes. This classification could be equally applied to other cities using such simple terms as *public space*, *planned space*, and *regenerated areas*. But it seems that in Belfast it is important to forcefully superimpose the terms *shared* and *intervention* to create a political image of 'post-conflict reality'.

In similar fashion, Liam O'Dowd and Milena Komarova (2013) have described the public spaces of Belfast according to three ontological narratives that reflect three conditions of shareness in everyday perception and interaction: the 'new capitalist city', the 'shared city', and the 'contested city'. Of these, the story of the new capitalist city reflects the belief that a resolution to conflict can be found through neoliberal economics and the development of a powerful new centre of capitalism, produced through the injection of foreign investment into signature projects and the development of a thriving new job market (Murtagh, 2011). The Titanic Quarter and the Laganside Development in the north-east of the city have been interpreted as successful examples of such a new culture of business based on investments in the information economy and the creation of new high-paying jobs. However, the development of exclusive spaces for high-profile users, as in these projects, has had limited impact on socio-economic conditions in adjacent communities and neighbourhoods, whose residents lack the high-end qualifications for these jobs. The story thus represents a mismatch between the needs of a spatial economy of engagement and a new global economy to which the unskilled, unqualified classes have no access, with the result being that those in the city who remember the Troubles are intimidated by the newly created spaces (O'Dowd and Komarova, 2013). These public spaces of neoliberal provenance have thus introduced a new 'other' to the city: a workforce of strangers who are as alien to the original conditions of conflict as they are to the communities still divided by them. The capitalist city, in this regard, has created spaces that are even more removed from the lives of local people and society than they are to the conflict (Figure 3.2).

Similar to these new business quarters, new cultural quarters have been developed in Belfast that capitalise on the city's traditional, cultural, and

Figure 3.2 The Titanic Building, the centrepiece of the Titanic Quarter, a large-scale waterfront regeneration project in North-East Belfast.

even political assets. But these projects have largely taken the form of branded tourist developments, rather than providing a catalyst for shared engagement by local people with the city's public spaces (Murtagh, 2011). Thriving on seasonal festivities and designated cultural events, for which no admission fee is charged, these new quarters are rarely visited in a meaningful way by residents throughout the year. The Cathedral Quarter, for example, is largely disconnected from its surrounding communities by giant civic office buildings (the St Anne's Square development), shopping centres and high-street outlets, and the University of Ulster campus – all of which close after 6 p.m. Such conditions limit the ability of its interlocking lanes and alleyways to serve as viable, active spaces of engagement, which might otherwise help ensure its security, safety, and sociability. To a large extent, this limited vision of branded neoliberal capitalism and physically determined regeneration overlooks key prerequisites for these spaces to survive as living organisms (Lee, 2013). And the social logic of space, in Henri Lefebvre's terms, is almost totally missing, since these regenerated areas afford neither the layering of activities nor the possibilities for engagement that might allow them to mediate ongoing socio-spatial pulses from nearby residential areas.

The spatial practices enabled by these new, open, modern spaces thus remain mostly alien to those inherent to the city's older built fabric and urban culture. Life in the spaces of any city requires a certain knowledge of local culturally accepted norms of behaviour. This implies a social code of accepted norms about how one should behave in public spaces, such as streets, squares and parks, and 'defying this code is to make a tiny, sting-ing cut in the social contract' (Tonkiss, 2005). Stevenson (2010) relates this to the expression of individual identity, noting that people will generally modify their behaviour and actions to fit what they deem appropriate for their physical surroundings. By ignoring local precedents in the practice of public space, these new spaces thus largely forfeit any chance they might have represented to advance attitudes of shareness in public space.

Between individual liberty and the collective social contract, public spaces may be measured against their capacity for being shared or exclusive. For example, an insular residential neighbourhood would enforce a code of con-duct for local streets. Hence, the understanding of such context in relation to individual expressions of identity can contribute to conflict resolution, as different understandings of space cannot only facilitate different ways of expressing and regulating identity but also potentially facilitate coexistence between opposing communities (Stevenson, 2010). By contrast, Gaffikin et al. (2010) argue that public spaces provide activity space for mixing and learning about other traditions through chance encounters which can 'help break barriers' and thus potentially contribute to 'reconciliation and inte-gration'. By creating room for 'unexpected or surprise encounters, [they thus] illustrate both the potential and challenges of having a less segregated city' (CinC, 2012: p. 1). This potential is largely unfulfilled in the spaces of the new capitalist city, too.

The intangible condition of the interface area

Northern Ireland has officially been governed by the terms of a ceasefire since 1994. Despite experiencing considerable political development in the intervening years, residential segregation remains a significant and costly problem, especially in the vicinity of interface areas. According to the Bel-fast City Council (2011), '[t]he impact on relationships, labour markets, the inefficient use of services and facilities, significant urban blight and poverty are all characteristics of divided areas'. To understand the contin-ued problem of segregation, one needs to look no further than the 2001 Census, which showed that 70 percent of the population of the city lived in highly polarised areas, defined as places that were at least 81 percent Catholic or Protestant; by contrast, only a small percentage, 10.7 percent of Catholics and 7.0 percent of Protestants, lived in mixed communities. Such polarisation is highest in working-class areas and areas of social housing, which have limited access to shared public services and resources (Shirlow and Murtagh, 2006). Indeed, considering that 91 percent of social housing estates in the city are controlled by the Northern Ireland Housing Executive, which are strictly polarised by religion and community background, public housing in Belfast provides the most segregated residential environment in the country (Shuttleworth and Lloyd, 2007).

One key difficulty with such a pattern of divided territorial control is that new land cannot be created. Therefore, land cannot be 'won' unless there is a perceived 'loss' by the other side. This focuses the attention of both sides on the shared areas between territories, the control of which can lead to intercommunity disputes (Stevenson, 2010). And such disputes only generate further socio-spatial exclusion in the future (Schnell and Yoav, 2001). In such conditions, patterns of fear and intimidation extend beyond residential segregation to everyday interactions in public space (Madanipour, 2010). Separation and insular community behaviour thus have a circular effect, as myths propagated about the 'other side' reduce the desire for future integration (Goldie and Brid, 2010; Figure 3.3).

In contrast to these negative effects of population separation, everyday mixing and encounter in social space contribute to individual understanding of diversity. Of course, the opposite condition is that a lack of interaction between population groups in common spaces contributes to a 'mutual lack of information' between them (Buonfino and Hilder, 2006). Continual negotiation of diversity occurs chiefly through the local 'micro-politics' of everyday interaction between individuals and groups. While acknowledging 'habitual contact in itself is no guarantor of cultural exchange', the mixing of individuals in shared environments with shared activities allows them to overcome the fear of the stranger and disrupts easy labelling of the stranger as an enemy and initiates new attachments (Amin, 2002).

Figure 3.3 'There's more in common . . . than what divides us', Peaceline wall, Belfast.

The possibility of social change, hence, may be tested through everyday practices in mixed neighbourhoods, workplaces, schools, leisure sites, and public spaces. Everyday social dynamics offers a valuable form of contact, presenting the opportunity for informal exchanges or marginal encounters with 'others' in an undemanding, casual manner. This can create positive experiences and may lead to other, higher-intensity interactions. According to Jan Gehl (2011), 'these modest "see and hear contacts (pp. 15)" must be considered in relation to other forms of contact and as part of a whole range of social activities, from simple and noncommittal contacts to complex and emotionally involved connections'. Daily interaction and presence within crowds, in particular, builds 'studied trust' and shared perspectives in urban multiplicity, and such increased trust and integration can build a sense of a shared society. Thus, feeling safe and secure in space is a vital precursor to fostering trust and encouraging new uses (Lownsbrough and Beunderm, 2007).

In the divided context, Gaffikin et al. (2010) argue that the provision of space for mixing and chance encounters can support reconciliation and integration. Positive actions of mixing have likewise been found to create room for unexpected encounters and illustrate both the potential and challenges of having a less segregated city (CinC, 2012). Komarova (2010) further emphasises the importance of sharing space as a social resource, noting that such spaces may otherwise be subject to factors which limit accessibility and inclusivity and limit its ability to play a positive role in healing. Key factors affecting inclusivity are discussed individually in the following four sections on 'Territorial ownership: between the physical and physiological', 'Spatial economy and urban regeneration', 'The discursive condition of the inaccessible city', and 'The micro-politics of the everyday contact'.

Territorial ownership: between the physical and spatial domains of influence

Residential segregation has been entrenched in the history of Belfast since its foundation and has rendered the city land of territories. People are born, educated, medically treated, and buried in the same locations as their ancestors in a culture that survives through the reproduction of division (O'Dowd and Komarova, 2013). Limited accessibility to border areas reduces freedom of mobility and produces patterns of spatial intimidation through community surveillance (Belfast City Council, 2011; Goldie and Brid, 2010). Yet such territorialisation is as much a practice as an imposed geography, which lives on both through physical walls and barriers and the display of flags and emblems and the power of mental maps.

In such conditions of division physical barriers may be used to stop or reduce tensions between the parties. Such a technique is evident in such cities as Nicosia, Mostar, Beirut, and Belfast. From manually constructed temporary barriers to permanent walls as high as 14 metres, these barriers have emerged as substantial signifiers of spatial experience in Belfast and remarkable landmarks in the urban fabric. The most prominent of these 'Peace Lines' divides the Nationalist Falls area from the Unionist Shankill area in West Belfast. At 800 metres in length and 10.8 metres in height, it was built in 1969 as an 'act of desperation' by a community in extreme conflict (Jarman, 2012). At that time, such partitions immediately reduced the threat of violence, yet by so doing, they justified paranoia and fear of the 'other side', and ever since, communities behind the walls have developed stereotyped fears of the 'unknown other' that have had a 'toxic' effect on social coexistence (Ibid.: p. 76). This form of physical separation is also a hindrance and chronic obstacle to normalisation between communities (Harbottle, 1970). Yet the presence of some 99 such discrete physical barriers across the city, one-third of which have been constructed since the ceasefire, provides telling evidence of how physically interwoven the city's communities traditionally were and how entrenched in everyday practice the notion of division now is (Jarman, 2012).

Visual markers such as flags, murals, and the painting of kerbstones and lampposts are further territorial indicators, used as expressions of cultural identity and claims to each community's 'right' to such manners of expression (Bryan et al., 2010). In fact, 'everyday spatial behaviour of people in Northern Irish towns and cities is dictated by the demarcation of public space through flags, murals and kerbstone painting' (Ibid.). And, following almost daily protests since December 2012, the failure of the US-led political process in December 2013 to arrange a deal to curtail the flying of the Unionist flag over City Hall provided evidence of the continued significance of flags as revered symbols of community identity (BBC News, 2012).

Physiological barriers are maps of fear that destabilise the popular perception of space, leading individuals to develop 'coping strategies' to help avoid perceived danger. These include mental maps of spaces seen to offer safe routes of travel, developed mainly through personal experience and community knowledge (Jarman and Bell, 2009). As guides to the use of space, these may then be passed down through generations, reproducing everyday spatial understandings and navigation strategies in younger generations and perpetuating the cycle of conflict (Anderson, 2004). It is this insularity which contributes to the lack of positive intercommunity relationships, which, in turn, can be an obstacle to shared space (Goldie and Brid, 2010; Figure 3.4).

Spatial economy and urban regeneration

There is a credible argument that processes of privatisation and commercialisation may compromise access to public space and increase social stratification (Baird, 2011). Nevertheless, Murtagh (2008) argues that the present wave of urban-regeneration projects appealed to Belfast authorities because it seemed to provide new workplaces and dwellings free of existing

Figure 3.4 The Peaceline Wall that divides Shankill Road from Falls Road, Belfast.

ownership structures and sectarian claims; they could thus be classified as 'neutral' or 'corporate' spaces, as opposed to traditionally 'Protestant' or 'Catholic' territories. Adopting a new imagery of 'low risk, glitzy and specu-lator sites' was also key to marketing such spaces to investors and tourists (CinC, 2012).

Some argue, however, that these city-centre regeneration projects are alienating and that members of the city's working-class communities are excluded from them. The high-profile Titanic Quarter is particularly seen as an example of a project intended to increase shared space in the city which has only further compromised the public realm by implicitly excluding large parts of the Belfast population along a socio-economic divide (Ibid.: p. 58). In a counterargument, however, Iveson writes that there has been no such loss of public life; instead, the publicness that such places supposedly dimin-ish is, in fact, a 'phantom . . . never actually realised in history but haunting the frameworks for understanding the present' (Iveson, 2007: p. 6).

Kelly (2012: p. 60), nevertheless, criticises the neoliberal economic approach to this form of development and highlights the irony that despite the significant amount of public money invested in the creation of a Titanic museum, the high price of entrance tickets excludes most working-class families from visiting it. Being located on the city's periphery, the Titanic Quarter would also seem to need to offer a series of public attractions to encourage families and young people to make the long journey out to it. But aside from the museum and neighbouring commercial facilities and shopping centres, there are arguably no spaces for average working-class families to engage with. Such new 'public' space, therefore, remains isolated from the everyday experience of working-class people, indicating how, through processes of gentrification, it has only produced new territories of exclusion (Kelly, 2012).

From another viewpoint, however, this only represents a normalisation of the condition of Belfast as a modern capitalist city whose public spaces are reliant on private investment. Murtagh (2011: p. 218), for example, writes that 'in reality, Belfast has caught up with the neo-liberalisation of the urban space familiar in other late capitalist cities but in more selective and potential unstable ways'. There is no more obvious sign of this condition than the series of bank buildings surrounding Belfast City Hall, whose overly protective and inaccessible ground-floor facades provide a measure of security for the invested capital they represent. While justified on security grounds, such designs are intimidating and unengaging. In fact, public space in Belfast's city centre is largely designed according to three interlocked spatial-optimisation concerns: to facilitate processes of capital exchange based on commercial and financial communication, to minimise security risks to business establishments, and to minimise direct contact between historic residential areas and the city centre. The labyrinth of streets and access routes around the Castlecourt Shopping Centre are thus carefully designed to turn it into a wall around which it is impossible to walk or drive.

The appearance of Writers Square, a supposedly well-designed public space opposite the historic St Anne's Church, is similarly intimidating. Although the design of surrounding buildings, such as those on William Street and Church Street, attempt to relate to it as a public open space, many of the businesses formerly occupying their ground-floor areas have closed down or relocated, replacing a lively public edge with a defensive border of graffiti-stained shutters. Furthermore, one full edge of this square is dominated by the massive Police Ombudsman office building, whose ground-floor facade is blocked off to prevent any possible engagement with passersby. Writers Square has thus fallen victim to its location at an edge of conflict in a border area.

Discursive condition of the inaccessible city

Unsurprisingly, the creation of an 'Accessible and Connected City' remains a main strategic objective of the Masterplan for Belfast (2012–2015), with a stated focus on 'enhancing accessibility and connectivity internationally, regionally and locally'. While segregation and physical and social inequality are intertwined on several levels, urban segregation can generally be considered a spatial manifestation of social polarisation (Madanipour, 2010). Thus, groups living in segregated communities typically experience limitations in terms of access to publicly funded local services. Indeed, Shirlow and Murtagh found that 78 percent of Belfast's population did not use their nearest public facilities because these were located on the 'wrong side' of a community boundary. Thus, more than 75 percent of individuals fail to use their local health centre, and in the Ardoyne and Upper Ardoyne interface area, 82 percent do not use the nearest leisure centre, opting instead to travel to another part of the city to one frequented by members of their own ethnonational group (Shirlow and Murtagh, 2006).

While segregation permeates many of the city's sectors and zones, with greater incidence in the northern and eastern sections, it is also divided around 'the commuter belt', where economic development generally follows a series of corridors, such as Titanic & Harbour, City Centre, and University. The heavy reliance on car transport and clusters of inwardly focused residential enclaves here has also created a number of voids in the built fabric that generate an unfriendly environment for pedestrians and cyclists. Yet, with more than half of all households in inner-city areas not having cars, the city's pedestrian network needs to be improved to create a better-connected city (Gaffikin et al., 2008). However, such a project is currently impeded not only by social exclusion but also by class stratification. Thus, mothers from segregated communities in the inner city may not be able to visit more outlying districts due to lack of economic resources and the difficulties in transporting young children to the area (CinC, 2012).

Group and individual mobility thus affects people's ability to access, use, and interact with each other in shared spaces. And in this regard Gaffikin and Morrissey (2011) note that a number of communities in contact with the city's inner belt display an 'acute relationship between deprivation, residential segregation and violence'. This has been heightened by the development of a 'twin speed city', which evolved with the economic boom, and according to which groups with skills and education excel, while those without such advantages remain tied to their estates (Murtagh, 2010). The report 'Crossing the Line' likewise asserts that 'education and skills deficit lead to a situation of no skills, no job, no reason to travel', which limits the 'freedom of movement' of residents of interface communities (Goldie and Brid, 2010: p. 32). Moreover, people who lack qualifications and skills see themselves as more vulnerable in external engagements with others and, as a result, withdraw more into their locality. This eventually results in a situation whereby 'the insularity of segregated communities obstructs the creation of shared physical, psychological and organisational space' (Ibid.: p. 32).

A further problem in Belfast is that municipal policies related to the condition of shared space remain fragmented due to the number of departments involved in this multidimensional issue; there is not even a precise definition of what shared space is (Komarova, 2010). Relationships between community groups and government agencies suffer from this lack of coherent, unified policies, 'with the consequence that some policies tend to reinforce separatist lifestyles and segregated spaces' (Gaffikin et al., 2008: p. vi). And poor channels of communication provide a further disincentive for community groups to work with public bodies (Goldie and Brid, 2010).

In order to realise positive change, governmental initiatives need to focus on a clear strategy that increases the extent of shared space, extends it beyond the narrow suburban connectivity belt, and improves its accessibility. This would encourage a spreading of intercommunity tolerance that might provide a catalyst for change (Jones and Boujenko, 2011) But who is the actual owner of such space and the de-facto decision-maker in matters related to it – the communities in which it exists, the state, or the public at large? Ownership of space is indeed a key feature in ethnic-national conflict, and processes related to the planning and programming of such areas may play a valuable role in helping the city heal. According to Gaffikin et al. (2010: p. 2), 'since space is so central to the overall conflict, and planning is the main instrument for social shaping of space, planning is unavoidably central to the conflict's resolution'. Constructive engagement between communities in this process could help break down barriers and potentially contribute to integration. But for this to occur, planning policy needs to account for the issue of segregation in zoning policy, land-use decisions, and the design of transport infrastructure and thus grapple directly with the way spatial and interaction patterns are currently affected by ethnonational divides (Shirlow and Murtagh, 2006).

If such conditions prevailed, the process of physical urban development could be a benefit to social cohesion, as development projects could bring together different groups in a process of negotiation where the discussion of individual projects allowed a forum for the mediation of larger conflicts (Bollens, 2007). In recognition of this condition, in 2012 the research group Planning for Spatial Reconciliation insisted that community collaboration be integrated into planning processes as a way to not only to improve the urban design by addressing community needs but also to improve community relations. One positive step in this direction has been a new 'duty of community planning' on the part of local councils. Since 2015 these councils have been required to consult local communities on decisions related to the delivery of local public services, allowing them to shape projects that affect everyday life (BBC News, 2012). While this has been hailed as a constructive move and welcomed by the Institute of Royal Town Planners Northern Ireland, this group has expressed concern about the lack of detail in associated legislation. It specifically pointed out that it is the very interactive nature of the new relationship between communities and the planning process that must be stressed if this initiative is to avoid creating further community fragmentation (Sore, 2011).

The micro-politics of the everyday public space

Typically overlooked by politicians and strategic planners alike, the design of everyday environments may provide a significant tool for improving knowledge about other groups, playing down mutual prejudices, and helping reintegrate the population. It is through everyday exchanges in public spaces, and buildings that the demonised other may be naturalised as similarly peaceful human beings. Such everyday intercommunity communication takes place most frequently in relation to public services, in the city's shopping areas and employment centres, and in proximity to homes and domestic environments. Admittedly, research shows that no clear line may be drawn between the public and private spheres (Sheller and Urry, 2003). Yet three different types of shared space have been shown to accommodate most everyday urban interactions. First are traditionally understood sites of shared urban space, such as the square, the piazza, and the park, which represent collective belonging and in relation to which all members of the public have equal spatial ownership rights. The second type is representative of social exchange, which comprises an arena of encounter, discussion, and debate, regardless of whether particular sites are publicly or privately owned. The café and theatre are two such typical physical spaces, while media and the internet represent non-physical forms.

Informal encounters in everyday life describe the third type of shared space, which may be understood as a de facto space of shareness, as in the street or on a public bus. Jan Gehl (2011) states that daily interactions in these de facto spaces of shareness provide multiple possibilities for an individual to experience the functioning of others in various situations, by means simply of seeing and hearing them. While such contact may be of low intensity, casual interactions may significantly improve cognition of others as equally human, creating positive associations that may open the way to higher-intensity interactions. These spaces are, in fact, more complex than they first appear, Indeed, 'these modest "see and hear contacts" must be considered in relation to other forms of contact and as part of the whole range of social activities, from simple and noncommittal contacts to complex and emotionally involved connections' (Gehl, 2011: p. 15; Sore, 2011).

In a way, everyday exchanges on the order of 'seeing and hearing others' in social spaces may do much to advance understanding of diversity; in particular, it may help diminish the fears and harsh expectations of encounter that emerge at the physical barriers of interface zones. In the quest to overcoming difference, such continual negotiation of diversity might even constitute a local 'micro-politics' of everyday encounter between individuals and groups. Habitual contact may thus be no 'guarantor of cultural exchange', but when individuals make contact in shared environments by means of shared activities, it may help them overcome fear of the other and so develop new attachments (Amin, 2002). In line with Amin's theory, Lofland acknowledges that

> incidental interactions among strangers do draw upon and constitute shared meanings, common values and cooperation for collective purposes. People accomplish this by learning, negotiating and reproducing overarching principles for stranger interaction and basic, albeit unspoken, modes of civility.
>
> (Vertovec, 2007a: p. 6)

After all, public space is generally the place where individuals become aware of others, helping them to avoid doing harm to one another based simply on 'judgements of difference' (Ibid.).

The process of daily interaction with (and presence in) crowds, in particular, may help build 'studied trust' in conditions of urban multiplicity, leading to the development of a sense of security, which may encourage the development of further possibilities of exchange (Lownsbrough and Beunderman, 2007). Placing people in living settings where engagement with strangers seems natural may also disrupt the easy labelling of the stranger as an enemy (Ibid.). One fruitful strategy by which to create new venues for change and intervention in conditions of urban division might thus simply be to increase opportunities for people to engage in everyday practices of cultural exchange in the design of such places as workplaces, schools, nurseries, health centres, and leisure sites.

Part II

Architecture and spatial memory in rural and urban environments

4 The architecture of the linen mills and the social history of Ulster's industrial villages

Introduction

In *Words and Buildings: A Vocabulary of Modern Architecture*, Adrian Forty (2000) cites the theories of the phenomenologist philosopher Christian Norberg-Schulz, suggesting that the two fundamentals of architecture are 'space' and 'character'. According to Forty (Ibid.: p. 120), Norberg-Schulz stressed how '[s]pace, or whatever is enclosed, is where man is; while character, denoted by adjectives, is what satisfies man's need to identify himself with the environment, to know how he is in a certain place'. To Forty, 'character' represents both 'a general comprehending atmosphere, and [. . .] the concrete form and substance of the space-defining element'. In light of these observations, a critical element of identity in Ulster is its picturesque rural landscape, against which the architecture of its towns and cities seems an elegant addition in an otherwise virgin paradise. Yet the contrast between unity and division must also be recognised in this landscape, because its quiet, natural beauty has been the result of sometimes fierce weather conditions and a long-standing history of polarisation.

Northern Ireland's Neolithic settlements, such as those uncovered along the River Erne and at Mountsandel on the Bann, once merged with dense forest (MacGabhann and McAllister, 2013). Later, fortifications such as Carrickfergus Castle were erected to guard key sites of access to inland areas from the sea. According to MacGabhann and McAllister (2013), until the 17th century, the west of Scotland and the east of Ulster constituted the former Dalriada kingdom, parts of which later became the territory of the MacDonalds of the Isles. The area thus had a long history of being connected, rather than separated, by the sea, a condition that produced similarities in language, music, and architecture.

Because of this historic orientation, coastal villages provide a distinctive figure in Ulster's landscape. Within this tradition, the quiet town of Portrush and its northern 'rock' offer a particularly striking image. Flanked on both sides by sandy beaches, Portrush developed partly on a peninsula shaped by the same geological forces that underlie the nearby Giant's Causeway, whose 40,000 basalt columns were created by an ancient volcanic fissure.

Against the force of the wind off the Northern Sea, Portrush's distinct coastal architecture takes the form of colourful terrace houses and small hotels, uniquely designed to offer cues to visiting sailors as to where to land (Abdelmonem, 2013).

The rugged natural character of Portrush is more the rule than the exception on Ireland's north coast, and coastal settlements in Ulster, in general, developed in response to this condition (Abdelmonem, 2013). Indeed, the outlook of the vernacular architecture of towns and other more remote places here makes them feel more like settlements at the water's boundary than the edge of the land. This has included the development of forms to support bathing in all its forms, from ancient ritual sweathouses to Victorian public baths erected for sanitary purposes, contemporary therapeutic seaweed and sulphur baths, lidos, modern swimming pools for leisure and sport, and spas both old and new (Larmour, 2013). Indeed, the tradition of open-sea bathing, developed in the Victorian era to promote health and well-being, still persists at Portrush in sites for 'ladies' and 'men's' bathing on the beaches of East Strand, West Strand, and Whiterocks (Ibid.).

Architects, artists, and musicians have all been inspired by this coastline and the fresh and authentic experience of confrontation it provides with weather and water. For architecture, the challenge has been to create places where people can enjoy and understand themselves between the familiar and the wild, on the edge of the land looking out to sea (Larmour, 2013). In coastal towns, however, this meant conforming to typical styles and patterns, whose modest scale was originally limited by the span of a pitched slate roof between rough, white-rendered, load-bearing walls (Ibid.). Commercial activities were concentrated along a high street/main street, with local residential streets developing around it in response to the distinctive topography and geology of each site.

One of the most distinctive experiences in Ulster today is the coastal railway journey that weaves through and around the rugged mountains that border the sea and that offers dramatic, fleeting views of the Ulster shoreline. This scenic quality has also led to towns with beaches and strands such as Portrush, Bangor, and Newcastle becoming significant touristic destinations. The tourist economy eventually brought a new scale of waterfront settlement to these places, originally in the form of Victorian terraces but more recently as high-end mansions. However, nothing catches the eye today along Northern Ireland's coast more than the extended-stay colonies of holiday caravans.

Yet, while rural Ulster has long been characterised by such outward-looking patterns of settlement, it also has a long tradition of farming and contains many inland villages, mostly developed around rivers, canals, and lakes. While Portrush, Bangor, and Newcastle may be representative of the former, Lisburn and Antrim are representative of the latter. And while this brief description serves to give a sense of its waterfront landscape, we now turn to our primary focus: the development of its inland industrial villages.

Figure 4.1 The extended waterfront of Portrush peninsula showing dense and topographical housing overlooking the harbour.

Figure 4.2 Holiday caravans site on the Northern Ireland coast, in Ballycastle.

Industrial evolution of linen mills in rural Ulster

Rural Ulster has been associated for three centuries with the linen indus-try, and the history of its many hamlets, villages, and towns owes much to the growth in demand for its highly sought-after production. Beginning in the late 18th century, the need to support this emerging industry and its essential infrastructure created the need for new forms of architecture and planning. Even today the imprint of this transformation remains evident in the form of ruined mills and chimneys (Thompson, 2012). The sheer size of these mills created centres of activity that defined the character of their localities through the flow of labour, capital, and products. Spatially and aesthetically, they were also formed according to an identifiable new lan-guage of industry with its own proportions, defined by an elegant rhythm and an array of openings over several storeys. Physically, their grandeur, boldness, and towering chimneys created prominent symbols in an other-wise rural landscape.

Northern Ireland has been synonymous with the production of linen for centuries. Indeed, linen industry was for a long time the main regional trade, at one stage employing more than 40 percent of the working popu-lation. But the decline of this industry has now resulted in most of its mills being closed or left in ruins. From the two-centuries-old Templemoyle Mills of the Dinsmore family (1791–2007) to Ulster Carpets in Portadown to one of the few surviving manufacturers, Thomas Ferguson Linen Mills in Banbridge, the Irish linen industry once flourished and shaped the Ulster landscape. At its peak, the mills at the heart of the Irish textile industry employed 70,000 people on 37,000 looms. Most towns and villages in Ulster had a mill or a factory linked to some other aspect of this industry, and many of them owed their existence to the evolution of a single family-owned business. At the height of production in 1955, there were 55 linen spinning mills in Northern Ireland, but none now remain open, with the last one having closed in 2009. More interestingly, these mill complexes were once central to the development of industrial villages and to a char-acteristic architecture of streets lined with terraced houses that developed around them.

A Department of Environment report (2011) has acknowledged the promi-nent effect that linen manufacturers had on the development of both rural set-tlements and urban structures in Northern Ireland and in Ulster, in particular. Linen and clothing factories fuelled the development of many small villages in the north throughout the 19th century, with mill sheds dominating the skyline until the late 20th century. The industry emerged following the decline of the farming economy in the 18th and 19th centuries and led to a transformation of many rural settlements (Thompson, 2012). Due to the development of a mill economy and associated flows of goods, many such settlements boomed, growing from villages of a few hundred residents into well-populated towns with a few thousand residents. In these new industrial villages. dense arrays of new houses coalesced to form streets, along which new structures also appeared to accommodate necessary local services and amenities (Evans and Patton, 1987). Rural Ulster today has, according to The Northern Ireland Statistics and Research Agency (2008a), 650,342 people residing in 22 intermediate settlements, of which there are a total of 48 villages and 26 small villages and hamlets. Most of these experienced boom times connected to the Industrial Revolution at some point in their history over the past two centuries.

Such mill towns displayed similar patterns of growth, as they splayed outward to provide areas of housing for workers and to access canals or railway lines for transport. Such a new pattern of settlement developed mainly between 1830 and 1870 (Macneice, 1981). And it was accompanied by the development of a distinctive regional transportation infrastructure based around a network of waterways, similar to that of England, and comprising many buildings, locks, and bridges (Rothery, 1997: p. 193). The new industrial economy eventually allowed inland settlements like Portadown and Banbridge to grow into major towns. But across the undulating green landscape, a combination of mill roofs, chimneys, and clusters of pitched-roof houses provided a picturesque image of togetherness and a coherent blending of man, industry, and nature, in some ways similar to the region's coastal settlements (Evans and Patton, 1987).

In such an evolving rural-scape, mill owners and early industrialists played an important role, which has been largely overlooked in the literature on Ulster. The mill owners, by definition, made decisions as to where to construct their mills, what forms they would take, and what associated infrastructure would be built to house workers and enable the transportation of materials. At a time when farming was in decline, these people were praised for making investments that offered jobs for the rural population and provided them access to services and amenities (Gill, 1964). Yet their developments also affected Ulster's cities, which grew as connecting nodes for this new industry.

According to McDermott (1975: p. 99), older forms of Georgian planning gave way at this time to new gridiron forms in which factories, mills, and warehouses were surrounded by streets of identical red-brick houses that offered a minimum, yet decent standard of living. It was also during this period that the red-brick character of Northern Ireland's cities was established, a tradition that contemporary architects have had to address in modern designs to maintain coherence and resonance with the past. This tradition may still be seen in Belfast in recent buildings such as the Lyric Theatre and in the new development along Ridgeway Street that is nestled at the bottom of a row of red-brick terrace houses. As the industrial population grew, the demand for shared services also grew, leading to the construction of churches, bigger schools, and hospitals, and it likewise prompted a need for new administrative structures and sites of management such as public buildings, markets, courthouses, banks, shops, colleges, and libraries (Dixon, 1973).

The linen industry continued to develop into the 20th century, such that in 1921, 70,000 people were directly employed in it, representing 40 percent of the population of Northern Ireland. But by 1949, only 20 percent of the population was employed either directly or indirectly in it. The industry had provided an essential basis for the growth of cities like Lisburn, known as the site of the first linen mill in Ulster. In 1821 the Census revealed that 4,684 persons resided there, and this number would eventually grow to 71,465 (Census, 2001). However, Lisburn's proximity to Belfast, the regional capital and chief port less than 10 miles away, also encouraged the development of other industries towards the end of the 19th century. Indeed, by 1880, the linen industry was not even the most prosperous in Ireland (Harrison, 2008). It had also always been a precarious endeavour, as economic uncertainty prevailed from the 1860s to the early 20th century. Thus, following periods of stagnation, depression, and mild prosperity, toward the end of the century the mills started to close one after another as a result of competition from producers in the Far East, Europe, and America.

The decline in textile and linen manufacturing has had an especially adverse impact on the character and environment of rural villages since the early 2000s, as these places can no longer support the communities they were built to serve. In 'Travels around Northern Ireland', Fletcher (2000) thus noted the coexistence of beauty and ugliness in the region: 'The beauty of what was, and the ugliness it has become'. The Department of Culture, Arts and Leisure of Northern Ireland (2006: p. 4) has similarly stressed how industrial decline and insensitive development have left additional scars on the grim and mediocre architecture of Ulster, a condition compounded by the political instability of the Troubles. Many Georgian and Victorian mills thus today stand derelict and in such a state of disrepair that they are at risk of demolition (Thompson, 2012). For the past two decades there has been virtually no investment in these mills. Despite their prominence as landmarks, this rich industrial heritage has been largely abandoned, despite the many voices calling for its preservation (Rothery, 1997).

Through an examination of several of these industrial villages, we now explore how the Irish linen industry helped shape the rural environment of Ulster. And we analyse how their closure and abandonment is once again transforming it.

Architecture of memory and the social narratives

Mill villages such as Gilford in County Down, Sion Mills in County Tyrone, and Bessbrook in County Armagh were predominantly once all of similar size, scale, and population and generally formed within a few decades of each other. Developed and funded by mill owners as sites for their businesses, they expanded outward as nodes of production in a larger industrial web. Yet even though they once employed as much as 85 percent of the local population, as in Gilford, the mills at their centres all lie derelict today (Cairns, 2002: p. 54). Attempts have since been made to transform these structures into outlet shopping malls or hotels, but many of these efforts have failed, with the result being that the population has also now lost its memories of active industry and the former associated sense of community.

To understand the evolution of Gilford and its decline, it is instructive to compare figure-ground drawings of it at different eras. A comparison of 1804, 1834, and 1928 provides particularly revealing insights on the impact of its flax spinning mill on its form (Figure 4.3). From the kernel of a small, irregular village, the new industrial settlement eventually came to be ordered in a Y shape parallel to the River Bann, which was flanked by industrial buildings and local shops. The village had emerged in the 18th century based on the location of several small corn mills, and thus, its main street was always called Mill Street. In 1804 the town also included a number of barns, haylofts, and shops and other amenities for residents. Some 30 years

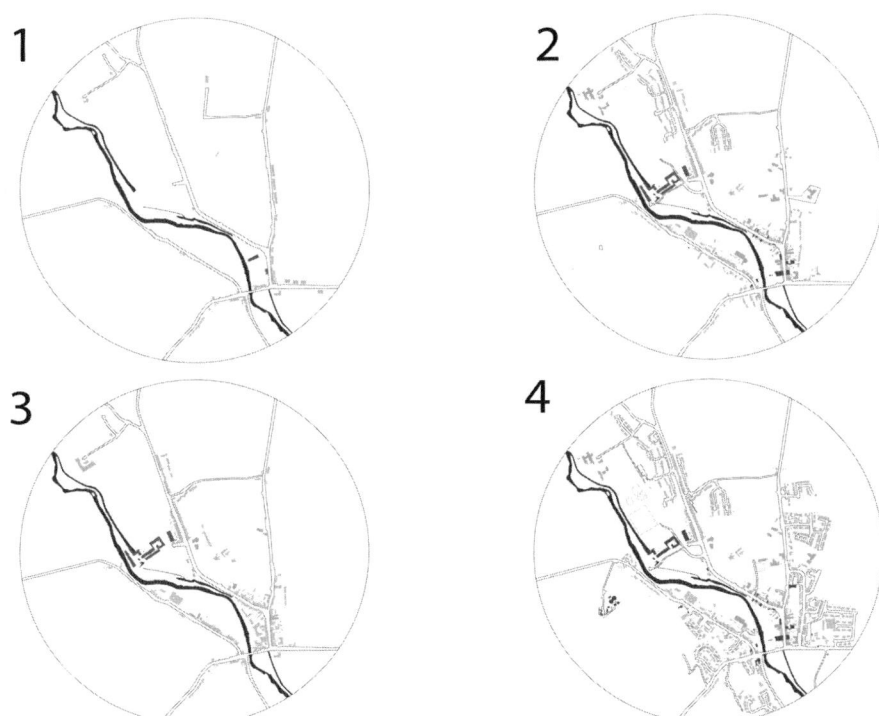

Figure 4.3 The evolution of Gilford Village: (1) 1834 map of Gilford; (2) 1928 map of Gilford; (3) 1974 map; (4) 2012 map.

Source: Developed by the authors from Ordinance Survey Northern Ireland (OSNI) Maps.

later, however, the village had become a small town. Indeed, the Ordnance Survey Memoirs of 1834 described Gilford as

> a small town . . . only two streets – narrow and irregular. The houses consist of seventy-five of one storey, twenty-three of two storeys and two of three storeys. They are mostly stone and brick; a few are made solely of brick. Cottages . . . generally stone, mostly thatched with three or four rooms on the ground floor.
>
> (Day, 1990; Macneice, 1981: p. 175)

At this time, the housing seems to have been quite organised – not scattered as would have been typical for a purely agricultural settlement but spread along the main roads, giving them a sense of purpose. The relatively poor, uneven local road network leading from the village, composed largely of dirt tracks for horses and carts, was augmented by the limited opportunity for travel and transport on the River Bann. But there were no public buildings or places of worship, as the residents, who were recorded as 529, travelled to nearby villages for recreation, religious services, and other needs (Bassett, 1886: p. 263).

The building of a large mill in Gilford in 1839, however, caused the town to grow rapidly into one of the largest centres of linen manufacturing in the world (Logan, 1999: p. 78) (Figure 4.4). Industrial production eventually led to the employment of around 1,600 persons, requiring the construction of a significant number of new houses, many of which were built between 1870 and 1915 (Macneice, 1981: p. 173). The Dunbar family, the owners of the local mill complex, raised enough money to build these houses to the north-east of the industrial facilities, creating a series of local streets and communities, including Ann Street, Bann Street, Bannview Terrace, Connors Row, Sandy Row, Prospect Terrace, High Street, and Hill Street. In the decade of World War II, the number of these houses then trebled again, from 104 in 1941 to 333 in 1951.

Due to economic cycles, famine, and emigration to the United States, the population of Gilford fluctuated through the 19th and 20th centuries, from a peak of 2,892 in 1861 to just 832 in 1937, according to the Census in those years. And to provide for the needs of this population, the Dunbar family constructed religious and other buildings on land they owned, including St Paul's Church of Ireland and an adjacent school directly opposite the mill gates, as well as a Presbyterian Church and St John's Roman Catholic Chapel. A courthouse was built on Dunbarton Street, and Dunbarton House, a secluded grand Georgian mansion for the Dunbar family, was constructed on picturesque grounds surrounded by forests and fields. A second school was later constructed on the main street, Mill Street, flanked by public houses, a cinema for silent films, a post office, a fever hospital, and other industrial buildings. Another feature of the mature development of the town was a large, swan-inhabited pond, designed as an attractive feature in front of the mill. Madden Railway Station was also built a mile away, on the main Belfast–Dublin railway corridor, to facilitate the mobility of labour

Figure 4.4 Gilford Mills Complex, Gilford, Co Down: (a) aerial view of the complex, undated; (b) view of the abandoned and run-down mills today.

Source: (a) Courtesy of Henry Clark; (b) Courtesy of Paul Allen.

and the shipment of products from the Gilford mill. Through the 1970s the village remained a centre of population, with 1,619 recorded residents in 1971 and 1,541 in 1981. But most new housing development and growth at this time took place outside the old town centre, most notably as a result of the development of Dunbarton Bungalows to the north and Woodlands to the south. The train station was closed in 1965.

The Gilford mill has now stood empty since its closure in 1986, an event that had a significant impact on the village. An overall decline in business and trade activity there has thus led to several other buildings in the centre of town and on its outskirts becoming similarly rundown. Indeed, Gilford's spectacular Georgian architecture and historically significant industrial village fabric are facing erasure in the face of new development, an outcome that would have a devastating impact on the memory of historic patterns of settlement in the region. Evidence of such loss had already become apparent in 1947 when the Northern Ireland Planning Advisory Board (1947: p. 23) observed that 'new housing schemes alone will take up many hundreds of acres, and if these new estates become permanent, scars of ugliness will remain on the face of the countryside'. Gilford has since been listed on the Northern Ireland Multiple Deprivation Measure as being in much need of investment and regeneration and redevelopment.

Sion Mills provides another example of the linen industry's impact on the architectural development of Ulster but from a different perspective. Alongside the River Mourne, in the far west of Ulster, it was recognised as a favourable site for a linen mill and employment centre early in the 19th century. Ferguson (2005: p. 27) has documented historical accounts of the location and the initial vision of its development by the Herdman family. Thus, in a letter to Andrew Mulholland on 10 August 1835, James Herdman wrote,

> [W]e drove along the river this morning from Omagh, a distance of 15 miles, and the country appears to be one of the best situated for manufactures in Ireland. The more I see of this fine country, the more can I see the vast importance of having a branch in it.
>
> (Ferguson, 2005: p. 27)

Eventually the industrial development in Sion Mills under the direction of the Herdman family came to feature a more explicit version of the Tudor/Elizabethan style with an Irish character. And for this reason it is more representative than Gilford of the architecture of Ulster villages (Ferguson, 2005). Perhaps more significantly, however, the Herdman family adopted an explicit policy of non-discrimination between sects and denominations, providing work, housing, and schooling for all.

Early settlement at Sion Mills, as was the case in Gilford, had been based on a corn mill, which attracted a small population of workers. The form of the town was also defined as an edge between the main road and the River Mourne, which ran parallel to it. As it later developed under the Herdmans, Sion Mills continued to be dominated by this straight road. But it was also rigorously structured according to a series of other roads that reached out to connect to other, more scattered areas of settlement, typical of the area's agricultural economy before the arrival of the linen industry.

After the initial construction of its linen mill in 1835 (Figure 4.5), the village was given further straight edges through the decision to build a railway

Figure 4.5 Herdman's Mill, Sion Mills, 15 August 1935: (a) exterior view of the Herdman's Mill complex; (b) interior of the Reeling Room.

Source: By Robert John Welch (1859–1936). Courtesy of © National Museums NI, Collection Ulster Museum, ref: BELUM.Y.W.09.51.1.

line to it and construct a train station there in 1852. This created a dividing edge between the area of industrial activity and nearby residential areas. (Fig. 4.6) The Herdmans also encouraged people from outside the area to move to the village for work, especially those uninterested in living in conditions of sectarian division, as in Ulster's cities. Ultimately, the town came to be structured around its mill complex. This was significantly redeveloped between 1884 and 1888 through the construction of a two-storey extension built from greystone with a slate roof. In 1907, a second three-storey extension was completed, using yellow and red brick. And at the turn of the century, the Herdmans added public spaces and services to the complex, including a bowling green and tennis courts, in an effort to establish a greater sense of community amongst the town's diverse population.

Housing in the village initially consisted of one-storey, terraced cottages for workers. But with heightened demand for production and a booming trade in Irish linens around the turn of the 20th century, second storeys were added to many of these structures to accommodate an expanded

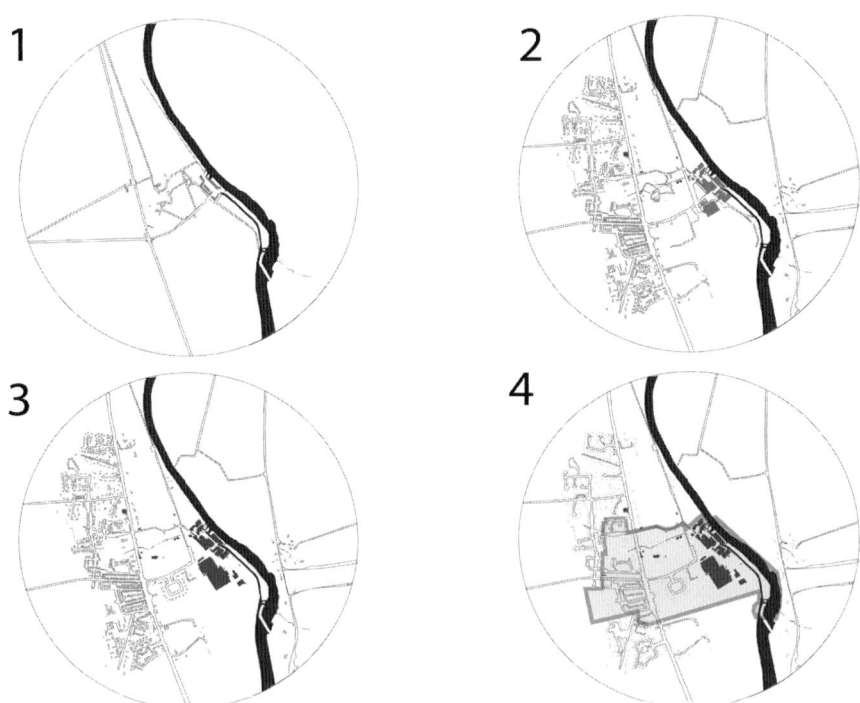

Figure 4.6 The evolution of Sion Mills: (1) Sion Mills 1854 map; (2) 1976 map; (3) 2012 Sion Mills; (4) Sion Mills Building Preservation Trust.

Source: Developed from Ordinance Survey Northern Ireland (OSNI) Maps. Courtesy of Paul Allen.

labour force (Ferguson, 2005). This and the construction of public buildings accentuated the sense of order in the layout of the village, a characteristic strengthened by the main street as a built edge in the landscape. The train station also grew in size, and the local school was replaced with a new one in 1879. The architecture of the entire ensemble was distinctive and truthful to its age and level of development. The schoolhouse was particularly distinctive, built in stone with Gothic gables, timber bargeboards, and a slate roof. It also featured a prominent chimney that faced the road and replicated the mill chimney on a smaller scale. Sion House, home to the mill owners, was also designed by the well-known English architect William Unsworth in 1883 in a manner different from other square Irish country homes of the time, taking the form of a well-crafted large, half-timbered, partly plastered, Elizabethan mansion with verandas and balconies (DOE, 1977).

By 1976, further extensions were made to the industrial buildings in Sion Mills to accommodate larger machines, warehouses, and factory space. During this new period of investment, more housing was added, and a better lifestyle was created through a progressive and more tolerant working and living atmosphere. Public facilities at the time came to include imitation Tudor and Elizabethan buildings housing such local institutions as pubs and church halls. However, a rise in private automobile ownership and the use of trucks to transport goods right to the door of this innovative factory led to the demolition of the railway station. Nevertheless, there remains a sense of rhythm on entering the village today, established through its rows of houses and the unified scale of its public buildings set around large green spaces. This character is further maintained in the streetscape by means of distinctive streetlights, bus stops, and a town clock.

The Sion Mills linen mill, however, which dated to 1835 and once employed more than 1,000 people, ceased production in 2004. At the centre of the town, it is now part of a conservation area with more than 40 listed buildings. Since it closed, the mill has unfortunately also been subject to almost yearly arson attacks, mainly in 2011, 2014, 2015, 2016, and 2017, which have caused significant damage to its architectural features. It remains a mystery why this historic building, which embodies a memory of tolerance and cohesive community development, has been so actively targeted. But other efforts to restore such structures to their original glory within important conservation areas have also been hampered by attempts to eliminate the traces of memory they provide (Thompson, 2012).

Gilford and Sion Mills provide insights into the development of other, similar Ulster villages. Most of these also have long histories of socio-economic development occasioned by individual investors motivated by a vision of connectivity, mobility, and production in the rural landscape. Development of facilities for the production of linen thus provided catalysts for community building and internal migration, and at times they allowed a high level of art and craft that provided these towns with a distinctive character, history, and architecture. According to Crawford (1972: p. 26), it was evident that 'the linen industry was to a great extent responsible for the rapid growth of the population in the country'.

The village of Bessbrook in County Armagh provides a third interesting case study within this larger history of industrial villages. However, what makes it particularly germane to our investigation is that it was initially developed as a non-sectarian 'model town' (Ritchie, 1876: p. 6). The irony of the situation is that, despite its success at maintaining this characteristic for more than a century, when its mill closed in 1987 it was transformed into a British Army base.

Located on the Dublin to Belfast corridor just outside of Newry, Bessbrook was ideally located in the emerging 19th-century rural Ulster landscape of production. It had good access to several ports and was nestled in a natural landscape of mountains and hills. At the time, Ritchie (1876: p. 12) provided an idyllic account of its mill: 'By night the place looks like a palace of glass, as the cheerful light, eloquent of labour and capital and intelligence, shines out of thousands of windows'. Moreover, the social experiment to produce an ideal industrial village, with no sectarian division, also meant the town had no need for public houses, pawn shops, or even a police station. And apart from the police station, which was introduced recently, the formal qualities of this ideal vision remain intact today.

Typical in form and structure to other villages, Bessbrook was developed around its mills and an associated transportation network. Houses emerged along its streets as a reaction to the arrival of waves of workers who were employed either in its mills or at a nearby granite quarry. The construction of Richardson's linen mill in 1845, in particular, brought substantial growth, and the town's population jumped from 207 (1841) to 544 (1851) and later to 674. By 1878, the mill grew to employ 1,532 people, resulting in a sevenfold increase in population in three decades (Harrison, 2008: p. 123). And with the increase of its population, the need arose for public buildings such as churches, schools, and community buildings. The opening of the Bessbrook and Newry Railway Company in October 1885, with a station directly opposite the mill, improved the transportation of goods to and from Newry (Adams and White, 1945: p. 39).

Such public infrastructure grew in size and type to include a distinguished town hall, designed by the architect William Watson and constructed in 1886, which remains today. According to the 15 March 1886 issue of *The Building News*,

> [owing to] the rapid increase of the population of this model village, consequent upon the yearly extension of Messrs. Richardson and Co.'s linen manufactories, Mrs Richardson, several years ago, decided that the erection of a town-hall would be a boon, and at the same time meet a great public want.

Figure 4.7 Mount Caulfield, Bessbrook, nd, by W. A. Green.

Source: Courtesy of National Museums NI, Collection Ulster Folk & Transport Museum; ref: HOYFM.WAG.2539. Courtesy of Paul Allen.

The town Hall stood at the heart of the village overlooking the school playground and was built almost entirely from Bessbrook granite. Immediately behind it was also a large hall designed for public entertainments, which could comfortably seat 800 people. The first floor of this building provided a lecture hall, a large billiard room, a lavatory, and sleeping apartments. According to *The Building News* (15 March 1886), its luxurious finishing was a testimony to the care and craft spent on the image of the town, which was reflective of the care for their environment exhibited of workers at Richardson Mills.

Originally built as a residence for the mill owners, the historic Mount Caulfield House was another notable structure in the town (Fig. 4.7). A three-storey house, it was located to the south of the mill. Today it is a listed building and still stands in reasonably good condition, with a projecting gable at one end and a curvilinear gable at the other. The village itself was also designated a Conservation Area in 1983, and as such, it has avoided the deterioration that has been the fate of so many other villages. However, the conservation area does not include the mill – only its pond, workers' cottages to the north, and the open grounds around it that help preserve its identity. Abandoned in 2007 after being used as an army barracks for two decades, the mill is now surrounded by a 15-foot-high barbed-wire fence and security cameras. It lost much of its character with the destruction of its most identifiable element, its chimney, and thus appears today as a large, empty warehouse. Nevertheless, it has been listed on the register of 'Buildings at Risk' as a former army barracks (DOE, 2012a).

Departure from memory: the emergence of neo-architecture of tourism in non-industrial Ulster

The case studies above show that visionary business owners and the demand for labour were the primary drivers of in the creation of active new communities around Ulster's rural linen mills. Some of these business owners were essentially town planners who set out to create ideal villages and tolerant communities. However, the decline of these mills and associated businesses today has had a detrimental effect on these places and the lives and social aspirations of their remaining residents. With no central economic raison d'etre or outside flow of investment, their houses and shops have gone into decline, and their historic public and commercial structures have in most instances become derelict. Yet Ulster's rural architecture once signalled the area's economic power. It is thus important to understand how this heritage still provides a shared memory distinct from the post-conflict condition of its cities.

This rich history of mill towns and villages, however, is at risk of disappearing entirely. Far from the circuits of the new urban economy, many historical landmarks have deteriorated to the point where they may not be salvageable. Several attempts have been made to restore mills or rebrand them as retail, business, or shopping centres, but these have largely failed. The fate of these once noble structures has also been clouded by arson attacks against several of the most historic of them, such as Herdman's Mill in Sion Mills. Significant sociocultural memories are still evident in the tangibility of this architecture. But as these buildings continue to collapse, so does this memory fade. Ultimately, however, the resurrection of this architecture can only come with a rejuvenation of these villages as relevant nodes in the contemporary Northern Ireland economy.

New forces are at work in the landscape of Ulster that may be paving the way for just such an architectural revival, however. In particular, tourism has emerged as a potential new economic driver, as visits from across Europe and North America have grown significantly since the beginning of the Northern Ireland peace process and the signing of the Good Friday Agreement. International competitions, races, and golf tournaments have also attracted many more visitors to the area in the last decade than in the previous 100 years. To date, it has been the North Coast that has attracted most of these visits. But tourism could be developed to address the potential of other areas of Ulster as well.

Interestingly, contemporary architecture has attempted to play a part in this new vision through new buildings that build on the artistic skills and crafts of the region, while introducing modern materials that capitalise

Figure 4.8 The Giant's Causeway Visitor Centre, County Antrim, by Heneghan Peng Architects: (a) external view showing the integration with natural landscape and green topography; (b) interior view of the busy visitor centre.

on its natural beauty. One example that might be cited here is Heneghan Peng Architects' Giant's Causeway Visitor Information Centre. The Giant's Causeway is a most challenging site due to its sharp topography and vast size. Instead of trying to compete with this quality, the architects chose to (Fig. 4.8) embed most of the building in the ground, leaving it visible only from the roadside. Covered with a sustainable green roof and walkways, most visitors will never notice the sheer volume of the building below, and its long black wall blades, designed to deflect the northern wind, provide further evidence of how such a building may be successfully integrated into this spectacular landscape.

5 Defensive architecture and the shaping of the urban experience

Introduction: permeability in public space

For the past century, urban space in Northern Ireland has been steeped in traditions of both diversification and segregation. Yet, while much of recent literature focuses on the last 40 years and conditions related to the Troubles, the fact that during the first half of the 20th century these spaces evolved as an active social domain and space of civic contestation has largely been overlooked. Most urban spaces in Northern Ireland grew organically, and it was not until the 1960s that Belfast's built environment was subject to significant changes under the effect of 'the restructuring plan for the Belfast sub-region, known as the Matthew Plan' (Sterrett et al., 2011: pp.102). For decades prior to this plan, however, Belfast's public spaces and squares had produced a considerable sense of civility, with the proliferation of pedestrian paths and walkways improving the quality of life in the city centre. To a large extent, such spaces still exist and continue to shape urban experience in Northern Ireland; however, their rehabilitation according to fresh design perspectives will be central to continuing to improve the post-conflict urban condition. In this regard, it must be remembered that the experience of a city through its streets and other public spaces can only be unlocked through continuing engagement. Thus, according to Pike (1981: p. 9),

> [t]he inhabitant or visitor experiences the city as a labyrinth, although one with which he may be familiar. He cannot see the whole of a labyrinth at once, except above, when it becomes a map. Therefore, his impression of it at street level at any given moment will be fragmentary and limited: rooms, buildings, streets. These impressions are primarily visual, but involve the other senses as well, together with a crowd of memories and associations.

If one reflects on public space in Belfast's city centre today, it is clear that its condition is indicative of broader political changes since the 1960s. More interestingly, however, is the realisation that the condition of this space may be a precursor to, if not a driver of, future political change. By looking at how civic space is actually used, it may therefore be possible to develop a more informed understanding of how different types of 'shared public space' can alter people's attitudes towards safe passage, socialisation, and cross-community engagement. During the later decades of the 20th century, however, it must be remembered that much of this space was boarded up and barricaded due to ongoing fear of violence and arson. And traces of such an unwelcome history remain embedded in the way public spaces are inherited, organised, and even designed. In particular, the buildings that surround these spaces and that frame them have for years been deliberately designed to prevent them from being damaged as a result of politically motivated attacks, even when such events were only a remote possibility.

It is in this context that we here seek to appraise the current condition of public spaces in Belfast's city centre and, particularly, how the design of building facades there affects the quality of the pedestrian experience and the possibility of safe and social engagement in an atmosphere of *shareness*. The condition of public spaces, in this sense, can help reveal how successful recent planning initiatives and architectural designs have been in transforming what was once the most vicious and insecure urban centre in Europe. This chapter thus emphasises how different methods, strategies, and decision-making processes, especially as related to facade design at the ground level, could be a powerful tool for re-creating a well-populated and socially active public realm in Belfast.

Civic space in Northern Ireland: a history of troubled public space

Ever since Northern Ireland came into existence in 1921 out of a state of conflict and division, public demonstrations have played a strong role in defining issues of identity in shared spaces (Bryan, 2015). And as an expression of dominance within its borders, Unionist groups have long employed civic space as a forum for parades and the display of their orange banners. Meanwhile, symbols and rituals of Irish nationalism have assumed equal prominence in spaces dominated by Nationalist groups. Policing and emergency legislation were instrumental in maintaining such a pattern of calculated political rivalry for decades (Ibid.). Moreover, because the public sphere is inherently political, the planning of public spaces in the cities of Northern Ireland also proceeded according to sectarian principles (Gaffikin et al., 2010).

Intrinsic political rivalry also meant that the everyday experience of civic space in large cities such as Belfast and Derry included occasional riots sparked by a range of provocative commemorations and symbolic displays. And the prevalence of such practices has long coloured the public sphere with the green and orange hues that symbolised conditions of dominance and contestation (Graham and Nash, 2006). The practice of parading, in particular, transformed the civic spaces of Belfast into a venue for political engagement. As a statement of symbolic territorial control, parading emerged among Unionist groups as early as the second half of the 19th century, but it was reinforced following the separation of the north and the south in 1921 (Nagle, 2009; Bryan, 2000). While public authorities never funded these public demonstrations directly, they provided massive indirect support through the use of police and other resources to protect them. Unionist politicians thus claimed a right to define the nature of the civic realm. And at the height of the Troubles, their dominance of urban space allowed them to create 'no-go' areas under paramilitary control (Wilson and Stapleton, 2016a).

In the pre-Troubles era, events such as the Lord Mayor's Show in the 1960s, organised by the Junior Chamber of Commerce, might thus contain 100 floats representing a broad spectrum of civic life, including charities, major local companies, and various military groups and associations (Bryan, 2009). Such an event was clearly intended to symbolise an espousal of Unionist values in the very fabric of civic space. But this condition was brutally upended during the height of subsequent conflict and economic decline in the 1970s and 1980s. At that time, the city centre was subject to a campaign of bombings orchestrated by the Irish Republican Army (IRA) and the Ulster Volunteer Force. Security measures subsequently escalated both on the part of the state and individual property owners. A person's mere presence in the public spaces of the city at this time also posed a risk, as many of the city's streets and walkways were barricaded by the army. The former civic qualities of public space were thus replaced by the presence of heavily armoured local police and British Army counterterrorism squads.

One consequence of these conditions was a huge decline in the urban population as well as a pronounced pattern of internal migration away from the political violence at the city's centre (Gaffikin et al., 2010). The trend also carried through to working-class residential communities surrounding the centre, which became increasingly polarised into self-identifying ethnoreligious communities. And no structures materialised this pattern of increased territorial separation more clearly than the permanent erection of Peaceline walls. The 360-metre-long, 10-metre-high Cupar Street wall, for example, illustrated the extent to which city residents would go to reinforce their sense of security and segregation from their ethnopolitical other. (Mulholland et al., 2014; Abdelmonem and McWhinney, 2015).

In the first decade following the Good Friday Agreement in 1998, several laws were passed relating directly to the management of demonstrations and parades in public spaces. But this state-led approach to the transformation of conflict proved mostly contradictory and even counterproductive (Nagle, 2009; Wilson and Stapleton, 2016a). One reason was it attempted to address the post-conflict condition of the city's public spaces only through capital investment and cultural regeneration and branding, including the encouragement of cosmopolitan notions of 'civic identity' (Nagle, 2009). Local planning authorities meanwhile attempted to establish designated 'interface' areas, in which the policies of 'A Shared Future' were mandated in an attempt to normalise daily interaction in safe and politics-free environments (Bryan, 2015). However, explorations of the character of public spaces in Belfast since the Good Friday Agreement later revealed that these steps, in many cases, only heightened the sense of division and led to an increase in the number of active interface areas (Shirlow and Murtagh, 2006).

As a condition of the Good Friday Agreement several other large-scale schemes have been attempted as a means to secure support from the two communities for the regeneration of public space. One of these was a scheme, called 'Westside District', within Belfast's city centre, developed by the Department of Social Development (DSD). By separating a particular segregated quarter for 'social, economic and physical regeneration', it set out to 'redress the disadvantage' by providing new public spaces with a 'Sense of Place' (DSD, 2003a). One of the major initiatives within the proposal was the promotion of independent, small-scale retailers as opposed to large-scale complexes, with an eye to develop a cafe culture and reduce the isolating impact of desolate car parks. In the end, however, this heavily capitalised effort to improve the quality of public space was heavily criticised and lacked enough public support to be implemented.

Spatial practice in civic spaces: urban thresholds in Belfast public space

> Urban life seems to flow to sectors with more activity: people attract people.
> – Gehl et al. (2005: p. 72)

Active civic spaces typically thrive on a sense of congestion, in which movement is facilitated by permeable thresholds that allow people to pass unhindered in and out of a variety of spaces. According to William Whyte (1980), flows of people in and out of buildings provide a particularly strong sense of security and help eradicate hostile conditions of emptiness. According to Jan Gehl (2006), one vital measure of a successful public space is the length of time people remain there; a lengthy stay, whether standing, sitting, or chatting with others, thus corresponds to dynamic characteristics of liveability. In this regard, it is important to underline Jane Jacobs's (1961) view that busy, active residential streets are the principal components of active communities and safe public spaces. Within such a view, however, it is also possible to differentiate between 'spaces for walking' and 'spaces for staying' (Gehl et al., 2005). And as a catalyst for the creation of successful public spaces, it is particularly important to note the characteristics of the latter. A series of factors may be involved here, including visual stimulation and a pleasing aesthetic quality at eye level, typically the ground floor of surrounding buildings. Indeed, the closer a person moves to a building, the more its upper floors disappear from view, until only its ground-floor facade remains visible (Gehl et al., 2005).

The public squares in the centre of a city are typically designed to act as civic spaces, and in contemporary contexts, it may also be common to limit or prohibit vehicle traffic on nearby streets to increase the number and vitality of retail and entertainment outlets. Measurements of the quality and extent of pedestrian activity in such areas may inform understanding of the nature of shared space in a city. And to understand the use and perception of such spaces as settings for a future attitude of shareness in Northern Ireland, we chose to analyse the current condition of politically 'neutral' areas in the well-capitalised centre of Belfast – those which are generally recognised as being accessible and secure for both communities in the current context. Our purpose was thus not to engage with notions of ethnic division but to evaluate modes of spatial design that might encourage public engagement in shared civic space. For the better part of the past two decades, the business, touristic, and retail character of Belfast's city centre, as well as of the adjoining Cathedral Quarter/Cultural District, has enabled it to become a diverse and safe zone. We thus deliberately limited our investigation to understanding how certain design strategies might encourage or inhibit the shared use of civic spaces, including pedestrian routes and public squares, in the context of ongoing ethnic-religious separation elsewhere in the city.

William Whyte has written that to engage with space, pedestrians must first be able to see it. Thus, '[u]nless there is a very compelling reason, open space should never be sunk. With two or three notable exceptions, sunken plazas are dead spaces' (Whyte, 1980). Such a view of the significance of visibility in the perception of public space is backed up by Gehl et al. (2005: p. 71):

> While sight and hearing are our remote senses, smell, touch and taste are activated at a closer distance . . . Ground-floor //s have a far greater emotional impact on us than our perceptions of the rest of the building and the street.

Evidence for this view is also provided by the relative success of Ricardo Bofill's design of new public spaces in Montpellier, France, which emphasises a complementary relationship between ground-floor facades and adjacent public space (Gehl and Gemzoe, 2000). Such interactive facades drive spatial sequences through building voids and make the pedestrian experience far livelier. A similar case is Gehl and Gemzoe's (2004) designs for public spaces in Copenhagen, Berlin, and Shanghai, whose user-friendliness and active character derive from the attention paid to approachable sightlines.

In such a design strategy, the presence of arcades and mid-block passages may divert people's attention from pedestrian streets and public squares. And low buildings around a space have also been found to provide a greater sense of harmony and a more intimate scale. The human brain is generally able to process sensory impressions of the surrounding physical environment while travelling at speeds of up to about 5 km/h (Gehl, 2010). A crucial element of city-centre architecture is thus its ability to respond to this relatively slow speed of perception. Interesting, provoking ground-floor facades, in this sense, can have a positive impact on the quality of pedestrian experience by relating activities inside a building to those outside, to their mutual enrichment. Gehl et al. (2005: p. 72) reiterate this argument:

> Modern cities have much confusion between these two scales. Pedestrians are often forced to walk in 60 km/h urban landscapes, while new urban buildings are designed as boring and sterile 60 km/h buildings on traditional 5 km/h streets . . . The need for good 5 km/h architecture along pedestrian routes remains unchanged.

Gehl and Gemzoe (2004: p. 32) used interviews and spatial analysis techniques to explore people's perceptions and reaction to different typologies of building facades around public spaces and squares. They found that a majority of people asserted that unattractive facades typically were characterised by 'large units with few or no doors, no visible variation in function, closed or passive facades and/or monotonous facades with lack of detail; nothing interesting to look at' (p. 32). As part of the same analysis, 'new buildings and poor design' was number three on a list of qualities users typically disliked about city centres. By contrast this seems to indicate that a healthy, positive relationship exists between older, more detailed and ornate buildings and the pedestrian activity in public spaces they border. Wiedenhoeft (1981: p. 26) has also asserted that older buildings are more engaging to pedestrians, possibly due to the amount of detail, craftsmanship, colour, and texture required to satisfy a basic level of psychological interest. As he explained, '[o]ne of the most serious problems of urban development has been its persistent obliviousness to the human scale in new construction' (p. 26).

Fear in disguise: the architecture of safety in Belfast's city centre

> A disembodied terrace from Sandy Row forms its own signifying system and must proclaim aloud the values it embodies precisely because the city from which it has been taken occupies a paradoxical intersection in spatial and temporal development mist clearly marked by silence. To write the city, to make it visible, is to stress its place in spatial territory yet also to perceive its contemporaneity through narrative within the process of a fragmented history.
> – Kirkland (1996: p. 35)

As a political and financial centre, Belfast is home to a number of trading, business, and financial institutions, whose offices cluster in its core district.

Due to the history of the Troubles and difficulty in providing security in more outlying areas, this city centre also came during the later decades of the 20th century to contain most of Belfast's commercial outlets. However, many of the public spaces here also developed a pattern of vacant desolation at times other than during business hours in a typical working week. As a result of frequent political unrest during and after the Troubles, the structures in the city centre also developed a more inward-facing character. Nevertheless, protecting the commercial centre of the city from the violence forces arising in its surrounding residential communities also became a main concern of government authorities during these times.

Narratives of violence and memories of fear, however, are by no means distant to the structure of the post-conflict city centre. To a certain extent they remain embedded in the overwhelming, inward-facing structures that were once intended to protect civic life during a time of threatened violence but which deny it to the reborn public realm of today. The damage caused by the uninviting, threatening facades of these buildings is clearly evident in the reduced level of social activity in the pedestrian spaces around them.

The Castlecourt Complex's stretches of tinted security glass displaying advertisements and the fact it had only one entrance off the street clearly indicated that security and isolation from its surroundings had been the primary driver of its design. Thus, its disengaged facades eliminated any chance of social interaction with the streets around it, and these spaces, even today, are mainly used as a commuter route for vehicles entering and exiting the city centre and as a means to access its 1,600 secure parking spaces. Spatially, this almost entirely internalised 'public' structure also acts as a massive barrier limiting points access between Royal Avenue and the Nationalist-dominated Shankill Road community north of the M1. The building also shuts down at 6 p.m., effectively closing one of the city centre's main interface gates. And even on the inside, its commercially driven spaces and retail outlets offer only the image rather than the practice of engagement, effectively eliminating any sense of shareness.

Jan Gehl has shed light on such practices of designed isolation. As he stresses, '[b]ig buildings with long facades, few entrances and few visitors mean an effective dispersal of events. The principle, in contrast, should be narrow units and many doors' (Gehl, 2006: p. 93). In the design of spaces for engagement, he instead emphasises the need for a relationship between ground-floor space and pedestrian use of adjoining public space. The narrow, lively alleyways and street cafes of Brussels provide a good example of this condition (Figure 5.1). Here many small storefronts and individual doorways make even relatively long journeys seem interesting and enjoyable, and therefore less taxing. Because there are few visual barriers, a sense of continuity of engagement prevails. When the threshold between the street and adjoining interior spaces vanishes, spatial and social spheres may be joined to form a complex, three-dimensional urban landscape (Abdelmonem, 2016) (Figure 5.2).

Figure 5.1 The conjoined, uninterrupted landscape of street restaurants in the city centre of Brussels.

Figure 5.2 Busy pedestrian street used as an outdoor extension of an Irish pub on a Saturday evening in the Cathedral Quarter.

In this sense, the small storefronts of Brussels provide a series of interesting and stimulating physical spaces, vistas, and human interactions that are far more rewarding than the those typically found in pedestrian spaces adjoining a large shopping centre or office block. In general, if urban districts are designed with engaging ground-floor facades that populate the edges of public space, they will by their very nature attract pedestrians and create a high level of social engagement. Establishing these qualities is critical to the design of any city centre.

Violence and design of public spaces

During the period between 1969, when the British Army was first deployed on the streets of Belfast, until the official end of the conflict in 1998, architects were faced with the dilemma of how to respond to conditions of strict social segregation and an ever-present threat of political violence. At the height of the Troubles in the early 1970s, temporary defensive structures were even installed to protect administrative buildings from attack. But as noted by Stollard (1984: p. 24), as the Irish Republican Army campaign to break the economy of the province evolved (and it corollary effort to undermine confidence in its central authorities), any building connected to the economic life of the city became a potential target. This led to the implementation of a series of modifications to the architecture of buildings to increase their security and protect them from attack. But the most damaging of these from a design standpoint was the reduction of openings to pedestrian space, because such disengagement only increased the deserted condition of surrounding spaces and made urban life seem even more dangerous. However, as Stollard (1984: p. 33) explains,

> [e]very architect working in Northern Ireland became conscious that any of the buildings he was designing might be attacked. So there was, developed of necessity, a whole new series of forms, ideas and techniques to cope with the problem. For the many buildings that were potential targets, or in dangerous locations, anti-terrorist design became very important.

The architectural impact of the Troubles may be most evident in the design of the British Telecom (BT) building. As a symbol of British authority, a new BT building would naturally have been a prime target for attack, and for protection, it adopted a fortress-like, defensive design. It is on the ground floor that the effects of this overriding concern for security are most prominent. Its principal pedestrian entrance is almost entirely hidden, located in a separate single-storey structure to one side of the main building. And its windowless facade is separated from adjacent public space by a set of chained concrete bollards, which line the entire length of the building in an effort to keep all vehicles – as potential mobile bombs – a clear distance away from it.

Unsurprisingly, the stark lack of openings on the ground floor and the line of bollards created a totally uninviting street facade. And the complete lack of attempt in the design to engage with pedestrian life creates a threatening atmosphere. Such a blatant approach of safety-first design, while seeking to proclaim strength and durability, only imparts a sense of barrenness to the surrounding public realm. As Stollard (1984: p. 38) notes, '[c]ertainly this is not the most attractive area of Belfast, but it is very close to the city centre and could have been designed more sympathetically . . . at the most one's only reaction to the building is to drive past it quickly'.

Interrogating the public spaces of Belfast city centre

This study, took place between 2012 and 2015, in a period that was relatively peaceful for active intercommunity engagement and 'spatial reconciliation' (Gaffikin et al., 2010). We selected three public squares and one pedestrian street for investigation based on several criteria: similar scale with pedestrian capacity, function and level of public amenities, similar patterns of paving and ground cover, and equal proximity to attractions and transportation links (Figure 5.3). The chosen spaces were Custom House Square, Writer's Square, St Anne's Square, and Fountain Street. Because all were located in Belfast's busy city centre, we also able to study patterns of

Figure 5.3 Figure-ground drawing of Belfast City Centre, illustrating the location of the investigated public spaces.

activity and occupation in them both during the day and as part of the city's nightlife. Their broad level of comparability also allowed us to investigate the impact of building facades on the quality of the pedestrian areas fronting them, including qualities of permeability, variety and number of openings, materiality and detailing, and potential for visual contact between their interiors and exteriors.

Our study of these spaces did not exclude other essential factors that might have affected the experience of these areas, such as their surrounding contexts, proximity to the territories of each community, or history of past violence. Our intent rather was to generate and analyse empirical data on present overall pedestrian activity within them, which may be read as a complement to historical narratives of contestation in Northern Ireland. This information was derived through detailed and methodical observation of pedestrian use in each space, the times at which it was used, and the purposes of its use. For our observations to be as representational as possible, we carried them out at various times during a typical working day: in the morning, at lunchtime, and in the afternoon. This allowed us to evaluate the effects of the great influx of pedestrians to the centre of Belfast each day as a consequence of the extensive development of business and commercial facilities there. However, we deemed it equally important to carry out our observations during the evening (post-6 p.m.) and on weekends in order to explore the qualities of these spaces as a result of the city centre's active nightlife – but also when they were relatively empty.

In particular, we set out to assess the effect of different physical aspects of the building facades that surrounded these spaces, particularly how the designed appearance and physical accessibility of spaces on their ground floors might influence pedestrian attitudes. While this information may be limited in its ability to reflect personal experience, it did provide an overview of how different aspects of architecture, when combined with memories of the recent past, may either enable or disable engagement with others in civic space. Our investigations in this regard also included setting up video cameras in each of the spaces to understand the main routes of movement through them. This photographic data offered the chance to produce a real-time pedestrian map of the space and its relation to the condition of particular building facades.

To understand the behavioural patterns we mapped, we also undertook a series of interviews in each of the four public spaces, in the form of short, multiple-choice questionnaires designed to elicit more detailed, personal accounts of the experience of public space. A total of 174 such street interviews were completed within a typical working week, which were further divided into four weekday interview periods – morning, lunchtime, afternoon, and evening – and one weekend time, Saturday afternoon. This plan ensured that we would sample the opinions of the broadest possible range of users of the four spaces. Overall, our intent was to understand the factors that infused each space with a sense of safety, that made it accessible for use, that attracted pedestrians to it, and that encouraged people to stay in it for longer periods of socio-spatial interaction.

Custom House Square

A prominent public space within the city centre, Custom House Square is located directly in front of Belfast's historic Customs House, a Victorian building designed by Sir Charles Lanyon, and the Albert Memorial Clock designed by W. J. Barre (Figures 5.4–5.6). The square's formal design, in combination with these architectural landmarks, the work of two of Belfast's most influential architects, cements its position within Belfast's history and culture. Before our study began, the square had been redeveloped in 2005 to restore its former public qualities by removing car traffic and re-establishing its use as a 'speakers' corner'. The restoration included the installation of a life-sized bronze statue of *The Speaker* on the steps of the Customs House itself and, directly opposite, several large lighting fixtures with copper bases intended to represent 'The Hecklers'. A significant water feature was also constructed in the centre of the square as a symbol of the former historical Calder Fountain once located there.

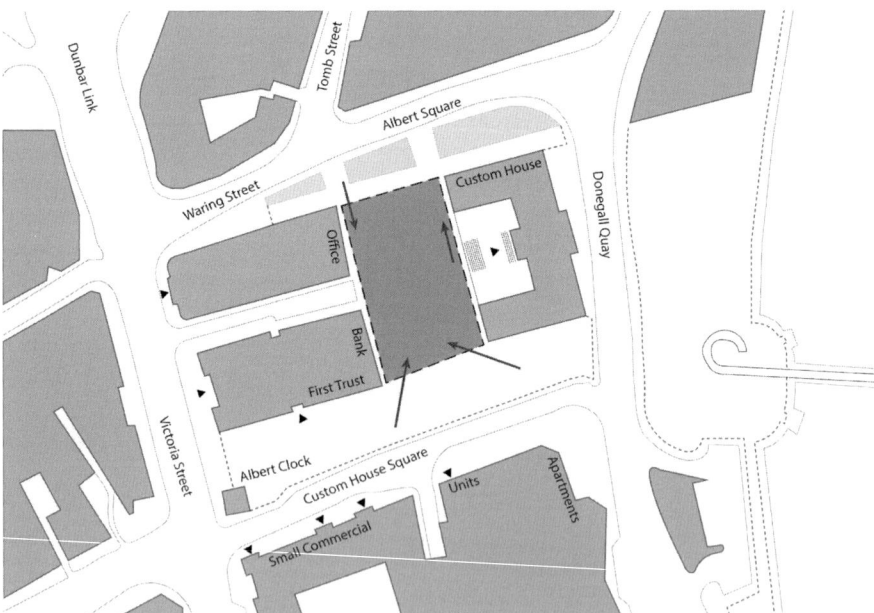

Figure 5.4 Custom House Square (area: 5,500 sq. m; average number of users: 5–10 per min).

Figure 5.5 Customs House facade facing onto public space.

Figure 5.6 Facade edge of Custom House Square, First Trust Bank building in foreground.

In its current configuration, this public space benefits from proximity to several recent commercial developments, including the Waterfront Conference Centre, Odyssey Arena, and the Boat Office and Apartment Complex. Its location thus also places it within Belfast's developing commercial core, which bridges the two sides of River Lagan. Despite this central location, however, there is almost no connection between this public space and ground-floor spaces in surrounding buildings, with the result that it is vacant and deserted most of the year. Specifically, one side of the space is bordered by the inaccessible and impermeable stone facade of the historic Customs House, whose only relieving feature is a series of small, eye-level windows covered with iron bars. The entrance to this historic structure is even less engaging, being pushed back and elevated above a pedestrian's line of sight. The opposite side of the square, meanwhile, is dominated by the recently designed First Trust Bank building and a large-scale office block of contrasting modern appearance. Yet, while their facades may be more transparent, they provide equally little public interest to occupants of the square. Similar to the Custom House, they present very few active openings or permeable thresholds. Instead, their large spans of tinted plate glass create a completely disengaging and unappealing edge to the public space (Figure 5.7).

Such disinterested ground-floor facades fail to provoke any response from pedestrians and, instead, increase their sense of being lost and isolated in an empty, oversized public space. And although this space has been refurbished to host outdoor events, it lacks the intimacy needed to make it appealing on a daily basis. Indeed, it is mainly unused throughout a typical week, with a majority of pedestrians merely passing through it on their way in and out of surrounding buildings. Furthermore, as might be expected based on the prevalence of commercial and office structures in its vicinity, even this activity declines after 5 p.m. However, since there are also many bars,

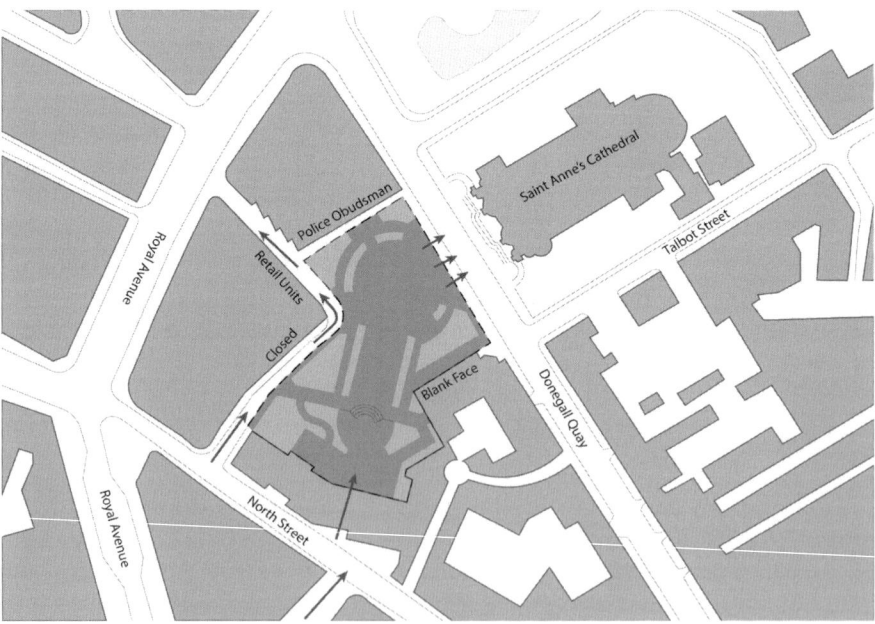

Figure 5.7 Writer's Square (area: 3,400 sq. m; average number of users – 5 per min).

restaurants, and clubs nearby, and because it is adequately lit and hence secure, the average number of users remains relatively unchanged in the evenings and on weekends.

Writer's Square

A central element of the city's historic Cathedral Quarter, Writers' Square has received considerable design attention in recent years as part of a conscious effort to restore pedestrian life to the area and eliminate anti-social behaviour. Close to Royal Avenue and with clear public access off North Street and Donegall Street, the space also benefits from having been entirely pedestrianised. Its proximity to a range of bars, restaurants, and cafes as well as public buildings such as Belfast Central Library, the University of Ulster, and the Metropolitan Art Centre further ensures an active public life, with an uninterrupted, diverse flow of pedestrians throughout the day. The space is also located in front of St Anne's Cathedral, one of the city's most historic architectural icons, which was restored in 2002. Moreover, as part of the Writer's Square redevelopment, the Laganside Corporation placed great emphasis on the materiality and nature of its paving, which now incorporates a series of inspiring literary inscriptions from Irish writers. In 2002, Laganside's chief executive, Mike Smith, even claimed that '[l]iterary inscriptions will ensure that Writer's Square is welcomed as somewhere to enjoy and a place to gather inspiration rather than pass through'.

Architectural students in design studios we have taught have often developed cultural and design activities that engage a public audience in the square, which benefits from being on most pedestrian routes to and from the cathedral. Similar to several other newly redesigned public spaces in the city, however, residual fear of arson attacks or bombings was embedded in the process of its redesign so that the structures around it maintain only a limited permeability. In particular, the shops located on William Street and Church Street maintain only a peripheral connection to the redesigned open areas, and they eventually failed to capitalise on the revived public quality of the area at all. Indeed, many eventually closed down, so that graffiti-stained shutters came to predominate along this edge. Other ground-floor facades of buildings around the space, including main entrances, also present an appearance of large expanses of opaque glass, offering little potential for public interaction and leading pedestrians to pass by them as quickly as possible. Instead of providing a social hub, in which people might pause and relax, the space thus tends to deter pedestrian activity, reducing its potential for being an active and interesting passageway through the city centre. One conspicuous result of these conditions is that the average number of pedestrians using the space declines markedly after 5 p.m., when its stretches of shuttered, black facades create an intimidating and unsafe public space (Figure 5.8).

Figure 5.8 View from North Street into Writer's Square, St Anne's Cathedral in the background.

St Anne's Square

Conceived as part of a brownfield redevelopment completed in 2009, St Anne's Square is the central public space of Belfast's Cathedral Quarter and one of Belfast's newest public areas. It is located within walking distance of the commercial core along Royal Avenue and is positioned directly behind St Anne's Cathedral (Figures 5.9 and 5.10). The location ensures its relation both to Belfast's historical culture as well as to its developing

Figure 5.9 St. Anne's Square (area: 1,300 sq. m; average number of users – 5–10 per min).

urban fabric. However, its inward-oriented nature as an open courtyard surrounded by new buildings endows it with a sense of isolation and exclusivity so that it maintains very little integration or connection to pedestrian life in the city around it. Indeed, the square has become in many ways a destination in itself.

In terms of design, the influence of the Italian piazza inspires its neoclassical form and architectonics. Although it could be argued that this approach creates little of architectural merit, it has resulted in a colonnaded entrance that not only attracts pedestrians into the space but also provides shelter from Belfast's temperamental climate. The catalytic effect of this design element is particularly noticeable at ground level, where pedestrians experience the full effect of its double-height, oversized columns and other decorative features. Overlooking the space, meanwhile, are restaurants/cafes, an apartment building, a gym, and the Metropolitan Arts Centre (MAC), all of which create significant potential for social interaction. All these buildings were designed with multiple openings to the central public area, both pedestrian entrances and windows, increasing the sense of interaction within it. The MAC design by Hackett Hall McKnight, in particular, affords a combination of materials, offset openings, and changes of level and height that produce a highly interactive facade facing out to this public space.

Figure 5.10 (a) The colonnaded entrance to St Anne's Square towards St Anne's Cathedral; (b) view of the square from the Metropolitan Arts Centre.

Figure 5.10 (Continued)

Adding to its use as a social hub, the courtyard was designed to enable outdoor seating at restaurants and cafes, which increases levels of pedestrian interaction and results in a lively, attractive, engaging space. Furthermore, as a result of its restaurants, cafes, and an apartment building – and a spillover effect from the Cathedral Quarter, which is an area of active nightlife – the average number of users stays fairly constant throughout the day, evening, and on weekends. The prevailing sense of security here is arguably also heightened by the presence of surrounding inhabited buildings, all of which emit much-needed light into its spaces.

Fountain Street

In recent years Fountain Street has become one of the main pedestrian routes through Belfast's city centre (Figure 5.11 & 5.12). A pedestrian-only thoroughfare, it runs parallel to Donegall Place and Royal Avenue and may be directly accessed from Donegall Square. This location ensures its status as a main feature of Belfast's commercial core. It is also proximate to many lines of public transport, large retail centres, and office buildings, ensuring that it benefits from a significant flow of pedestrians. Being located near Belfast City Hall as well as Linen Hall Library, this narrow public space is

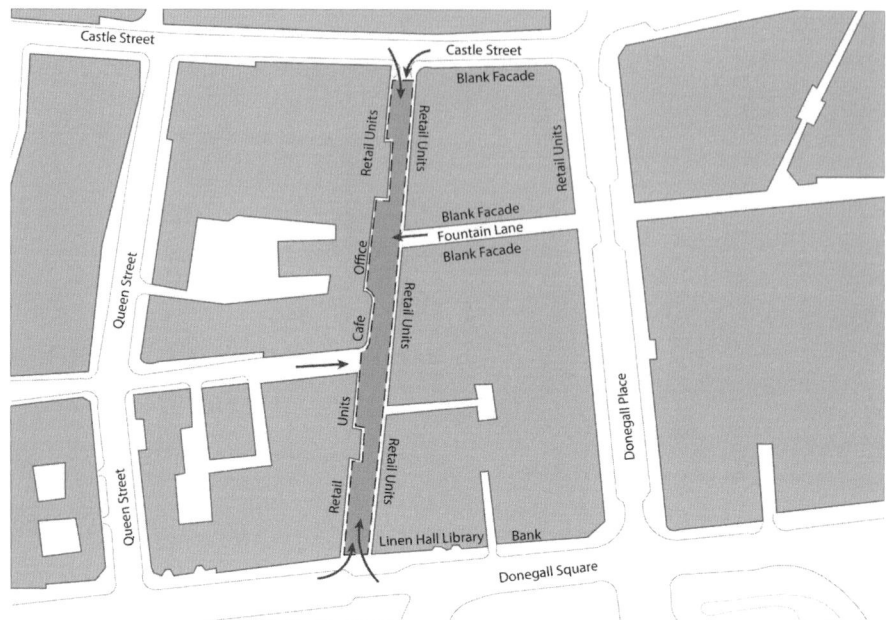

Figure 5.11 Fountain Street (area: 2,100 sq. m; a heavily used pedestrian route).

also cemented in Belfast's historical culture and heritage, and thus benefits from a high flow of tourists, which adds to its appeal.

In terms of physical character, Fountain Street benefits tremendously from being lined on both sides by highly permeable, engaging storefronts which do much to activate it. This interactive character ensures a pleasant, interesting experience, uninterrupted by noisy and hazardous traffic. Shops running the entire length of the space also provide a variety of facade treatments and functions, creating considerable permeability and social interaction between their interiors and the public space outside. Only a small number of these shops have chosen to face the street with plate-glass displays and advertising posters, leading pedestrians to pass by them quickly instead of stopping frequently to engage with their architectural features and commercial displays.

Cafes and other eateries, some of which provide their own outdoor seating, further encourage a 'stop and stay' culture at different locations along this street. The pattern of use is reinforced by the presence of public benches at varying intervals. The sum of these attributes creates a high level of pedestrian activity along the full length of the space, which is made even more rewarding by a high level of interpersonal interaction. However, as this public space is heavily dependent on its retail outlets and on walk-through traffic related to nearby office buildings, its usage drops off considerably after

Figure 5.12 Fountain Street's ground-floor facades, as seen from Donegall Square.

5 p.m. Another reason for this may be that it lacks nightlife in the form of pubs, restaurants, and clubs. Moreover, many of its shops are completely closed off and protected at night by shutters, with the result that it then assumes a defensive and somewhat threatening appearance, with very little light being emitted into it from adjacent ground-floor spaces.

Analysis and summary of findings

Based on the sample interviews, we found that 80 percent of pedestrians who use Fountain Street live within the borough of Belfast, with 20 percent coming from outside the city. This number was quite low in comparison to

Writer's Square, where we found that 35 percent of pedestrians were visitors from outside Belfast. Of these visitors, we also found that two-thirds were foreign tourists, highlighting the relative importance of St Anne's Cathedral as an adjacent attraction. The percentage of users from outside Belfast was generally comparable at St Anne's Square and Custom House Square, although fewer were foreigners. At St Anne's Square, however, the percentage of users living nearby was relatively high because it included an apartment block as part of its private development.

A large number of pedestrians we interviewed at all four public spaces lived in areas surrounding the city centre considered to be entirely or almost entirely segregated on ethno-religious lines. Of the four spaces, Custom House Square exhibited the greatest number (84 percent) of users living in such segregated areas, with only 4 percent of those interviewed living in areas considered 'neutral' – that is, not predominantly Protestant or Catholic. Although the percentage of people visiting the other spaces from such areas was lower than Custom House Square, the overall percentage of pedestrian users living in completely or almost completely segregated areas outside the city centre was relatively high: 64 percent. However, St Anne's Square reported the highest number (24 percent) of interviewees who might be classified as living in a 'neutral' area. This may reflect its popularity as a destination for young professionals and the fact that those living in the apartment building that is part of the project are classified as living in a neutral area.

Across the four public spaces a minimum of two-thirds of pedestrians who identified themselves as living in segregated areas lived in areas where Protestant ethno-religious groups predominate. This might reflect their greater confidence socialising in the city centre, an area of power characterised by a prominent police presence. Custom House Square and Writer's Square reported the highest level of segregation, with 80 percent and 81 percent respectively of those interviewed answering that they lived in areas that were predominantly Protestant. Although a majority of pedestrians in all four public spaces reported living in an area dominated by Protestant

Table 5.1 Demographic analysis of users and interviewees

Interviewees		St Anne's Square (%)	Writers Square (%)	Custom House Square (%)	Fountain Street (%)
Gender	Male	60	47	55	54
	Female	40	53	45	46
Age Groups	15–24	18	29	38	21
	25–34	42	32	29	40
	35–50	38	18	26	28
	51–65	0	0	0	2
	>66	2	21	7	9

Table 5.2 Place of residence of the respondents and ethno-religious orientation of those residing within segregated areas surrounding Belfast's city centre

Respondents Demography		St Anne's Square (%)	Writers Square (%)	Custom House Square (%)	Fountain Street (%)
Place of Residence	City Centre	16	12	12	5
	Surrounding Areas	56	53	57	75
	North Belfast	28	22	38	6
	South Belfast	24	22	8	22
	East Belfast	0	78	46	47
	West Belfast	48	3	8	25
	Outside Belfast	28	35	31	20
Ethno-religious segregation areas (% of Catholics in area)	0%–20% (less Cath)	45	53	67	46
	20%–40%	0	12	0	12
	40%–60%	27	17	5	19
	60%–80%	14	6	11	0
	80%–100% (less Pro)	14	12	17	23

Table 5.3 Main purpose for visiting the public space and frequency

Respondents Type of Activities		St Anne's Square (%)	Writers Square (%)	Custom House Square (%)	Fountain Street (%)
Purpose	Work	4	6	31	14
	Leisure	67	50	38	30
	Passers-by	18	44	31	19
	Shopping	0	0	0	37
	Living	11	0	0	0
Frequency	>3 times/week	36	38	67	30
	1–2 times/week	31	15	4	40
	1–3 times/month	22	20	14	28
	>1 time/month	11	27	14	2

ethno-religious groups, one-third of those interviewed along Fountain Street identified themselves as living within areas that were predominantly Catholic.

Interviews further revealed that there was a direct relationship between the purpose of people's visits to each space and the frequency of their visits. Both Custom House Square and St Anne's Square, which are dominated by office/bank buildings, public-service venues, and places for leisure activities, exhibited a significantly higher proportion of regular visitors coming for work (the former) and living (the latter). Indeed, two-thirds of all those interviewed within Custom House Square visited it more than three times a week. Compared to the other three public spaces, Writer's Square experienced the least frequent visits, with 27 percent of those interviewed visiting it less than once a month. The responses also indicated that the space is frequented by many foreign tourists and other visitors who come to see St Anne's Cathedral on a one-time basis. The deterioration of shopping/retail around its edges also seemed to be related to its location adjacent to a segregated area with a history of violence, resulting in a lack of interest among shoppers in visiting it.

Finally, we noted on the basis of the interviews that Fountain Street particularly benefits from its location close to the city's commercial and retail hub, and thus a significant portion of ground-floor spaces adjacent to it are occupied by shops. Of the four public spaces studied, it also exhibited the most mixed-community presence, a result perhaps of its predominant pattern of commercial, shopping, and leisure usage. Indeed, a majority of all those interviewed here responded that they used the space for 'shopping'. As a result, the pattern of frequency of visits reflected a more even spread between those who came there more than three times a week, once/twice a week, or once/twice a fortnight. This also helped explain why Fountain Street experienced the most significant decline in pedestrian use after 6 p.m.

Ground-floor aspect

Our study confirmed that the permeability of an urban space's boundaries, as evident in the frequency and pattern of openings in surrounding facades, has a positive impact on the number of pedestrian journeys through it and people's length of stay (Figures 5.13 and 5.14). This finding may arguably be relevant to many other city centres. However, in Northern Ireland, in general, and Belfast, in particular, these spaces and the designs of the buildings around them have long carried memories of violence and reflected a fear of being alone in vacant space. The historic lack of permeability of the building facades around these spaces may thus be interpreted as a result of this history of violence, which, in return, has infused a sense of vacancy and desertion into much contemporary public space. In this respect, architecture, particularly building facades may act as an agent of memories, helping to lock public space into a reciprocal cycle of commemoration and fear.

In the case of St Anne's Square, a high percentage (67 percent) of interviewed pedestrian users visited the space for the purpose of 'leisure'. This was explained by two factors: the high number of ground-floor restaurants and cafes, and the presence of the MAC and a large gymnasium. Indeed, a majority of interviewees described the space as being predominantly 'cafe/restaurant'. The same percentage suggested that these ground-floor outlets were likely to encourage them to stay to read 'outdoor menus', chat, or take shelter. The MAC was the most visited space, eliciting a nearly constant flow of movement as a consequence of its exhibitions, theatre, and cafe, and more interestingly, its architecture. In this respect, the design of

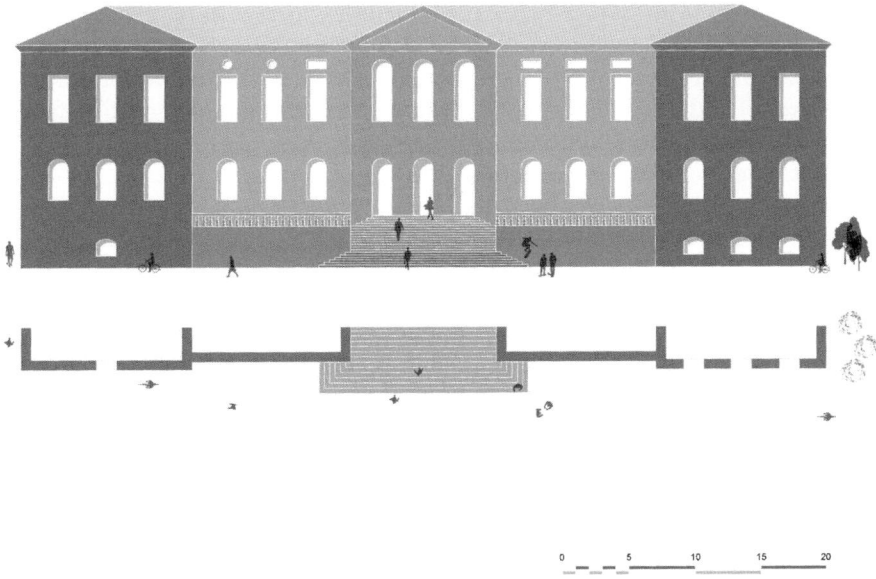

Figure 5.13 Diagrammatic analysis of the permeability of ground-floor facades at Custom House Square.

Figure 5.14 Diagrammatic analysis of the permeability of ground-floor facades in Fountain Street.

the MAC was notable in that it broke with the stagnant, disengaged design of many other buildings in the city centre, and thus produced a higher level of pedestrian satisfaction. But in this regard, it is important not to overlook the inward-looking design of the square itself, which establishes a protective, sheltered urban space, with only a few, controlled points of entry.

A significant percentage of those interviewed felt that this space, however, would benefit from 'gallery space' or facilities for outdoor performances that might link it more directly to activities at the MAC. Such a view surely benefits from its enclosure as a courtyard, with many overlooking semi-public retail and other areas above. Such a protected spatial condition facilitates interpersonal interaction by, in effect, transforming public space into a semi-private domain. Of the pedestrians we interviewed, others stated that the space would benefit from a 'workshop gallery', which would increase interaction between pedestrians and interior spaces. There was also interest in additional services such as 'retail shops', 'a convenience shop', and 'an ATM'. It is also worth noting that people's comfort in the space was supported by a stated preference for more outdoor seating.

Writer's Square, on the other hand, has become quite underused and even neglected, with several vacant storefronts along its edges. This has had a substantial adverse effect on public perceptions of it (half of those interviewed), and we observed many people simply crossing it without any effort to 'stop and stay' and enjoy any aspect of it. St Anne's Cathedral, opposite the square, did provide a substantial attraction, drawing people to the square, but this was a factor mainly for tourists and visitors – although it did encourage its occasional use by large groups. In addition, its relative popularity in the morning was offset by a sense of evening hostility as the consequence of an 'undesirable' minority of residents of a housing block on its edge who were witnessed engaging in such antisocial behaviour as drinking. Such conditions have created a stigma about the space that has discouraged pedestrian journeys through it, particularly at night. As part of its designed renovation, it was hoped that the square's relationship to Belfast's culture and history, as well as the high rate of tourism associated with the cathedral, might encourage other activities to develop there, increasing the flow of pedestrians and enlivening the Cathedral Quarter as part a broader effort to revive the centre city. However, these hopes have been undercut by the failure of the retail spaces around its edges, which have remained vacant or barely used. In this sense, the history of the space and the limited new opportunities afforded by its redesign have combined to undermine its long-term prospects.

Fountain Street was the most successful public space amongst those we sampled, largely as a result of its busy pattern of daytime use. In this regard it benefitted directly from the significant amount of commercial and retail pedestrian traffic generated by other facilities in the area, including Belfast City Hall. However, a majority of journeys by shoppers had a larger impact, as many interviewees explained that they spent considerable time either within its shops or in its coffee shops and other food establishments. Indeed, these were identified as the two main catalysts of activity in its public spaces. Such a busy shopping environment increased the number of workers in nearby buildings who also visited it, reinforcing a pattern of activity throughout the day, from early morning arrivals to those who visited at lunch and other meal times, to those who stopped there for after-work drinks. In addition, the large number of short, varied, and engaging ground-floor facades, coupled with eye-catching and somewhat interactive window displays, further encouraged pedestrians to stop and engage with the built environment, creating an even greater sense of safety and social interest. And although many of its stores closed after 6 p.m., the presence of restaurants and bars nearby ensured a continuing level of interaction at night, even though the space itself was not nearly as welcoming.

By contrast to these other spaces, pedestrian use of Custom House Square was primarily connected to 'leisure' interest in the two of Belfast's most iconic and highly regarded architectural landmarks, which directly adjoin it. Indeed, a majority of interviewees here were tourists visiting the space as part of tour groups. This invigorating architecture, as well as ample opportunity for public seating, helped generate a 'stop and stay' culture among out of town visitors to the space. Local pedestrians, however, generally responded that they were there either for 'work' or simply 'passing through', with a majority listing 'business/bank' as the principal reason for their visits. The use of its bus stop was a second popular reason. During the period of observation, it also became clear that the size and overall nature of Customs House Square made it attractive to a minority of youths who used it for recreational purposes, most notably skateboarding.

Reciprocal production of memory in public space

Weavers Cross is a flagship transportation-hub project in Belfast, planning for which began in late 2016. The design foresees a new integrated transit hub as part of a larger 8-hectare development comprising more than 100,000 square metres of commercial, residential, and amenity spaces. The area targeted for this redevelopment was once a centre of the linen industry in the city, and a key crossing point over the Blackstaff River (Translink, 2017). The project is one of many planned in the city in recent years to support urban mobility and promote alternatives to the use of private vehicles. It is also designed to counter the stigmatisation of Belfast as a hostile environment for pedestrians. The developer has thus argued that it will benefit a rundown area adjacent to the city centre by means of 'regeneration through reconnection'. It is also intended to create a 'new city neighbourhood that brings life to the area's past, regenerates its present and reimagines its future' (Ibid.). However, an underlying concern with regard to this and similar projects is how young people will interact with the spaces created at times other than during the working day. In other words, will antisocial behaviour and antagonistic practices adversely affect the experience of these space at night-time and on weekends? Thus, while a transportation hub may indeed do much to populate the new space, like other public spaces in Belfast, its success as a generator of shared encounter may have more to do with its success at creating an engaging environment as a way to ward off undesirable social practices. And, as the preceding discussion has shown, this may have a lot more to do with its design, the activities it enables, and the interactive quality of its facades, particularly those on the ground floor.

Similar schemes have claimed to create such new lively public spaces in the past with little apparent success. For example, the Forum for Alternative Belfast, a community-led organisation, proposed a regeneration project for Divis Street, one of five former urban arteries across which the Westlink Motorway was constructed. Left empty and uninviting to walk or cycle along, the proposal aimed to regenerate this stretch of road and nearby streets connecting to the city centre, creating new value for building owners and improving the local environment to the benefit of their users and residents (FAB, 2015). The scheme relied on a set of principles, including repopulating the edges of this broad street with small, interesting, and varied commercial outlets. A vision of how to enliven public space in Belfast has never been more precise, yet its success has been limited by a combination of conditions. On one side, this included a condition of fear based on memories of past; on the other, it involved a condition of limited creative architectural and development vision. In fact, these two conditions have a record of reproducing and feeding each other.

Judgements as to the success or failure of such design proposals are multifaceted, however. And it would be misleading to claim that design issues alone affect the use of redesigned spaces by the public or their ability to create active venues for social exchange. Other implicit, yet critical, factors also influence the ways that people use public space in a city like Belfast. Yet there is no doubt that the planning and design of public space, including the nature of building facades, have direct effects on pedestrian activity. The facade of a building, especially at ground level, creates an edge which largely determines the quality of a pedestrian's visual and spatial experience in the adjacent public domain. For a space to be lively, be it a public square or a pedestrian street, it must have a lively edge. And in this regard, if it is lively enough to attract some people, it is likely that those people will attract others. However, in Belfast, such a premise always begs another question: Which people will it attract? It may be a particularly difficult condition of post-conflict cities that the hostile attitudes or antisocial behaviours of a small group of users may drive away many more ordinary ones. And proximity to the spaces of one community may limit the potential of interventions designed to encourage new sociocultural attitudes or attract a more general population.

Clearly, the Troubles have had an enduring impact on public spaces in Belfast. That particular era also created a shadow that continues to haunt urban design attitudes and architectural production in the city. However, as the city looks for a new direction forward, its leaders should also realise that the concern for safety embodied in the architecture of the city centre over the last half century has in many cases produced the exact opposite effect. Thus, the fortress-like nature of many building designs only created threatening new public spaces. As Jan Gehl (2006: pp. 24–25) has observed, '*[f]irst life, then spaces, then buildings – the other way around never works*'.

6 Community architecture and the question of spatial agency

Community architecture and the living environments: from experiments to real-life practice

The notion of architects being *'agents of change'* can be seen throughout the history of the built environments with changing living conditions, industrialisation and the most recent digital age. When architecture considers the real-life practices at the design stage, the immediate impact on design will appear in the general nature of the complete form. Users' actions and interaction with buildings are not predictable; however, the dynamic nature of human–building interaction should give space for alternative developments and improvements. Therefore, such dynamics should be reflected in the organisation of social spheres which appears in the spatial organisation. Socio-spatial architecture is a long and complex task, which appears to involve an extended and unpredictable process of interaction and association between the residents/occupiers and their homes. According to Thomas Dutton (1989: p. 3),

> [o]ur strength and skills (the architects) lie in our capacity to generate spatial form and architectural expression for institutions, peoples and groups, but we tend to be one-sided: we reproduce and manifest the practices and spatial requirements of the dominant culture. What we need to do more, is a link with struggling cultures already present to help create spaces of cultural transformation: spaces of resistance that are linked to transformative cultural practices.

Tatjana Schneider and Jeremy Till looked at architects as agents of change in a kind of architectural practice they branded as *spatial agency* across the 20th century. Architects in this spatial agency deliver a different view of the architect's mission that challenges the nature of the contemporary professional practice's reliance on the design and delivery of buildings which hold little relevance to the process of making a home (Abdelmonem 2016). Instead, architecture, or possibly the 'spatial agency' for Schneider and Till, opens up to dynamic continuity and open-ended elaboration on inhabitants' lives, rituals, and activities, even after the building has been taken over. Architecture does not finish with the very moment of handing over a building to the users/clients. Instead, the transformation and development of its socio-spatial environments and domains start to take effect.

As Tatjana Schneider and Jeremy Till (2009: p. 97) highlights, the concept of the architect as an agent is inherent to the nature of the profession, arguing that this word is frequently misused by stating 'agency just denotes "acting on behalf of": a contractor, a client, a developer, etcetera'. Becoming an agent to a local community is just another aspect of an inclusive multifaceted profession. Architects do not just design a building or space in isolation of its environment, they, in fact, provide a significant change and intervention in reshaping the urban or rural fabric every time their design become a factual component of the built environment.

The 'spatial' as 'relating to space' (Oxford Dictionary, 2017), on the other hand, focuses on space as an object that creates and manipulate space in relation to the events within this space. According to Henri Lefebvre space is produced, space is inhabited, and then space is reproduced, revealing that space is constantly adapted. Its production is a shared enterprise, meaning that the process of producing social space includes the input of others and is not solely beheld with the architect (Awan et al., 2011). In this sense, the spatial production is part of an evolving sequence, with no fixed start or finish, and that multiple actors contribute at various stages. Magnifying such influence, a single architect could exert on the landscape of a city, we need to look at Le Corbusier vision on the dynamics of change in everyday life. He always envisions his mission as the collective and sequential acts of change, as to him, great things are made out of a multitude of little things that follow one upon another every day (Le Corbusier, 1982).

Architecture is, by definition, intrinsically connected to society's everyday life, where people shape their perception of their lives in connection to their surroundings and contextual realities, including culture, built environment and aspects of everyday socio-spatial practice (Abdelmonem, 2016). According to Steven Holl et al. (1994: p. 37),

> [t]he timeless task of architecture is to create embodied existential metaphors that concretize and structure man's being in the world. Images of architecture materialize our images of ideal life. Buildings and towns enable us to structure, understand and remember the shapeless flow of reality and, ultimately to recognize and remember who we are. The architecture enables us to place ourselves in the continuum of time.

People have this subconscious relationship with their surroundings; it helps to identify and provide a sense of emotional security and stability. Referring to the rebuilding of Parliament after its destruction by German bombers during the Second World War, Winston Churchill (1943: p. 358)

Figure 6.1 Hackett Hall McKnight's Metropolitan Arts Centre in Belfast, view from St Anne Square.

famously said, '[F]irst we shape our buildings, and afterwards our buildings shape us', reflecting on his belief that the rectangular plan of the old
chamber had directly influenced the creation of the two-party system that
defined British democracy. The 'spatial agent', however, could not be just
architects. Florian Kossak et al. (2010) stresses that realising the power
and transformative potential of connections, among subjects, disciplines,
and people, is key to understanding the act of agency. The spatial agent
is every person involved in the act of building an act of change, not solely
the architect.

However, this role of architects as agents of change poses a different
challenge to architects and designers in Northern Ireland than any other
parts of the UK or most of Europe. Their role starts with the very moment
they engage with the demand and context. The sociocultural and political knowledge is of paramount importance for any project to successfully
go through the process of negotiation, consultation, and buildings. The
prominent examples of the O'Donnell Toumey's Lyric Theatre in Belfast and Hackett Hall McKnight's Metropolitan Arts Centre in Belfast
(Figures 6.1 and 6.2) offer one view on how cultural buildings in neutral
areas of the city could be a success story to unify a divided community
around a shared interest in arts and cultural performances. In this chapter, we attempt to develop an analytical approach to the way architecture
could add strength to the notion of *shareness* in Northern Ireland, utilising
its power as an agency of change.

Societal challenges and the need for agents of change

> It is at the intersection of space and culture that architects can make signifi-
> cant contributions to urban social change
>
> – Dutton (1989: p. 3)

Architecture as a practice tends to focus on the search for the optimum
way to attend to people's needs (physical, psychological, spiritual, political, cultural, and social). These needs, however, are perceived by architects
differently according to time and context. In medieval cities and towns,
small parts of the built environment affected by architecture as a discipline
of professionals (architects; Kostof, 2000: p. 3). The distinction between
medieval and modern practice, the vernacular and the professional of any
time, lies in the process of production and how user and community needs
are met. During the post-war period, when the ordinary people's fundamental needs, such as housing and neighbourhoods, were set to drive the
architects' agenda, the production of homes moved towards the mass production of housing: with the prospective residents considered as subjects
with no role in the decision-making process. Although the period and situation may have justified this approach, it proved problematic in the long

Figure 6.2 Interior views of the Metropolitan Arts Centre with extensive use of red brick as the main features of the interiors.

term. As a result, design informed by architect–user interaction and mutual negotiation was lacking in much of architectural productions during the 20th century.

Architects are bound by two institutions: the formal organisation of the profession (regulations that control the practice in a systematic way, such as codes, standards, and specifications) and the informal sociocultural context of society within which the building will be produced (social analysis). In Northern Ireland, other factors influence how architecture is being practised, namely the sensitivity of intercommunity relationship. These aspects of the unique context of division and post-conflict have much say in the way each project is designed and produced. Several projects in the region fell out of favour due to the contentious politics that focus mainly on territoriality, community identity, and mutual benefits to each community. These issues resulted in a series of schemes being scrapped and others significantly delayed.

In such a context, architects struggle to situate themselves between two polar characters: architect as a *creator* or architect as a *collaborator/facilitator of designs*. The former means the building reflects the architect's creativity and personality while the meaning belongs to his or her concept and ideological thinking. The latter, on the other hand, means the product is a group effort, a process, in which the architect is more like an elaborator. To introduce such participation in the design process suggests a series of negotiations that at times had to go through parallel negotiations with both communities to ensure each side's requirements and demands have been met, as we discuss later. The building and its meaning, then, reflect the values and personality of the involved actors and the dominant culture of the community.

Schneider and Till (2009) used to refer to architects as technocrats whose technical knowledge and expertise elevate them above the mere building. Architects' knowledge, training, and expertise provide the tools to alter the settings of the built environment through creativity. Others chose to translate their philosophical and idealistic understanding of society or life into unique examples of architecture that impact the broader landscape. The work of deconstruction architects such as Zaha Hadid and Frank Gehry, in this sense, is widely perceived as exemplars of such a surrealist/sculptural approach that altered our way of practising architecture during late 20th and early 21st centuries (Jenks, 2005: p. 7). Le Corbusier, on the other hand, was a pure theorist with a determined ideology that utilised the urban environment to enforces his utopian vision of modern cities.

The understanding of the sociocultural context of Northern Ireland requires not only awareness of the general political issues and complex planning system. Instead, architects need to engage and become aware of the historical background of every street, locality, village, or community. Central to this understanding are mechanisms of interaction and the way locals elaborate their barriers and connections spatially and mentally. Such understanding requires social analysis of the users and the context to grasp social tensions, conflicts and real-life situations. Dealing with every-day matters and ordinary people necessarily requires an architect to oper-ate in a way that reflects an awareness of the social context and impact of his or her work. In this instance, the size, scale, and site are ideas only in the user's mind, not on the site plan. However, the architect does not have ultimate control over such extended environments; instead, he needs to cope with its parameters to elaborate the best environment from the user's perspective.

Architecture is a situated process and practice that is grounded into the sociocultural context of a particular site, community, or society and legitimate itself as a primary medium for dominant institutions to manifest forms and images. To practise, architecture is to elaborate the environment that governs such social interaction and communication. As the shaper of public space, architecture commands act of designing and building is an *'unavoidable social act'* (Hutcheon, 2003: pp. 180–181). The mechanism of socio-spatial architecture as an agency for change cannot be sufficiently considered as a design process. We argued before (Abdelmonem, 2016) that an architect is instead an act more than a noun. In this sense, the act of such spatial agency is architecting, the original act that is linguistically described as the action of the architect and, by definition, recognises the complexity of architecture as a situated practice that deals with space, buildings, users, and context.

To *architect* a space, is a process by which and the contextual environment is made to suit human needs within a particular sociocultural and economic situation (Abdelmonem, 2016). Users, in this sense, come as a priority, cen-tral characters around whom the building is constructed. Architecting a space is a generative and open-ended process, which could give results far different from the initial predictions and involves a continuous endeavour in which the users are key players as much as the architect. The product of architecting is an environment, a habitable space and place in time, whose value is more than its physical characteristics or spatial features. The spa-tial agency for change here acknowledges a different type of production, a product that is an essential innovation (Ibid.). Being a reproduction, devel-opment, or refurbishment, the outcome of the spatial agency is one which is flexible and enduring and could be reproduced through different forms.

Similarly, as we scrutinise the act of the architect as an agent for change, we need to revisit the notion and structure of the profession itself. There has always been a debate over the balance of science and art within architec-ture, with many architects distance themselves from others in the building industry as an elitist practice driven by its ambitions to serve specific sec-tors of society. To a certain extent, this was the case for much of the pre-modern era when architects were different from master builders, who were effectively doing the same job but for a few selective and wealthy clients, a practice dominated by economic power and affordability. However, in doing so, Margret Crawford describes architecture as 'a luxury rather than an indispensable service' (Crawford, 1991: p. 31), disengaging architects from social problems and cultural issues. Here, we interrogate a few projects, processes, and architects to understand how this practice for change has evolved in the post-conflict situations in Northern Ireland and to what extent the division has helped or countered the rise of architecture as a spatial agency for change.

Practices for change

There are many diverse practices around the world whose design philosophy revolves around responses to social change, both within their locality and elsewhere. Following are just of a few of listed practices which help shed light on the role of an architect in community regeneration. Each practice has a different philosophy and methodology to how they act out agency of change. Few examples of such agencies stood out to Schneider and Till (2009) to make a case for architecture as a socially and politically aware form of agency and critical of the social and economic formations of that context to engage better in a transformative manner. The London-based Feminist architects MUF committed to public sector projects in the mid-1990s, and the Spanish architect Santiago Cirugeda questioned the notion that the architect is the author and thereby the sole recognised designer. For Cirugeda, the architect acts as a catalyst of change for an unspecified period.

One of the recent exemplars of such practices is Teddy Cruz's San Diego–based research-led practice puts a clear emphasis on regenerating existing urban fabric in response to local communities living needs, traditions, and everyday life. His studio focuses on enhancing the voids and forgotten spaces of the micro scale of the neighbourhood, transforming it into the urban laboratory of the 21st century. For Cruz, the aim is to improve the quality of poor and neglected suburban. Cruz's work on the overlooked peripheral communities at the borders between the San Diego–Tijuana to develop 'Living Rooms at the Border' and 'Senior Housing with Childcare' offered a new visionary role for architecture to play and act to change. Through a thorough and comprehensive study of the area, Cruz discovered numerous unplanned spaces, through adaptations of garages and other outbuildings. Cruz's proposal derives from densification and multi-use strategies that are common south of the border and was inspired first from discussions and brainstorming sessions led by Cruz's Casa Familiar, showing his belief that to be an agent of change for a community.

Architects in such spatial agency for change deliver a different view of the architect's mission that introduces new obligations on engagement, understanding and being part of the context with which he is dealing. They challenge the contemporary professional practice's reliance on the design and delivery of buildings which hold little relevance to the process of making a home. Instead, architecture, or possibly the 'spatial agency' for Schneider and Till, opens up to dynamic continuity and open-ended elaboration on inhabitants' lives, rituals, and activities, even after the building has been taken over. Architecture does not finish with the very moment of handing over a building to the users/clients. Instead, the transformation and development of its socio-spatial environments and domains start to take effect.

Northern Ireland's agents of change

In the post-conflict condition littered with the manifestation of division, the protagonist and territorial contestation in Northern Ireland pose different challenges to architects wishing to challenge the status quo and introduce positive change. On the back of the troubles and associated decline in economic and industrial activities, the spread of deprivation in inner-city areas was epidemic in a manner that generated an overarching feeling of neglect towards the state and hostility towards other communities. This resulted in mass densification of red-brick terrace housing segregated into Protestant and Catholic streets, such as the Shankill and the Falls, mainly lived in by the working class, as the city grew the more affluent citizens moved out of the centre to form the suburbs. According to Boal, these areas, or 'territories', 'provide a source of identity, they are characterised by substantial degrees of exclusiveness, and they act to compartmentalise activity spatially' (Boal, 1969: p. 35), thus encouraging a negative impact on the city.

The effects of this conflict are visible throughout the region with most glaringly in Belfast in which must of the city's urban landscape suffered from vacant landscapes and spatial voids resisting the development of the fear of inequitable benefits between both communities. Post–Good Friday Agreement, consultation on development plans and projects must involve communities from both ethnic affiliations. In Belfast, one such effect is the residential segregation. During the Industrial Revolution, Belfast proliferated from the shipbuilding, and its associated engineering and linen industries, with population increases of approximately 1,745% over the span of the 19th century (Barakat, 1993: p. 13).

To act as agents of change, hence, architects need to work not only with the community but need to develop an agency of trust and evidence on neutrality and objectivity that is hard to gain in a divided society. To act as an agent of change in Northern Ireland in the post–Good Friday Agreement required the departure from the mindset of divisions and developed a unifying value system that target shared concerns, mutual benefits, and equity amongst disadvantaged communities. This requires long-term practices of negotiating preconception, hostility and overwhelming territorial concerns. Hence, examples of these practices are either rare or take the form of community or social enterprise that aim to serve a particular community. The Forum for Alternative Belfast (FAB), founded in 2004, by the group of activist architects and urban designers in Belfast aimed to shape a 'regeneration agenda for the city' with the goal to create a 'connected and shared city' (FAB, 2015). The forum set up its mission to engage with divisive and controversial agendas and to bring different groups to deal with the issues of conflict in the urban landscape of the city. There are also a few architectural practices that have a particular desire for community regeneration within Belfast.

While this need for change has to be tackled by many disciplines, and not just those within the built environment, it is essential to see how an architect can play their role in this change. With the recent recognition and subsequent emphasis from government and local councils that regeneration is needed in this inner city and interface communities, there are a few architectural practices in Northern Ireland jumping on board. Many practices in Northern Ireland have 'Community' in their portfolios, but this does not mean they are agents of change, only a small selection of practices address the community issues, as described previously, in any real or active way.

Todd Architects, for example, was highly involved in the regeneration of Belfast Dock's and Cathedral Quarter, and has worked closely with Belfast Health and Social Care Trust in delivering numerous Health and Wellbeing centres to areas with inadequate healthcare, such as The Arches centre at the Holywood Arches in East Belfast and Shankhill Road Health and Wellbeing Centre. Architects who engage with these situations are trained to capture such sensitivity of the changing aspects of living for different groups within society, be they ethnic minorities, divided communities, or special groups like older people. Many of them acknowledge the critical role they play to facilitated a better quality of life by working with their prospected users, occupants, and the public. If an architect can incorporate features that bring together the broader community, it will impact on morale within the home, create a positive atmosphere, and bring hope. In the following part of this chapter, we try to explore the way in which a few exemplars of architecture have developed such agency of change in different situations.

Weavers Cross transport hub

Designed as a new neighbourhood than a functional transportation hub, the new flagship project in Belfast, Weaver Cross neighbourhood is designed to reach out to the surrounding communities and aim to connect local communities for better living standards, accessibility and potential economic investment on 100,000 square metres of commercial space alongside significant residential and amenity space. Drawing on the industrial heritage and geography of the local areas, the name 'Weavers Cross' reflects what the designers call a unique identity for the distinctive and central city community as one of Belfast's linen industry centres (Translink, 2017). The project includes a railway link, a bus station, and residential and leisure space that were developed to meet multiple needs of different user groups and different patterns of activities.

According to the Transport Company's website, Translink asserts that '[a] key theme of this project is 'regeneration through reconnection' and that Weavers Cross represents a new city neighbourhood that brings life to the area's past, regenerates its present and reimagines its future to benefit the whole community'. The emphasis on the reproduction of the coherent (Fig. 6.3)

Figure 6.3 Weavers Cross, Belfast Transport Hub Proposal by John McAslan + Partners, together with ARUP.

Source: Photos of the public consultation exhibition at the Europa Station Exhibition.

memories of the past seems to be dominant in the public messages that being communicated to different communities. However, following the public consultation, concerns were raised towards aspects of accessibility such as 'access for people with impaired mobility; cycling infrastructure provision; contemporary versus traditional design; traffic congestion and parking provision in the vicinity; noise & air quality; construction impact and local history recognition' (Ibid.).

The £175 million Belfast Transport Hub was designed to support up to 400 jobs during construction and will serve as a main bus and train connection for all parts of Northern Ireland and as the main rail link to Dublin. The design is located on the 20-acre site of the existing Europa Buscentre and Great Victoria Street train station with construction to begin between 2019 and 2022. According to Translink CEO Chris Conway, the facility will be 'a catalyst for the regeneration of the local area and will play a pivotal role in making public transport 'your first choice for travel in Northern Ireland', connecting people and opportunities and connecting industrial heritage with a newly reimagined future (McKeown, 2017). The ambitious plans submitted have been developed following months of consultation with local stakeholders and the local community, including formal consultation, community briefings, and numerous face-to-face meetings with many interested parties.

O'Donnell + Tuomey architects: how memory is captured through materials

Known for their excellence in utilising the purity of materials and crafts to weave silent and memorable narratives within the built fabric, O'Donnell + Tuomey architects offer a distinctive understanding of contested Northern Ireland. Their buildings in both Derry and Belfast embody their striking and smart use of material binaries, fair-faced concrete and red brick. The modest and restraint and understated design of Cultúrlann building in Derry, completed in 2009, offered a unique way through which, John Tuomey and Sheila O'Donnell's expression of how Irish culture is vibrant yet embedded in strangled constraints of the Northern Irish political landscape. The interlocking plains of inner surfaces are only dynamic when met with day and sunlight within the multi-storey void that enables the users to reach each corner of the building visually. Accessibility, however, requires more negotiation with different plains and levels.

The Cultúrlann cost a mere £4 million to offer a contemporary validation of the powerful message of the modest forms and quiet fabric of buildings (Figures 6.4 and 6.5). Built on Great James Street in the old walled city, the building is fronted by subdued facade dominated by electric substation on a street of Victorian and Georgian terraced houses. It has a broken low-ceiling entrance that opens the way to a vast interior void that is rich in activity and hype but low in colours and material expression. Its excellence lies in it being joyful for children who keep exploring different spaces and voids as if it was a bouncy castle for entertainment. A power substation occupied a third of the

Figure 6.4 Exterior of Cultúrlann Uí Chanáin: Cultural Centre for Irish Language, Arts and Culture in Derry by O'Donnell + Toumey architects.

site's street frontage and had to feature in the facade. Moreover, there is only one entrance to the site – there's no view from the back of the building. O'Donnell + Tuomey's brilliance is in the subtlety of its spatial and material expression that speaks to the local community, fabric, and context through the non-intrusive but integrated addition of spaces that add to the memory of the area.

In Belfast, the architects' Lyric Theatre was another Stirling Prize–shortlisted building that was completed in 2012 within an entirely different context. While the Cultúrlann building was designed in the heart of a Victorian residential and urban neighbourhood in Derry, the Lyric Theatre enjoyed much of the natural landscape and frontage of the River Lagan from a wide angle that reaches almost three sides. The corner location of the building on a steep road leading to the river enables the multiplicity of floors and levels that both reach the sloped paved entrance from one side yet enjoy uninterrupted views of the river and the two lines of trees on the sides. The architects' sensitivity to the landscape ensures that the vast red-brick walls of the buildings gradually emerge from a modest scale on the sloped streets to enjoy a giant facade that meets the riverside for the studios and coffee shop on multiple levels. Being a cultural venue does not suggest community-led activities.

The matter of the fact that it is a familiar destination for every weekend morning coffee or a nice break from work at Queen's University where many colleagues used to meet. It emerged as the central hub for social engagement

Figure 6.5 Interlocking volumes and geometric forms of the interior spaces.

and recreation in the area, benefitting from its user-friendly red-brick facades that weaves its continuity into the adjacent the terraced houses. The building's interior is another bod poetry in material purity, in which the external context-led red-brick facades wrap opulent interiors of fair-faced concrete surfaces and timber interior of the auditorium. Perhaps, O'Donnell + Tuomey's architects are not known for their community engagement activities, yet their use of material and form expression reflects a sincere appreciation of the contextual fabric, community perception, and sensitivity towards a politically neutral and socially rich built environment.

Michael Whitley Architects

Founded in 1985 Michael Whitley Architects are specialised in working with local councils on community projects, such as the Craigavon Community Hub, which received a few awards for Community Benefit Design. Its project of the regeneration of Girdwood Barracks in North Belfast in the form of the proposed Girdwood Community Hub was the most challenging and somewhat controversial. Essential to this process is the engagement with Girdwood Community that Paul Griffith stresses that central to the project is getting people to share what will be iconic about the building and the way in which two communities could engage together in one building at the one time, not its shape or form (Griffith, 2013).

The regeneration of Girdwood Barracks and Crumlin Road Gaol in North Belfast has been on hold for some years over the placing of social housing on the site. When was put back on track in 2012, the then minister of social development, Nelson McCausland, to state a political message of reconciliation: 'They said that this area was too divided to ever come together around an agreed plan for shared development at Girdwood. . . . We are sending a powerful message that positive change is coming to north Belfast' (Bell, 2013). The site of Girdwood Barracks is one of the most contested locations in Belfast, the north of which was witness to most of the violent incidents during the Troubles, and segregation is still highly visible in the area. The Crumlin Masterplan 2007 describes the site as located at the most 'heightened and destructive at interface areas such as Clifton Park Avenue. The spatial grouping of Girdwood Barracks and the Goal creates a large physical divide within the area inhibiting the building of relationships between different sides of the community. It is the same area where the first Peace Line wall to be taken down as mentioned in Chapter 1, however. The site, nevertheless, created one of the most challenging conditions of divisions for a long time, and in 2012 the proposed project was considered a precedent of how to change divided areas and communities of Northern Ireland (Bell, 2013).

Michael Whitley Architects different yet inventive approach paved the way for other catalyst projects of conciliation in the city for a similar highly social building. By considering themselves as agents of change in the built environment rather than social engineers, the architects dismissed 'the usual binary social terms in Northern Ireland' taking more pragmatic approach to a design process that avoids anything political (Ibid.). They ended up with a politically neutral building; through setting a non-hierarchical approach, there is no emphasis placed on the entrance (Ibid.).

Donnelly O'Neill Architects

Donnelly O'Neill Architects' most recent community project, located on the Newtownards Road, 'Skainos' has created a stir among the media and attracted considerable attention. As lead architect Nial O'Neill's creation of a 'village' of residential, commercial, and community units; therefore, the scale of this project and the practice's dedication to community that earns this further exploration (Bell, 2013). While this project does not involve contested site, it does address the other pressing issue of Belfast inner-city areas such as the decline of the industrial boom and subsequent decline of the city's inner community and social degradation. As a neighbour to the Belfast docks, shipbuilding, and rope making, East Belfast was once at the heart of the industrial boom and Northern Ireland economy especially with the infamous Harland and Wolff and the Belfast Ropework Company. This was the area that was once vibrant and prosperous but now has fallen into such decline that is home to two of the ten most deprived electoral wards in the whole of Northern Ireland, with low educational attendance, poor health, and high unemployment rates.

Initiated by the East Belfast Mission back in 2000, the Skainos project is designed to provide shared space for community transformation and renewal; more than 12 years later, Skainos was officially opened on 23 November 2012. The project is centred around a civic courtyard with a new urban street that is not dominated by the history of the Troubles and providing shared space for all communities. It comprised retail and commercial office space, a café, a community hall and auditorium, social housing, and counselling services. The project incorporates various organisations and even artists into its design, with the enamelled panels on the Newtownards Road elevation and various glassworks throughout the development, creating an urban village.

Donnelly O'Neill Architects undertook various methods of consultation with the community, from meetings, workshops and presentations and community opinions were very highly valued and had an impacted the resulting design. Barbara Baird, the project architect, stresses that 'this is very much a building for the local community and we've been working very closely with the local community, if they don't buy into it, it won't work out' (Bell 2013). Much time and energy were spent consulting with the community and ensuring that they were kept involved at each stage of the design process. This project fully embraces the importance of community engagement, and in that it will continue to meet the needs of its users, it allows the building to develop as the community does.

The building does not appear to blend into its local surroundings directly, the three-storey grass wall is not exactly typical of its red-brick neighbours; however, the community is reflected through subtle references intended to evoke memory and pride through the use of yellow and galvanised steel with rivets. Listening to the stories of individual members of the community influenced the design process through the expression of these stories developing the building; the Newtownards Road elevation contains mixed sized panels arranged, according to O'Neill (2013) as 'timeline' that expresses 'the passing of time as rings in a tree', representing past. The ambiguous hints, such as the panels, leave people to make their interpretations and in doing so provide a personal connection with the building.

The agency of architecture in Northern Ireland

From the emerging discourse of architecture as an agency for change, architects are increasingly aware of their social responsibilities and that a change in the professional structure, and psyche, is emerging to place more emphasis on the end user over economic pressures or professional regulations and codes of conduct. As agents for progressive change, architects play a significant role in helping to regenerate communities as collective efforts that are centred on the local community members, their needs, and their input. Architects are better to facilitate intervention than drive it from a professional standpoint. Under this ethos of practice, architects undertake measures to engage with the community and provide them with a sense of ownership over the projects since the early phase of design. It is essentially research-led.

The encouraging sign in contemporary architecture and spatial politics of Northern Ireland is the increasing awareness of architects' roles as enablers for positive change. Several architectural practices, social enterprises or community-led efforts continue to contest a top-down approach to design, planning and urban development that disregard the community needs or the social-cultural context of the local groups. Northern Ireland practices hence started to embrace high community involvement in the projects and therefore affects the outcome of the project in a positive sense. Architects, hence, need to develop a relevant skill set to deal with such complex situations with communities, local authorities, and government bodies that invigorate innovative means of cross-community engagement, communication, and collaboration on shared interest.

7 Spatial voids and the integration of urban parks in divided Belfast

The landscape of sharing in a divided city[1]

Grounded in fragmentation and polarisation, the contemporary city is accustomed to the notion of division that is ingrained in the structural complexity of social hierarchy, in cultural diversity and the condition of coexistence. Layers of physical and social polarisation do exist in the urban fabric, services, infrastructures, and accessibility privileges (Mulholland et al., 2014). This polarisation becomes more evident in real inequalities in urban space, where the spatial expression of communities dominates the urban landscape (Amin, 2002). Groups with similar problems are forced to cluster into enclaves that offer support and protection in situations that would typically be the government's responsibility. Social groups attempt to overcome their sense of insecurity by fortressing behind physical boundaries that become part of their identities; the demolition of such boundaries becomes a non-tolerated offence. In these enclaves, myths about the 'other side' prosper and provoke fear that hinders the possibility of engagement (Goldie and Brid, 2010; Leonard and McKnight, 2011). Myths thrive on the way division and shareness stand in the collective memory of a group and become an ideology in a narrative form that communicates coherent social positions, norms, and fears (Lincoln, 1999). Divided infrastructures for housing, education, and other public services reflect layers of unspoken tensions and parallel lives that often do not overlap or have the capacity to promote meaningful exchange (The Cantle Report, 2001).

The nature of the division, be it ethnic, political, religious, or class, defines the structure of the city and the hierarchy of public spaces across the divide: pluralist, segregated, or contested (Gaffikin et al., 2010). The necessity of coexistence in public space leads groups to demarcate social and political territories based on gathering spots, patterns of sociability, and groups' defining features, such as dressing style, common food, art performance, or vocal expressions. The neighbouring Chinatown and Italian district in downtown San Francisco or Dubai's new developments present examples of distinctive identities that are a positive asset of a multicultural and diverse society. In contrast, Asian gatherings in Birming-ham or Algerian neighbourhoods in Paris are viewed as alien minority cultures in an increasingly divided society. While cities are formed out of the socio-spatial patterns of inevitable coexistence, the mix of ethnocul-tural groups and the rights and contributions of those groups in a collec-tive national society remain distinctively different (Parekh, 2000: p. 341; Gaffikin and Morrissey, 2011a).

Whether contestation among groups is perceived as good or bad, indi-viduals' attitudes towards shared living largely define the urban condition and shape the experience of public space. Hence, intercommunity exchange and contestation are a form of negotiation of power, dominance and space that outlasts the duration of the conflict. Long-term rivalry leaves memories and visual imprints that translate into a variety of physical forms, includ-ing walls, fences, murals, and even symbolic flags in extreme conditions (Calame and Charlesworth, 2009). According to Mike Morrissey and Frank Gaffikin (2006: p. 886), in these contexts, '[a] core aim would be to ensure that the contested city would contain more than just neutral spaces but shared public spaces. The peculiarities of locality will remain, but the chal-lenge is to make them inviting rather than threatening'.

Central to overcoming such a state of division is the ability to confront issues of particular identity and discriminative loyalty in public space in favour of collective belonging and shared commitment to socio-economic revival (Cunningham, 2001). Spatial division builds a lack of confidence in the political establishment and in administrative structures that foster unequal access to resources, protection, or opportunities (i.e., governance infused by divided loyalties and ethnic affiliations). The neutralisation of these spatial consequences can only ensue from restored confidence in the collective management of the city as equal for everyone. This idea helps us to understand the dynamics of the spatial landscape of 'shareness' in the modern city. According to Ralf Brand (2009a: p. 2674), contested cities are convenient cases from which to develop 'design conventions because they provide high-contrast scenarios where the variety of authors, power and enforcement mechanisms, rationales, forms of expression and degrees of socio-activity are clearly visible'. However, while the notion of division is researched exhaustively in post-conflict cities, the practice of shared living in everyday life remains understudied. Walls and partitions that exist to isolate opposing communities and prevent confrontation and violent offences are the same lines around which problems and suffering are primarily mirrored. Where they exist, lines of division harm as much as they protect. They act as negative urban features that hinder accessibility, walkability, and engage-ment and divert economic and job opportunities elsewhere.

In public space emerges an interplay of several spheres: physical (i.e., pri-vate and public), contextual (i.e., social and cultural), and global (i.e., vir-tual, media, social media, etc.). This interplay evokes tensions of collective memory, the search for the self, and the inevitable need to assert one's identity (Bauman, 2000). In this sense, narratives of territorial division in divided cities become a powerful tool for this assertion, as well as an ethnic protector and a self-defence strategy that often associates sacred meanings. The legitimacies of shared belonging are displaced by the politics of dominance, with an ever-present sense of underlying conflict between those who own the space and those who are alien in a continual reproduction of ancestral hostilities (Morrissey and Gaffikin, 2006). In these spaces of division, the undermined minority withdraws spatially, and the empowered majority expands in a manifestation of inequality. However, the account of minority/majority division is neither definitive nor detectable in terms of spatial representation or historical pedigrees unless this division is physically defined or forced by the political rivalry that attributes urban structure to inequality, privileged accessibility, and decision-making (Brand et al., 2008). In this sense, urban parks gain true significance as urban spaces where groups can react to the condition of coexistence and overcome boundaries of division in a quest to build a consensus of shared living; hence, urban parks are venues of 'shareness' per se.

Hence, urban parks come to the fore as places of exchange with a significant social role as a complex system of open socio-spatial engagement (Marcus et al., 1997). However, an urban park could be an irrelevant urban space to a community that depends on an active street life as a venue for local social networks. Low et al. (2009) argued that cultural diversity and mutual acceptance are expressed through behavioural patterns and the use of facilities in New York urban parks. Parks are therefore urban devices that tend to decode and shape sophisticated expressions of identity and power relationships in the city and to negotiate spatial relationships between the oppressor and the oppressed (Awan, 2008). Through its material design, space, and venues of interaction, the urban park interplays these tensions, where the antagonistic rivalry negotiates the thresholds of interface areas on a daily basis.

The park's essential elements of natural landscape, physical characteristics, and events, designers and planners generate a spatial system and accessibility privileges that either enhance engagement or foster division. A wooded forest, an artificial lake, or a set of functional playgrounds could quickly become a physical barrier if not integrated into an inclusive social system of shared venues and activities. The accessibility of venues and the timing of events could drive people away from using the park. These decisions have far more impact than the mere spatial rationale of aesthetic logic that may appear from two-dimensional drawings or maps. Equally central is to recognise the interest of each community/rival to extend their secure and exclusive territories into such shared venues, which are considered a territorial gain. Similar to home territories, communities prefer to have exclusive access to outdoor park spaces, when possible. Unless prevented through park design, rival communities would extend their dominance to reach a physical or natural barrier. Hence, spatial practices in the urban space emerge as reliable indicators of confidence in the public sphere and the city as a domain of cohabitation. Spaces, where people from different groups meet, become experimental environments that groups use to legitimise themselves through decisions of where to stay, gather, and socialise (McCann, 1999).

Belfast: urban structure of spatial division

As discussed before, the sectarian and territorial division has most shaped the history of Northern Ireland since long before the Troubles of the late 1960s (Leonard, 2006). Maps drawn as early as 1685 show clusters of segregated communities in Belfast, although it was not until 1969 that the relationship between the two communities turned into a militant rivalry due to the rapid growth of the Catholic community. Due to the industrial evolution of Belfast, the accelerated need for manual labour drew Catholic workers and families from rural Ireland to the flourishing city in the northeast, where they settled in either existing Irish communities or the western areas of the city (Brand, 2009b). The game of boundaries and the territorial demarcation between Northern Ireland and the newly independent Ireland in 1921–1922 was a discrete attempt to maintain certain majority/minority domination (Smyth, 1996). The violent troubles of 1969 triggered the move of thousands of families towards more exclusive community zones, where they sought protection and safety. Physical segregation resulted in interface areas, with separation walls, streets and parks as buffer zones that created 'no go' areas and influenced the deeply rooted 'cultural expectation' of territoriality (Leonard and McKnight, 2011). According to Jarman (2005), this division is 'a product of a process of contest over domination of social space and this contest contains the fear, threat or actual use of physical forms of violence', where communities defend their space against trespassers (Brand et al., 2008).

However problematic, segregation fosters inner community cohesion, solidarity, and sociocultural obligations towards local community institutions, which, in turn, consolidate and maintain the local system of authority (Darby, 2003). In fact, an abundance of research on public ritual in Northern Ireland suggests that community groups share similar attitudes and behavioural patterns despite differences in political orientation and ideology (Kearney, 1997; Keirsey and Gatrell, 2001; Shirlow, 1997). Such similarity translates into common spatial practices that mirror physical attributes of segregation in daily negotiations of power, domination, and presence in split public services. These practices are most evident around the Peaceline walls that started as temporary structures to isolate an incident of conflict at Shankill Road (Catholic)/Falls Roads (Protestant) in 1969 and grew into

99 walls that divide more than 55% of the population in concentrated communities (90% or more of the same sect) over the past 45 years. The mirroring of services on both sides of the divide costs the public purse more than £1.5 billion per annum (Deloitte, 2007). Due to the inaccessibility of facilities, communities lack drive and ambition for education and employment, affecting public attitudes towards the state and its flagship integrated and cross-community spaces.

The majority of planning measures in Belfast tend to either promote desegregation and the removal of existing physical boundaries or manage the provision of services across the separation lines in an attempt to confront inequality as a primary means of eliminating violence and conflict (Bollens, 1998; Boal, 1995; Birrell, 1994). The magic word *integrated* dominated much of the discourse and occupied a prominent place in all political initiatives and planning policies in the city; this word was used to brand newly introduced projects as being accessible to both communities and to counter the prejudice of considering public spaces as part of either community's domain. The central devices of this integration are urban parks that were developed in intercommunity areas with the expectation that members of both communities would mingle or use these parks on a daily basis. To some extent, these parks were meant to be temporary venues of peace conciliation that would gradually lead to public acceptance of a new spatial structure in a pluralist city.

However, the result of these projects and public interventions is mostly unimpressive. Instead, problems intensified. According to Gaffikin et al. (2010), the urban architecture has unintentionally reinforced the existing problems between the communities. Since the ceasefire in 1994, no Peaceline walls have been removed. Instead, 18 new walls have been built, extended, or raised (Jarman, 2005), raising questions about the effectiveness of political and planning intervention (Carmona et al., 2003) without a background culture of 'shareness'. Integration is more likely to be achieved if communities share values, morals and a work ethic (Smyth, 1996), avoid the 'culture of blame', and stop holding the rival community responsible for violence (Smyth, 1996; Jarman, 1999). How could the design of venues of spatial engagement be a key factor in fostering or alienating this notion of 'shareness'?

A rejuvenated vision of public space in Northern Ireland appears to escape this state of conflict by recognising the precondition of diversity as a democratic space that is not neutral but open and non-hostile (i.e., 'a place where different forms of cultural heritage can be expressed in an environment that is safe, welcoming, good quality and accessible for all members of society'; Belfast City Council, 2011: p. 5). Such a space is free from territorial and sectarian claims, impartial, and accommodates differences, not hostility. McKeown et al. (2012) categorise three types of shared space in the divided context of Northern Ireland. The first is 'naturally shared environments'

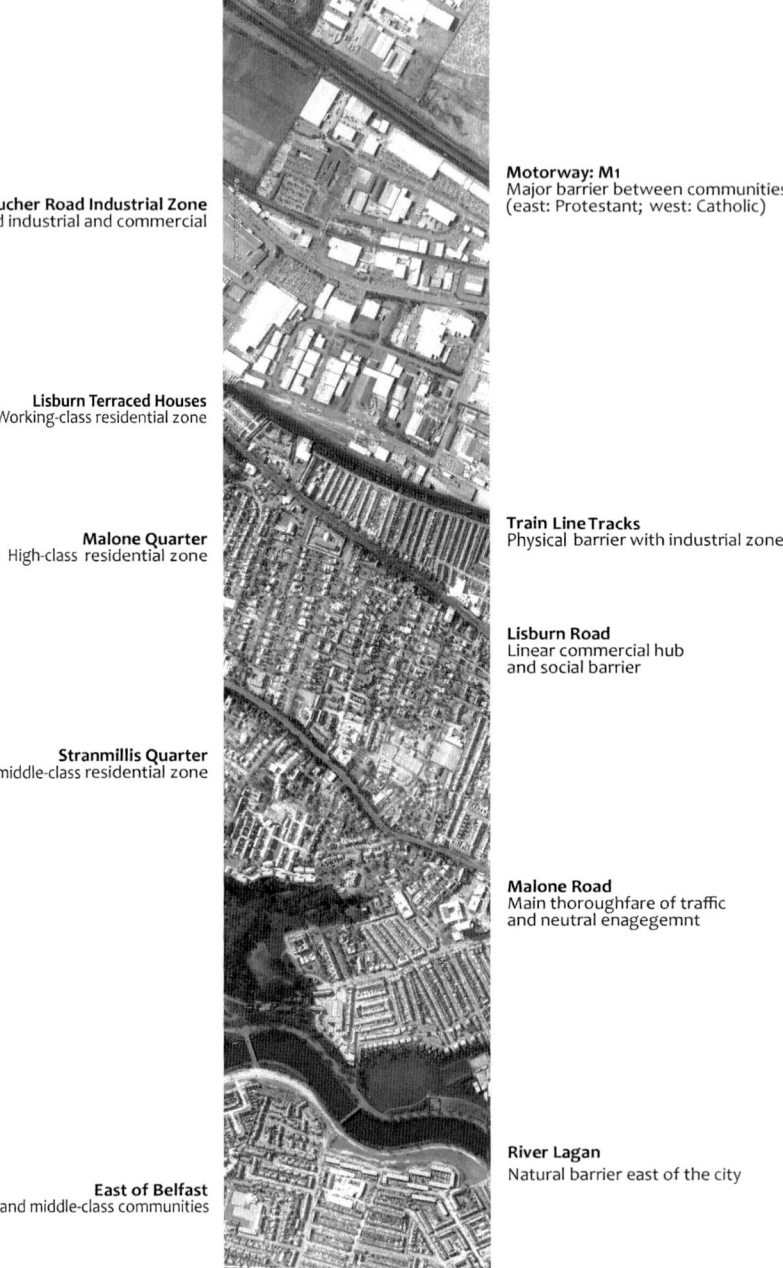

Boucher Road Industrial Zone
Mixed industrial and commercial

Lisburn Terraced Houses
Working-class residential zone

Malone Quarter
High-class residential zone

Stranmillis Quarter
A middle-class residential zone

East of Belfast
Working- and middle-class communities

Motorway: M1
Major barrier between communities
(east: Protestant; west: Catholic)

Train Line Tracks
Physical barrier with industrial zone

Lisburn Road
Linear commercial hub
and social barrier

Malone Road
Main thoroughfare of traffic
and neutral enagegemnt

River Lagan
Natural barrier east of the city

Figure 7.1 Spatial partitioning of Belfast: section of South-West Belfast that shows the spatial partitioning of the city's urban structure around natural and infrastructural barriers.

Figure 7.2 Defensive planning of business developments: Riverside Office Park on New Forge Lane, which is accessible only through a residential area in South Belfast and outside the city centre or accessible routes.

(i.e., everyday melting pots). The second is 'policy-driven shared environments', where spaces are created as deliberately shared spaces, such as integrated schools. The third is 'field interventions', which are generally short-term projects (e.g., cross-community programmes). This classification could also be applied to other cities with simple terms, such as *public space*, *planned space*, and *regenerated area*. However, the terms *shared* and *intervention* appear to be forcefully superimposed to deliver on the political image of 'post-conflict reality'. In addition, while the new liberal economy and associated economic structures have contributed to the emergence of neutral middle-class zones, these factors have done little to address the existing structures of division (Murtagh, 2002). In some cases, new business developments tend to be protected within a locality of dominance and away from violent public routes (Figure 7.2).

Integrated parks as urban devices for sharing

To determine the causal relationship between park design, spatial settings from one side, and the spatial patterns and everyday practices of local users and communities, a triangulated method of data gathering and analysis was applied. First, the physical characteristics, spatial organisation, and natural and hard landscape of the park space were mapped and documented with regard to the surrounding communities and area of dominance using a spatial survey. Second, interviews were conducted with users from both communities and casual/neutral users to map individual perceptions of the park and their reactions to implicit sociopolitical imbalances. The maps were demarcated to reflect the sense of belonging, safety, and privacy in territory that reflected a sense of community. This qualitative data was later compared with a third data set (i.e., the field observations of the researchers) based on specific durations and timing, which was designed to verify the reality of spatial practices, actions, and engagement with spaces, nature, and facilities. Hence, cognitive mapping was introduced to evaluate the intensity of the mentality of fear/risk of engagement and the extent to which this mentality determines individuals' actions within the park.

Overlaying these qualitatively driven data sets is the only way to gain more insights into the way the perception of division in polarised environments may drive actions and spatial practice or deceive the reality of active engagement with urban space. Hence, to obtain credible findings, four different typologies of open spaces, comprising two integrated community spaces, an integrated public space, and a private community space, were used as case studies in Belfast (Table 7.1). All parks were surveyed socially and spatially to determine actual and practical strategies for practising privacy in a demonstration of superior control (Figure 7.3). The case studies were selected to represent a variety of forms, scales, and conditions of contestation in the

Table 7.1 Locations and characteristics of selected case study parks in Belfast

Name	Location	Year of construction	Nature of activity	Majority/ minority dynamics	Inclusion of peace walls
Alexandra Park	North Belfast	1882	Recreational	Balanced: Catholic (eastern)/ Protestant (west)	3 metre-high across the park (1994)
Waterworks Park	North Belfast	1840s	Recreational/ sports facility	Catholic-dominated/ minority Protestant	No internal peace walls
Botanic Gardens	South Belfast	1828	Recreational/ public facilities	Balanced: Student-dominated	No internal peace walls
Cregagh Estate	South-East Belfast	1946–1947	Private recreational/ sports facility	Exclusively Protestant	No internal peace walls

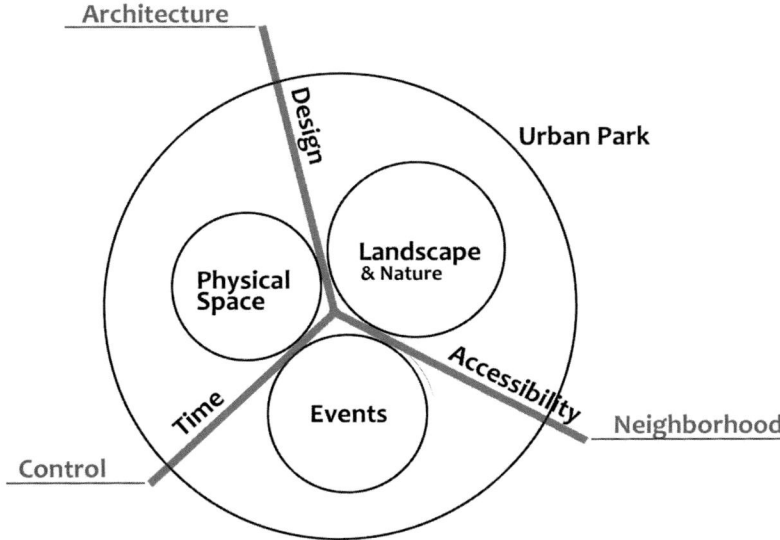

Figure 7.3 Urban park design: principal factors and settings of the contemporary urban park.

city that would collectively portray an overarching view of the design and challenges of the urban park in such a contested environment and hence inform the research findings. The criteria for the analysis included the documentation of activity trends and patterns and attitudes towards inclusion/exclusion. Social grouping, engagement in sports and exercise, children's freedom of play and movement, and fishing, among other factors, were at the centre of our analysis.

Using the spatial practice of private activities and patterns of control as indicators of active engagement with the park space and its power politics, the empirical data were analysed during the following stages:

1 Patterns of control in Belfast public spaces were reviewed through a sample investigation and analysis of official actions (i.e., planning and design) and the implications of a state of the division for the use of park space.

2 The four shared public spaces were chosen from parts of Belfast, where the division is an everyday reality: North, South, and South-East. Each case has a different majority/minority balance between the two communities, with different provisions for accessibility. One-on-one interviews were a sufficient qualitative tool for providing a sensitive perspective on the exploration of the subjects' everyday routines and

broader perceptions (Miller and Dingwall, 1997). Ninety-three community members and residents from both communities were interviewed, either in the public space under study or at their homes adjacent to these public spaces. These community members included 51 males and 42 females (refer to for gender grouping and age distribution in the different areas). The interviewees were asked to draw the boundaries in the shared spaces and public parks beyond which they did not feel safe, empowered, or even confident enough to walk freely.

3   This analysis was paralleled with periodic observations of groups' spatial practices within the park spaces at different times of the day. Observations were documented through photographs, maps and sketches, and interviews with members of the public and community representatives.

Based on the interviews, observations and spatial analysis, cognitive maps were produced using 'Decision Explorer' (Banxia, 2011) to identify and analyse people's activities in each of these public spaces. The information gathered was manually arranged into categories: Activities, Challenges, Strategies, Objectives, and Outcomes. Links between these categories were identified; for example, a particular challenge could be improved using a strategy and had spatial practice consequences. Gradually, a visual web of interpreted links was developed for each case study, and the process was repeated to create a final map of combined information that allowed the most-cited issues or the issues with the most links to be extracted from the main map through Domain, Central, and Cluster analysis. These individual cluster maps were further analysed to acquire the most common issues between the communities and the case studies.[1]

Spatial behaviour in the divided park-scape

Our fieldwork findings suggest that there is a fundamental need for creative design tools that address adverse reaction towards the principles of shared public space, as suggested by Morrissey and Gaffikin (2006). Four main issues emerged that have discrete impacts on behaviour and spatial patterns within integrated urban parks in Belfast. Analysing these issues will advance our knowledge and understanding concerning the attributes of an active and integrated urban park in a divided city and facilitate principles of good design. These issues are discussed under the following headings: a. Decision-making and spatial control; b. Spatial order and designing for shareness; c. Designing for blurred identities; and d. From the physical to the cognitive.

a. Decision-making and spatial control

The social fabric and ethnic topography of Belfast have resulted in disjointed communities with many sectarian struggles (Bollens, 1999a).

Urban parks, which are the crux of interface areas, were, unfortunately, utilised in such a way that difference is sustained (Leonard, 2006). Of surveyed inhabitants from the two main communities in Belfast (i.e., the Loyalist and the Nationalist communities), 86 percent would not enter an area dominated by the other group, while 79 percent would not travel through such an area at night, even by car (Shirlow, 2003). This division was further confirmed in our study, with nearly all participants confirming that they would not travel to the other edge of the park that separates them from the other community. The edges of the area that they consider safe to visit are identical and extend to the same natural or physical boundaries. These boundaries may be an artificial lake, a set of playgrounds, or a small forest of trees, depending on the park design. Parks that lack those definitive boundaries have several entrances, have pedestrian paths, and enjoy high traffic of neutral users appear to be effective and integrated park spaces. Public facilities and user destinations that are strategically located across far corners encourage stranger visitors and school tours that diffuse a sense of exclusive accessibility and privileges. To a certain extent, the model 'public' urban park that is an active destination for the whole city is far more successful than the one designed exclusively for local community engagement. The latter would naturally become an expansive field of territorial contestation.

In addition, villains assume control of the isolated spaces that result around division lines and physical barriers, leading to anti-social behaviour. By creating dead-end routes, the dividing wall develops a vacuum space for teenage drinking and violent confrontation, forcing the social activities of each community to withdraw from this territory. For example, sectarian confrontations in Alexandra Park in the 1990s led to the construction of a separation wall with a gate within what was supposed to be integrated recreational space, resulting in a dysfunctional recreation area (Jarman, 2004) (Figures 7.4 and 7.5). Daily observation and interviews highlighted underlying patterns of aggressive attitudes that contribute to the hostility around these Peaceline walls. These attitudes could be driven by vicious attacks or criminal offences, as well as by understudied planning decisions made by policymakers and the city's management.

Decision-making is a battle for control amongst adjacent communities that are motivated by self-interest, self-security, and local coherence. Only when a small building or facility becomes indispensable to the community does the reality of sharing become central to the process of conciliation and a catalyst for integration. The prominence of this process pervades issues of aesthetics in such instances and has somehow been absent from the planning perspective. An unplanned container shop in the Skegoneill/ Glandore interface area, which had a long history of intercommunity hostility, succeeded in attracting individuals from both communities. This shop provided an influx of local traffic that pushed offenders out while

Figure 7.4 Alexandra Park: the separation wall between the Protestant-driven eastern side and the Catholic-dominated western end.

Figure 7.5 View of the wall separating both communities.

combatting sectarianism more effectively than 'policy-driven' shared environments (Irish Times, 2010). However, the shop owner was consistently
denied planning permission due to the 'unsuitable aesthetics' of the shop,
and the shop was demolished amidst adverse reaction from the localities
(Meredith, 2011).

This case exemplifies the fact that a lack of understanding concerning the
dynamics of implicit patterns and attitudes could be damaging to the naturally developing practices of engagement. Successful integration has invariably
included an element of local self-interest in the planning and design stage, in
which both communities and their representatives are essential partners. The
Farset Community Farm and the Clovelly Street Redevelopment Area in Belfast, which was slated to become a shared space for both communities, failed
due to violent attacks and ingrained segregation habits (Brand, 2009a). Both
of these spaces fell victim to the inherited culture and a lack of support from
local communities. In contrast, the Stewartstown Road Regeneration Project
represents a success story of collaboration, negotiation, and work between
the Protestant enclave Suffolk and the Catholic Lenadoon in West Belfast
(Brand and Ferognese, 2013). The cross-community development model with
rented facilities and income-generating abilities has been replicated by the
Northern Ireland Housing Executive in Carran Crescent with mixed groups
of Protestant and Catholic residents.

b. Spatial order and designing for shareness

In the face of demographic imbalance around integrated urban parks, minority groups are more determined to seek psychological assurance through the
demarcation of territorial boundaries and the acknowledgement of de facto
ownership rights. The threshold is pushed further into the park to add space
to the group's domain of activities and privacy. That spatial divide between
the communities within the park space does not necessarily equate to pro-
portional dominance in the surrounding residential zones or accessibility.
However, dominant representation impacts the use of the park space, with
members of the majority group making full use of recreational spaces and
facilities alongside an equivalent spatial withdrawal of the minorities. This
scenario occurred in Waterworks Park, which is an integrated park in North
Belfast, with the Protestant community withdrawing spatially in the face of
the Catholic community's dominance: 'The majority of the park cannot be
used by Protestants' (R2-Prot). According to a community officer, '[t]here
are boundaries in the park, these go from the Cavehill Road entrance to the
bridge after the football pitch. The [Protestant] community will not go past
these' (R3-An). This observation confirms that Murtagh's (2002) observation that boundaries affect people both directly and indirectly by changing
the way they interact and move within the physical space appears to be
accurate in the urban park.

In community members' drawings, there was a common trend that the
Protestant community only felt comfortable using the triangular area

surrounded by the Cavehill Road entrance and a bridge below the Clift-
onville football grounds. Due to the perceived non-physical boundaries,
the facilities and activities are believed only to benefit the Catholic community. The Westland community was reluctant to participate in any
integrated activities (R4-Prot). A strategy involving the introduction of a
permanent fence or boundary blocking the Westland Community's access
to the park and effectively physically separating the park into two conflicting communities was proposed by the Council and Police Services of
Northern Ireland a decade ago. Luckily, this strategy was rejected (Jarman, 2004): '[I]t has brought about a sense of discrimination towards the
Protestant Community; they feel that it is biased towards the Catholic
group' (R3-An).

More profound is the dominant presence of a large lake that formed
another natural boundary and limited the level of interaction. With communities negotiating their boundaries, the physical presence of these elements
(i.e., the lake and the football playground) became undesired boundaries
that hindered potential engagement. Both of these elements allow individuals to mingle around their edges but prevent such engagement through their
space, making them adverse venues of engagement and 'social voids'. In
these voids, the psychology of fear reproduces the notion of barriers and
segregation, with little opportunity for free movement, social gathering, and
children's activities.

In areas where the park acts as the backyard for housing estates in both
communities, such spatial order has more significance, as it impacts families
in their own houses. For example, the Cregagh Estate is composed of a central, large open green space, small terrace housing, and blocks of flats with
a history of sectarian confrontations that caused tension over the shared
space (Darby, 1974; Figure 7.6). The separation of this space from public
access limited its users to the residents. Residents denoted 'smoking', 'having a cuppa', 'lying in the sun', 'kids playing', 'reading books and news-
papers', and 'gardening' as the private activities they pursue in the park
space adjacent to their homes. Due to the dominance of one community
(i.e., Protestant Ulster Scots), the residents felt relaxed to dominate the park
space as an extension of their community space and hold events and festivals. Events, such as the 'Festival of Ulster Scots', are typically orientated
towards the assertion of the identity of the community as a solid interconnected group (R9-Prot). Disputed sectarian murals are used in and around
the park as propaganda and expressions of identity rather than as pieces of
art (Buckley, 1998).

c. Designing for blurred identities

Spatial order that is associated with multi-user groups that have neither accessibility privileges nor exclusive occupation allows facilities
to become integral to the city at large, regardless of the surrounding

Figure 7.6 The Cregagh Estate's park, which is enclosed within the community and has limited access to outside users.

community affiliation. Situated in the multi-ethnic Queen's Quarter, with its vibrant student community, the Botanic Gardens enjoy a relatively neutral position in Belfast as a 'public' space per se. While the lack of accessibility to two adjacent ethnic communities has led to ongoing political and social issues (NISRA, 2001b), the public use of this space by the neutral student community, multiple access from three sides, the inclusion of the landmark Ulster Museum, and frequent visits by school groups, have made this space a very popular and trouble-free urban park (Figure 7.7). Nonetheless, the Botanic Gardens continued to be perceived by a community officer (R6-An) as a place of a sectarian divide with boundaries that discourage one community from using the space. Meanwhile, the large grassy areas, physical spaces such as the Glass House in the Winter Gardens and the Ulster Museum have all become activity destinations for families and children from different backgrounds. The distribution of buildings towards all corners, with routes from different entrances, has deliberately blurred local boundaries and diffused the potential sectarian divide that could have quickly developed around spatial voids and barriers.

Figure 7.7 Belfast Botanic Gardens: (a) location within the surrounding University
Grounds and student accommodation; (b) public activities and facilities
in the Botanic Gardens that are community-neutral.

In contrast, the design for blurred identities of more privately accessed
park spaces has proved somewhat problematic. The central issue in the
development of the exclusively accessed interface area between the Protestant Suffolk and the Catholic Brook (SLIG, 2008) was bringing representatives of both communities together to make decisions concerning the
design and spatial order of the park. Some consultation meetings were
conducted separately between the planners and members of each group.
In some instances, the two communities did not meet; instead, the communities separately put forward their ideas and proposals while the planners mediated the discussions. Despite some agreement, contestation over
ownership remained inevitable (R11-Prot). Hence, integration was limited
to a shared discussion over rights to the two sides of the barrier rather than
to the design of a single inclusive shared space with blurred boundaries.
Hence, the struggle of the negotiations was not over the space itself but
the power behind its management. In this context, the spatial design of the
space and facilities was a tool of negotiation that was used to gain more
access and space via integration. Under such conditions, the negotiation

over space and design means scarifying the very notion of blurred identities, which would negate the very notion of 'shareness': 'The community is not ready for the interfaces to be taken down; they may never be taken down. Instead, they have been replaced and renewed with something the community can benefit from' (R10-AN).

d. From the physical to the cognitive

Based on the documentation of respondents' interviews and responses, cognitive maps were developed and subsequently analysed based on the relationships that most commonly affect the assumption of spatial behaviour and practices in urban parks. This analysis provides links between common factors and factors that are of great influence (Banxia, 2011). While interviews and investigations determine people's actual behaviour, these maps help us to understand the cause of this behaviour and hence help to develop informed solutions. The central concepts related to spatial behaviour and control in the Urban Parks in Belfast can be seen in the way that these factors are linked to spatial division and issues of accessibility and constructed boundaries.

The perception of boundaries, whether physical or non-physical, contributes to the way communities use and interact in their outdoor park and landscape spaces. This effect makes accessibility a vital issue, as in the previously discussed case of the Botanic Gardens, where the positioning and aesthetic qualities of the entrance near Queen's Library have created a misconception that the land is private; thus, this design discourages the Donegall Pass community from using the space. Meanwhile, the Catholic community is discouraged from using the Cregagh Estate due to the surrounding Protestant context, proving that accessibility can be a mental perception of where space is located, and the Westland community is restricted to a specific area of the park due to perceived but non-existent boundaries. The external boundaries of outer fences fulfil a security function in both Waterworks Park and the Botanic Gardens, allowing the parks to be locked at night and discouraging the antisocial behaviour. Access in all of the investigated examples has likely been deterred by the psychological fear of 'not belonging' within a space rather than by physical obstacles. Here, the assumption of submission or vulnerability is a non-physical act that leads individuals to withdraw from unbalanced contestation. For example, the Waterworks Park in North Belfast provides great outdoor facilities for the community to use, but due to Westland's Protestant community's fear of being outnumbered and intimidated by the Catholic community, those individuals view the space and its facilities as inaccessible and are reluctant to engage in the available activities (Figures 7.8–7.10). Thus, it becomes apparent that the assumption of control encompasses the concept of making communities feel comfortable within a public space. It

Figure 7.8 Waterworks Park with highlighted boundaries for the Westland community.

has become a popular trend that communities extend their own claimed territories within a public urban space and public park to hold their exclusive social gatherings, activities, and festivities.

Based on the analysis of the interviewees' responses and interviews, we identified the main determinants of everyday interaction in urban parks using 'Decision Explorer'. Amongst the most common concepts (factors and issues that determine spatial practices and actions) that emerged from the responses are 'Boundaries', 'Accessibility', and 'unbalanced representation or population' within the urban parks, as per the following:

- Invisible/perceived boundaries – 25 from 53 concepts
- Make the space accessible to all – 25 from 47 concepts
- One community dominant or using the park more – 21 from 46 concepts
- Unbalanced population – 19 from 42 concepts

Figure 7.9 Intercommunity activities, including social running mornings at Waterworks Park.

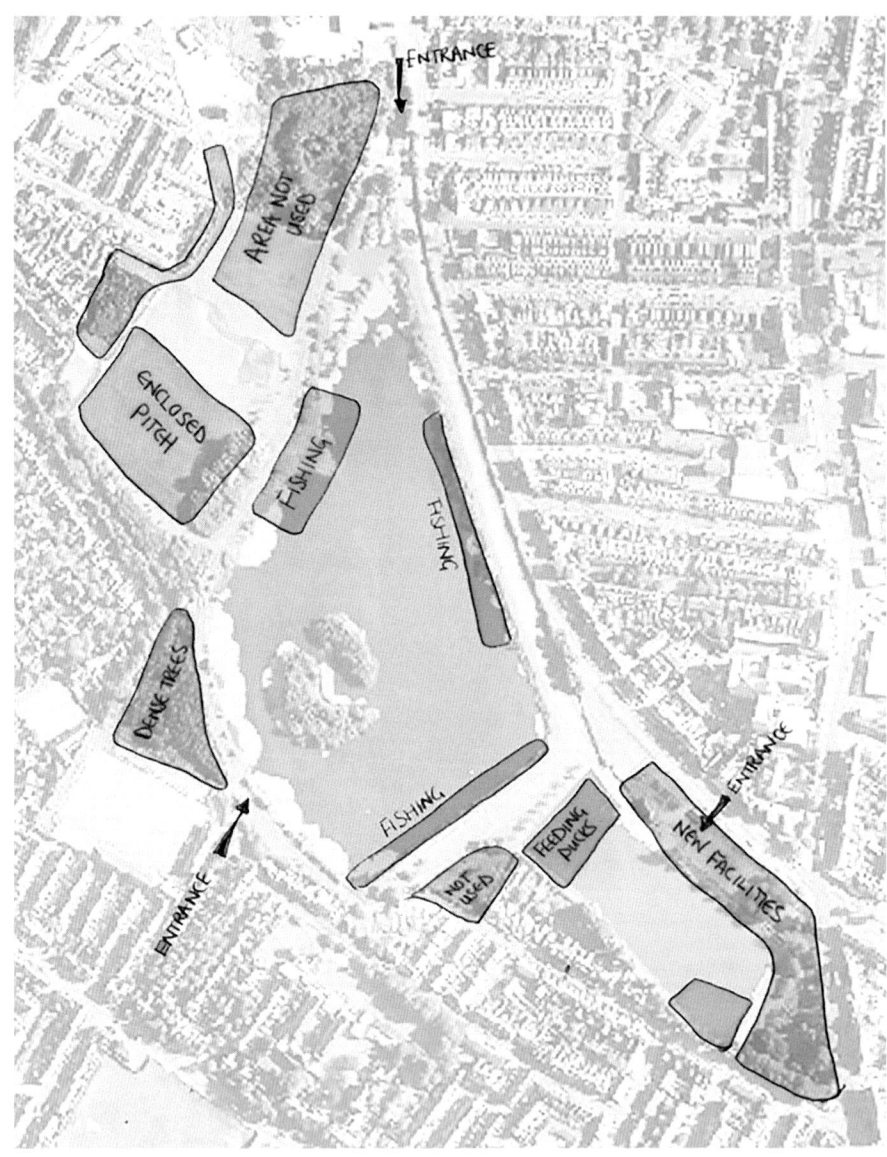

Figure 7.10 (a) Resident's sketch, highlighting the football pitch as a boundary between opposing communities; (b) resident's sketch of the perceived boundaries within which they can move freely.

Figure 7.10 (Continued)

Territorial division of urban parks in Belfast

In cities that are divided by ethnonational rivalry, public space and its architecture become the crucible of contestation related to ethnicity, territoriality and in particular cases, national identity. Physical barriers, such as Northern Ireland's Peaceline walls, materialise this paradoxical relationship of the edge as a line of separation and attachment, which is the inevitable reality of coexistence in a 'landscape of risk' (Leonard, 2006). Hence, this study of the spatial practices and patterns of activities carried out in four interface parks in Belfast has revealed the extent to which an atmosphere of prejudice is dictated by inherent tension over issues of identity, territorial gains and a contest over 'who controls the space' rather than by 'who uses the space'. The evidence indicates that the demand over territory is driven by a sense of insecurity on the minority group's side. Using their demographic dominance, groups expand beyond their perceived territory and make use of broad areas of integrated parks. An underlying aspect of urban parks is the ability of planners and designers to capture the dynamics of sociocultural and cognitive encounters that are essential elements of what should be investigative design processes. In such environments of division, conventional design principles do not work, as the dynamics of rivalry translate spatial configurations into territorial and political gains. Under the pressure of coexistence of rival groups, shared spaces are prone to becoming partitioned into non-physical territories where members of the other community feel intimidated.

Integrated parks with a soft landscape and a culturally neutral recreational atmosphere that have been offered by the state to ease and beautify these spatial relationships in a quest for gradual conciliations have suffered several setbacks and failed to bring proposals to reality. While the parks vary in their locations, conditions, scales, and designs, they were primarily driven by the vision of the designer and the planning authority, or its historical routes. Ironically, due to their spatial order, some integrated parks have expanded rather than limited the landscape of division. The architecture of the park that aims to encourage engagement and participation while trying

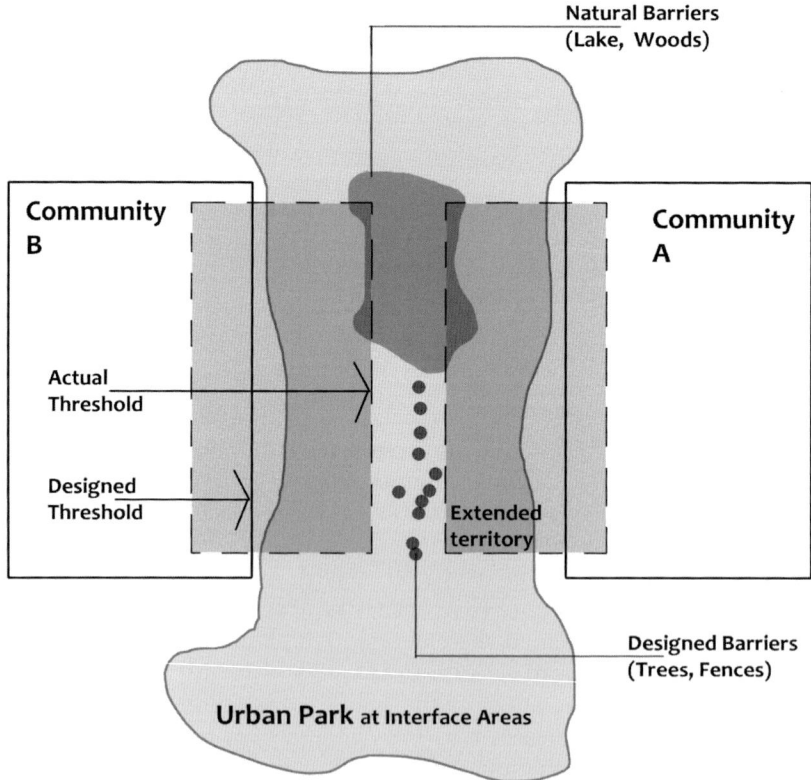

Figure 7.11 Patterns of territorial contestation in urban parks in Belfast.

to elude categorical identities has not always succeeded. In fact, through the presence of social voids, natural barriers or physical gaps, the spatial order, and the design of the park can become, in some cases, devices of further division. Figure 7.11 shows diagrammatically the way each community tends to extend their privileged spatial practices into the park space. Rather than acting as spaces of engagement, urban parks could offer rivals the opportunity to add to their territorial gains, using the park's physical and natural barriers and spatial layout.

Even though parks are designed to be integrative and accessible to all, the lack of a detailed and coherent spatial strategy that intends to stitch up the physical voids and fill socio-spatial gaps within the landscape of the park could have a damaging effect on the possibility of conciliation. We argued that a deep understanding of the modes and tools of spatial division is needed to develop models of socio-spatial behaviour that help to blur spatial and physical boundaries. Urban parks in divided landscapes require the social design of their components and physical elements if the objective is to allow people to engage with the park space and facilities while muting potential territorial claims. The strategic aim of the pluralist structuring of public space through equal access to services and facilities is not a solution to the cognitive psychology of division and prejudice towards the state, its planning authorities, and the culture of rival affiliations. Instead, a more sophisticated and multilayered approach to landscape planning and urban design is needed to focus on interweaved routes to essential facilities as a possible pathway towards spatial and social conciliation in both the public space and the city.

Part III

Understanding spatial practice and planning in divided cities

8 Landscape of difference

Encounters of contact, segregation, and urban justice in Derry/Londonderry

Living 'under siege' and encountering in the fountain estate

One of Northern Ireland's historic cities, Derry/Londonderry, is geographically divided by the River Foyle and man-made walls built between 1613 and 1618 as defences for early settlers from England and Scotland. The walls stretch about 1.5 kilometres in circumference and form a walkway around the inner city, which highlights the ethnic separation between the Catholic and Protestant communities. Following the famous Siege of Derry in 1689, it was classified a Protestant town, and Catholics resettled in the Templemore and Long Tower areas just outside the city walls, while wealthy Protestants moved out of the inner city and into the Waterside area. The Troubles of the 1960s marked obvious evidence that working-class Protestants and Catholics could not coexist, as previously mixed areas became exclusively one or the other. The people's political opinions were set in stone from this time on – a 'them and us' mindset (Murray, 2013); defensive walls and security barriers at interface zones have increased, isolating urban sections of Derry/Londonderry (O'Brien and Nolan, 1999: p. 557).

The Fountain estate is the last Protestant community living in the Cityside section on the west bank of the Foyle and surrounded by the predominantly Catholic areas of the Brandywell, Bogside, and Creggan. Population demographics show that the working-class estate houses approximately 500 residents living in blocks of terraced houses, many of which are managed by the Northern Ireland Housing Executive, the Fountain Primary School, and the Life Triumphant Church. The minority group is hemmed into a small area by means of Peaceline walls and barriers constructed on two sides along Bishop Street, Bennett Street, and to the rear of houses on Harding Street, while the historic Derry walls border the estate on a third side. The barrier along the Fountain interface and Bishop Street was erected in the 1990s to control access to the estate through a security gate that could easily connect or seal off both areas during times of tension and violence (Derry City Council, 2010). However, almost 40 years after the start of the Troubles, the walls and barriers remain intact and are used for what they were intended: to separate.

Politically motivated violence in Derry/Londonderry encouraged people to retreat to the 'security' of their enclaves or to create new ones, as '*mental divisions, through which the signified places are communally guarded and bounded, which often strengthen physical boundaries and vice versa*' (Kuusisto-Arponen, 2003: p. 73). Despite ongoing peace negotiations, started in 1997, new barriers have been constructed. On the other hand, division, combined with proximity to the Other, showed a heightened cultural self-definition and caused the distinctions between the two to be massively exaggerated, 'the narcissism of minor differences' (Ibid.: p. 22). The barriers also distorted travel patterns, as routes from one enclave to the other have been reduced or gated so that they can be closed off in times of high tension (Bevan, 2006). In a way, levels of social equality appear unbalanced under high measures of governing free movement and walkable routes.

Living in such settings is not without its troubles, on either side of the barriers. Flags, parades, and gable-end murals are all signs of distinct differences in Protestant and Catholic cultures, when, in fact, the differences between the two are very slight at the root (Bevan, 2006). The estate kerbstones and lampposts are emblazoned red, white, and blue to match the fluttering Union flags.[1] When walking around the Fountain; one cannot miss a well-known mural stating 'Londonderry West Bank Loyalists Still Under Siege No Surrender'. The mural widely evokes the sense of a wartime blockade and an attitude of defiance towards the invader. Even though Derry/Londonderry has been free of any ongoing battles for a while, the residents use metaphors like this to express how they feel about living on the estate and their thoughts about life beyond its borders. They mentally incorporate this meaning into their everyday encounters and behaviour, in which some people interestingly say, '*[W]e have a siege mentality . . . . but sometimes we feel that we are under real siege*' (R10). Indeed, the term *siege* brings to mind areas of attack and resistance in a battle, and therefore the militarisation of treatise implies the militarisation of thought and practice. Accordingly, people living 'under siege' probably tend to have their ways of protecting themselves, reacting, and progressing from day to day.

For the people living in the Fountain, the events of the Troubles remain stories handed down to the younger generations of both community groups. For generations facing conflict, learning about history is a significant challenge, not merely because 'it eventually surrounds them everywhere' (R1). As this chapter shows, their daily journey to schools and public amenities passes through memories of conflict, articulated in artefacts and murals displaying pain and distress. The Bogside Catholic murals, for example, communicate the British government's domination and the community's resistance since the 1960s. A caption on a gable wall, noting 'You are now entering free Derry', recalls the Bogside Battle in 1969. McCann (1993) claims that such assertions are reproduced differently by newer generations, who have traditionally received similar accounts from the past and demonstrate a particularly hostile attitude towards the Other, with a sense of belonging to one's group that knits people together.

The Fountain, similarly, displays murals on the walls, but they deliver different narratives displayed and told through its people. Murals in the Fountain not only express the loyalty of the Protestant groups to the British Crown, with flags extremely visible at the first glimpse, but also communicate accounts of their past experiences and solidarity (Rolston, 2010: p. 294). While these may be seen as intimidating, they allow ethnic groups in Derry/Londonderry to maintain their identity alongside that of their surrounding neighbours; many residents feel that, without these symbols, as Nationalist or Unionist neighbourhoods surround them, their cultural identity would eventually be diminished (Figure 8.1).

The geography literature documents examples of segregated neighbourhoods sectioned by conflict and rife with the struggle over different ways of doing and being in urban shared spaces (Watt and Stenson, 1998). The battle over space not only comprises ownership and control of public space among different ethnic groups but also 'among citizens of different ages – like tension between teenagers, who often feel unjustly marginalized in public space by adults, and the elderly who are commonly fearful of groups of young people'(Valentine, 2008: p. 328). Positive contact could be undermined by any manifestation of differences that could breed frustration and resentment at various scales and levels; however, the range of socio-spatial practices linked to segregation is vast.

Figure 8.1 The Fountain Estate housing units.

How could two ethnically segregated communities accept sharing public spaces, travelling routes to schools, health care, and public transport without jeopardising their safety and emotional wellbeing? Key answers to this question may critically reflect the history and politics of spatial segregation, which is undoubtedly relevant to social psychologists. Shirlow et al.'s study (2005) looked at the urban demographic decline of the Protestant population living in Derry/Londonderry, showing a 'reduction in violence that led to re-engagement with the shopping areas in the Cityside' (Shirlow et al., 2005: p. 4). In fact, Protestants were willing to interact regularly and socialise with non-Protestants. Nevertheless, they remained in a state of cultural uncertainty, which increased levels of marginalisation and a sense of inequality (Ibid.).

Physical, emotional, and ideological safety in the public realm was the key factor to drive development in Derry/Londonderry. Reclaiming shared space aimed to develop a town centre that was safe and welcoming and free from threat, aggression, and intimidation (A Shared Future Report, 2005). The minister of state for Northern Ireland, John Spellar, noted in 2005 that 'good relations must be based on partnership, equality and mutual respect and it must be built upon the significant progress that has been achieved to deliver equal opportunity rights across Northern Ireland' (Ibid.). However, Protestants in Derry/Londonderry generally feel that they were neglected during the development phases of Northern Ireland's nationalism, with 'minority representation at council levels' and fewer job opportunities (Shirlow and Graham, 2005: p. 9). Claims were also made about lower levels of availability and access to services. While it is not proven that employers discriminated against residents of the Fountain, some individuals believed that they did not have the same opportunities as people living in the Bogside, for example, 'just because they are from the Fountain's' (R7). Inequalities are often a burden on those in the post-education sector, particularly when 'putting on a job application identifying yourself as coming from the Fountain. It is just like a black mark; people get automatically refused because they are tainted with the name' (R8).

The physical proximity between both communities often aggravates comparisons when it comes to access to facilities. The Fountain community is in relatively low-income or insecure forms of employment, with either housing or health concerns. They told community-based narratives of social disparity, injustice, and victimhood, acknowledging that the barriers allow minimal contact with the outside and controlling their access and movement patterns, despite its significance to their safety or regardless of the sociocultural integration with the Catholics living nearby (R3). The fact that the entire estate is solely composed of housing units, with the exception of the school, the youth club, and the church, and lacks essential services raised their criticism. The estate, for example, has 'no newsagents, cafés or takeaway restaurants, so residents must travel outside the enclave for the most basic amenity, especially in the morning time when they feel safest' (R3).

In the past, small shops were available, but 'the migration of many people from the Fountain to the Waterside has resulted in their closure' (R5). Instead, residents have to visit shops on Carlisle Road, which is a 5-minute walk but outside the enclave borders. The construction of the Peace Bridge in 2011 along the river was a concrete manifestation that visualised a wider vision of integration and contact. Although it sought to improve connections on both sides of the river, movement patterns available to both groups diminish its social implications. These quotations from some of the focus group communities capture a sense of their persistence:

> There is no shared space for the Protestant community living in the estate; there is a park just adjacent to the Fountain at the bottom of the road, but our kids can't use that park. Anytime they try and use it they're stoned out. (R3)
>
> They are called Orange "B's" and all these terrible names. It's just a space we can't utilise at all. (R4)
>
> I couldn't name you a shared space on the Derry side at all. (R4)
>
> Our kids here are hemmed in. They can't even use the shopping centre unless there's a group of them together. They can't use the corner shop unless there's a group. There are no shops in the Fountain area. There's nowhere user-friendly for the young people here. (R2)

On the other hand, institutional spaces, such as schools and universities, would instigate amalgamation rather than separation, where contact and intercultural exchange are most likely to occur (Vanderbeck, 2007); hostility among groups, however, changes the equation. The negative side of this appears through social research outcomes showing higher levels of animosity in schools with a different class, gender, and religious practices (Valentine and Skelton, 2003). Orr (2012), for example, used a behavioural approach to test intergroup contact amongst young Protestant and Catholic individuals in schools, colleges, and community groups in Northern Ireland. He found that participants made self-segregating decisions in the early stages of interaction, based on both religious tradition and national identity (Ibid.). An elderly informant from the Fountain noted that 'I grew up in a mixed area of Catholics and Protestants. The only difference between us was that we went to different schools; although I didn't understand why' (R10). There was also a common belief among the Fountain community that institutional facilities must be separated because they 'would not feel safe walking to school through similar travelling routes with the Catholics' (R11), which is why most children attend the local Fountain Primary School on the estate or primary schools on the Waterside (R5). At the secondary education level, with the exception of Foyle College and a grammar school in the Pennyburn area, there are no non-Catholic secondary schools for the Fountain community on the river's west bank, so they attend Lisneal College on the outskirts of the city, which seems a convenient option because otherwise, 'they would always be worrying about their kids['] safety' (R6).

In such settings of subjective and communal anxiety, it is likely hard to have mutual respect and integration towards groups they perceive as a threat. At some times, being prejudiced could become an asset for some individuals by presenting them as victims of their failures. Being prejudiced, for example, could also provide them with a conferred interest in favouring intolerance, despite progressive individual encounters with the other community. As such, violence, incivility, and discourtesy between proximate communities become naturalised acts of everyday encounters. This was evident during the annual Orange Order Parades on the 12 July, for example. Carnivals often move from the Waterside, over the Craigavon Bridge, and into the Fountain, passing by the Diamond area in the city centre. Informants recall that they attended the parades 'the same as others and so aren't restricted from celebrating their culture' (R5). However, this is not without its difficulties. The parades are usually guarded, in certain areas, with a high police presence, to keep tensions at bay, although 'recent years have been relatively quiet' (R7). Similarly, community workers closely collaborate to ensure that young people from the other side are kept busy with activities organised during that time, or are taken to field trips away from any possible trouble.

However, even under high measures of precaution, attacks by young Catholics would frequently recall the Siege metaphor by the majority of older residents of the estate. Using public transport is always preferable. The youth club informants said that 'it is crucial not to walk in groups, but we prefer to take a bus to go anywhere, even on the shortest journeys' (R4, R9). An additional incident happened when a visit to the nearby Peace Bridge on foot was planned. On the return journey, young groups of a neighbouring community were waiting at notorious interface areas, and violence broke out (R12). Individuals feel victimised and powerless, in such cases, because they cannot walk freely between sections of the city, as a spatial practice that became opposed to collective modes of administration and politicisation (De Certeau, 1984: p. 96). Community groups from the Fountain were mostly in agreement while justifying their retaliatory violence against their attackers. Often in an aggrieved, or infrequently in a matter-of-fact, tone, they claim that they were defending themselves.

Ongoing cross-community schemes have been in place to listen to communities and promote contact (Murtagh, 1999), but even this initiative is problematic. On one occasion, the conflict was in place mainly 'when they allowed us to work face to face and youth boys from the Fountain were attacked after being recognised' (R2). It is necessary here to grasp discourses associated with the reproduction of social cultures, such as social relationships, identities, beliefs, and norms. By adhering to the discourse of feeling anxious and unsafe in the presence of members of the other community outside the Fountain's borders, although it might not be true, the informants build their sense of belonging with fellow Fountain residents and with their community. When a new play pitch was erected in 2012, apparently, all community members gathered there with their children while simultaneously keeping their frontiers with the other community closed, and the potential transformation intact.

However, there are certain levels of imbalance influenced by the physical location of the Fountain estate and its relationship with its outside neighbours. The fact that essential amenities are distanced from the estate highlights one form of instability and uncertainty; errands must take place at certain times of the day and, for some people, only in a group, revealing an increased version of the moral and political allegory of 'the Siege'. While the current economic climate may prevent any other facilities being brought into the Fountain, people are eager to walk and travel freely without the fear of attack from the Other side. The closure of the gate in the Bishop Street wall at night also fuels the 'siege' metaphor, where temporal and spatial dimensions of freedom are denied, and residents are 'hemmed in' and only allowed 'out' during the day (R11). However, it is believed that the physical presence of the gateway is indispensable to alleviate tensions, thus confirming the theory put forward by Calame and Charlesworth (2009) that, as long as the walls remain intact, fear and paranoia relating to the Other side would always remain (Figures 8.2 and 8.3).

Figure 8.2 Peaceline wall running alongside Bishop Street and the Fountain Estate.

Figure 8.3 Bishop Street gate that closes between 9 p.m. and 7:30 a.m.

To a certain extent, the Fountain community restructured their socio-spatial and contact practices according to the cognitive images of their rooted division. Vaneigem (1967) believes that direct communication between qualitative subjects is the end of the spectrum to which history leads people to become manipulated as passive objects in the absence of qualitative richness descended from proclaiming their complex distinctiveness. People in the Fountain rarely recall stories of the Troubles or probably have inherited little from the past (R5). As Vaneigem (1967: p. 231) argues, 'an ideology of history has one purpose only: to prevent people from making history . . . preventing them from coming to life, from rising from the dead and running once more through the streets of our daily lives'. What stood out in this context were the omnipresent signs of security and defence. There is no harm if one was caught in a fight, simply because 'everyone has done it and they are inevitable' (R15). Apter (1997: p. 1) claims that, in time, rooted and long-lasting violence tends to become a norm of the everyday reality, where individuals acquire defensive skills that live in them, although it is now occurring at much lower levels than in the past.

Regardless, people from the Fountain still believe that feuds and tensions between Catholics and Protestants are unavoidable 'just because of what they did to us long ago' (R2). In fact, younger generations from the Fountain did not witness the Troubles themselves: '[T]hey only reproduce the discourse of their community and what they were told by their families' (R8). 'The event is, so to speak, deep-frozen. It becomes illegal to retrieve it, remake it, complete it or attempt its transcendence. It is merely there, preserved forever in suspended animation, where the aesthetes can contemplate it at their ease' (Vaneigem, 1967: p. 234). They repeatedly express intertextual stories of the history of the Troubles in a way that recalls the fact that they have never lived with Catholic communities, although they simultaneously feel disconnected from the other side of the community. 'If you are raised in the Fountain, you will never have friends from the other side' (R14). These narratives became unconsciously 'repeatable' and mentally stored from the past, to become model actions to legitimise the future non-acceptance of the Other (Porter, 1986: p. 35). On occasions, the hostile attitudes towards the Other have developed from an apparent feeling of discrimination during the past while the struggle continues today.

Spatialising peace and interdependence

> To construct the present is to rectify the past, to change the psychogeography of our surroundings, to hew our unfulfilled dreams and wishes out of the veinstone that imprisons them, to let individual passions find harmonious collective expression. The time gap which separates the insurgents of 1525 from the Mulelist rebels, Spartacus from Pancho Villa, or Lucretius from Lautreamont, can be bridged only by my will to live.
> – Raoul Vaneigem (1967: p. 233)

Conflict incidences in Derry/Londonderry showed that proximity, on its own, is not sufficient to bring about social transformation; instead, more emphasis on building the next generation of peacemakers in Northern Ireland is crucial. Amin (2002) argued that it is essential to create spaces of interdependence to develop a mature intercultural understanding. However, if we need to get closer to others, what should we do? Is it a matter of mental confidences for peace, or should we raise the bar of our enthusiasm to develop platforms and paths of interaction and contact, with spaces that could help healing memories of the past to generate new hopes of futuristic peace and interdependence? As such, attempts from all sectors of the community to capitalise on this process appeared on the surface. In 1987, Antony Gormley designed a sculpture for Derry: a three-part statue in three particular locations on the Derry Walls; one sculpture sits on the east overlooking the Foyle River, one over the Bogside by the remains of the Walker Monument, and one on the Bastion overlooking the Fountain estate.

The sculptures represented Derry's two dominant religious communities, turning away from each other but paradoxically joined as one body.

Despite that both communities were separated by their religious, cultural, and political differences, the sculptures advocated that they are united in their Christianity and their shared location. The Arts Council of Northern Ireland organised another venture in 2011. The 'Re-Imaging Communities Programme' was supported by Derry City Council to produce some arte-facts designed by local children from schools and community groups in the area (Derry City Council, 2011). Non-competing endeavours like these are anticipated to bring communities and individuals together and to empower the 'recognition or acknowledgement of Otherness in situational specificity' rather than, for example, to constantly develop robust bonds of friendship (Wise, 2009: p. 35). It is also a long-term strategy to learn from the future through establishing social programmes set out to identify social niches through well-defined methods and processes of implementation (Huse, 2014: p. 189).

On the other hand, everyday interaction, it is argued by Christina Ho (2011), could be generated in the micro-publics of cross-cultural contact and encounters, where various social settings of everyday life take place, for example, workplaces, sports centres, communal parks, schools, and chil-dren and youth community participation schemes (Amin, 2002: p. 969). In the micro-publics, people with diverse backgrounds are brought together to negotiate new patterns of social and cultural exchange and to transcend cul-tural boundaries to transform the inherited relationships of the past (Ibid.). However, if we are asking how to spatialise micro-publics of peace in Derry/ Londonderry, the apparent response will be by removing the security bar-riers first. This holds long-term negations with Northern Ireland ministers and policymakers. In 2013, work started to take down 11 of the 16 gates, with the hope that this act would send a positive message about a city once blighted by some of the worst of violence during the 30-year conflict. In fact, earlier in the year, Derry/Londonderry held the title of UK City of Culture in 2013 and was designated one of the top 10 cities in the world to be visited, with the historic walls progressively welcoming tourists flocking into the city to enjoy the wealth of cultural events.

As noted by Northern Ireland justice minister David Ford, 'the walls can now be enjoyed without the imposing structures that point to our past rather than our future' (Dawson, 2007: p. 92). Working closely with stake-holders from both communities, this initiative was supported by the Peace Walls Programme (PWP) adopted across Northern Ireland to encourage both communities to overlook the past and to stop searching for differences. It also aimed to deliver and develop confidence and relationship-building interventions to help them reach a position where they feel safe to move on with the removal of their local Peaceline walls. With such an optimistic atmosphere, it may be hard for tourists to imagine the city's troubled past, which has been 'shaped by violent and traumatic conflict' (Dawson, 2007: p. 92).

Primary and secondary schools, as micro-public spaces with children segregated by ethnicity and religion from the age of 3 and educated separately until 18, are also realistic places to start desegregation. In 2013, 300 primary-school children from the Derry/Londonderry City Council area gathered on the iconic Peace Bridge to welcome Children in Crossfire's patron, His Holiness the Dalai Lama, to the city. The party engaged in a symbolic walk across the Peace Bridge, from the cityside to the waterside, chaperoned by the children who formed a guard of honour, singing 'Peace is flowing like a river'. The Serpentine of the Peace Bridge itself was designed as a structural handshake across the Foyle, creatively built to tackle the problem of the separated communities by creating genuine and unique shared space. Also, a newly installed all-weather play pitch opened in summer 2012 for children of the Fountain community, to form part of the landscape of the primary school and the youth club. 'Facilities like this, and improvements being made to housing, in the estate, have resulted in some new families moving into the area' (R5).

In the past, the closest recreational area was the Riverview Play Park, located in the Bogside and Brandywell areas, which were avoided by the Fountain residents, fearful of entering these neighbouring areas despite efforts for integration in place since 2011. Interestingly, the minority Protestant community from the Fountain rarely referred to their historical propositions to locate themselves in history, either to position and describe themselves in opposition to the majority of Catholics surrounding the Fountain in terms of historical successes or to present their community as victims of the past. Instead, as explained earlier, they presented their intertextual references to what has become more critical for them, as a matter of daily routine survival and belonging, which adds meaning for them to be more positively constructive about themselves. One explanation for this is that people lack robust ties with their modern history and repeatedly get confusing information about the past.

The core of Allport's contact theory is that when individuals of one group display negative behaviour towards the Other, this probably leads to a generalised negative impression towards the entire group. Dominant attitudes could also be represented in the context of positive encounters; however, evidence from this research showed that 'encounters never take place in a space free from history, material conditions, and power' (Valentine, 2008: p. 333), and these conditions are indeed evident in Derry/Londonderry. Conflict and tension between rival communities of Protestants and Catholics, Unionists and Nationalists, and Loyalists and Republicans are well-documented in the history of Derry and indeed the rest of Northern Ireland, and therefore the Fountain is no different. On the other hand, negative encounters tend to be generalised while positives only represent individual endeavours, and indeed, judgements from both sides will usually be based on their intertextual accounts of the Troubles that consequently develop into a model of actions that legitimise their future encounters. The geographies of the political and economic environment of division allow victimised groups to justify their encounters, and therefore, these groups tend to not acknowledge their behaviours as instituting prejudice but, rather, the freedom to express their grounded opinions in the course of the Troubles.

A possible resolution is the need to generate models of contact with innovative indexes that allow interactions among individuals. A fundamental start will be acknowledging equalities and the right to the city between all community groups, such as enabling even resource allocation, for example, job opportunities, affordable housing, and reasonable education. Only in such settings could different groups become less defensive or antagonised. It was reported in 2012, by the Northern Ireland Housing Executive (NIHE, 2012), that almost £200,000 would be invested in the homes of 170 residents of the Fountain Estate for much-needed renovation and improvement works. On the other hand, both communities started to have a close working relationship, initiated some years ago, to minimise interface trouble during the marching season. Further relations developed to create a number of cross-community programmes and activities supported by a dedicated team funded by the International Fund for Ireland (IFI) PWP. The programme aims to transform the enclave into a shared community asset to reduce the physical and physiological barriers surrounding the estate.

Along with this, a high level of appreciating the Other is crucial, which requires critical inquiries in human behaviours to deliver efficient frameworks to add values towards cultures and identities and to cut back discrimination or intimidation. Indeed, interviews with the Protestant community of the Fountain endorsed conclusions in relation to how the everyday encounters in a divided city impact the use of space, access to amenities, movement patterns, and sociocultural identity. Moreover, the security barriers, the city walls, and, indeed, the River Foyle all act as intimidating boundaries with lasting effects on the lives of residents, leading to a life of controlled movement and fear of the other side. It could be argued, however, that some positive aspects of divided communities were witnessed here: culture and identity, which are distinct from the Other, emerged in this small community, while the Fountain community spirit enables this identity to be zealously maintained. The creation of groups, such as the Cathedral Youth Club, enhances the community's opportunities to gain person-to-person contact with like-minded people and gives rise to positive influences on behaviour (Gordon and Monastiriotis, 2006). The work carried out by the community workers and their colleagues certainly backs up this claim, proving that the residents' welfare in the estate is of the utmost importance, so 'thinking outside the box' helps them to provide opportunities and enhance the lives of the residents.

Spatial improvements are also necessary for the Fountain to achieve social equality. The Peaceline walls around the estate have both positive and negative value: they provide security and alleviate tensions but, as highlighted by Bevan (2006), as long as these walls remain intact, paranoia and fear of the other side will remain, and full inclusion into the rest of society can never be achieved. Problems in Northern Ireland have continued for several decades, and so it is unlikely that any action will provide an overnight remedy. In fact, time is the most significant factor in bringing change to such communities. Current generations that experienced the full nature of violence and tension during the era of the Troubles find it challenging to change their views and attitudes towards such political matters, whereas the next generation of young people could be the key to providing a permanent change in Northern Ireland and eventual peace between currently separated communities. Attitudes are changing, with many people eager to move on with their lives; however, this is a slow process to show significant results. As long as there are political and cultural tensions in Northern Ireland, there will always be divided cities; as this research claims, it is likely that there will always be social inequality in one form or another.

9 Intertextual spaces

Young people's memories of segregation in Derry

Introduction: generation of post-conflict Derry

Conflict in Northern Ireland has placed an unequal and devastating burden on its young people. These youngsters are sons and daughters of the 1994-ceasefire generation who lived through and witnessed traumatic violence and experienced bereavement (Kilkelly et al., 2004; Gilligan, 2006). This was also a time when insecurity was a common feature of everyday experiences (Harland and McCready, 2012; Harland, 2011; Hansson, 2005). Desmond Bell (1990) explains that in the late 1960s, young people in Derry/Londonderry succeeded in developing their unique sense of ethnic identity – of being Ulster Protestant or Irish Catholic – in the midst of political crisis and sectarian confrontation. At that time, people faced unemployment conditions, segregated educational systems, and increased levels of ghettoised residential living (Ibid.). By the 1990s, discussions on the 'peace process', community differences, sectarian violence, and shared spaces were active, at times heated, and mostly drew on young people's own lived experience and the experience of their families and communities (McGrellis, 2010).

These communities' transition to peace has been slow and not without political or social challenges (McAlister et al., 2013). However, the peace process negotiations evinced a progressive turn in young people's lives and crossing the lines of division (McGrellis, 2010). A shift in the political landscape 'contributed to their [young people] biographical narratives of community, affiliation, identity and perceived opportunity in ways that either reflected new optimism and confidence or enduring fear and suspicion' (Ibid.: p. 764). It also endorsed practical opportunities for physical mobility into the territory of the Other to support stronger social bonds and new relationships (Caballero et al., 2008).

Young people from either side certainly still suffer from distrust of and prejudice towards the other community – the same attitudes that have burdened their parents for decades. Until today, they frequently engage in uncontrolled violence or verbal confrontations in the street. They are strictly attached to their local territories while cultivating their personal encounters against the Other. Young people garner important benefits 'from their ability to shape their identities by occupying public spaces' (Pickering et al., 2012: p. 945). Cummings et al. (2016), for example, explain that youths aged 11 to 14 living in high religious interface areas in North Belfast are at high risk of alcohol abuse, low self-esteem, anxiety, depressive feelings, and low mood. Their everyday space of encounters becomes a sharp chain of edges and borderlines in which stories of conflict are engrained. Byrne and Jarman (2011) note that between 1995 and 2003, young people were gradually *demonised* as the cause of the violence, particularly those connected with criminality, damage, and chaos. Such attitudes gave rise to young people being labelled as 'youths causing annoyance' and 'anti-social behaviour' within working-class communities in Northern Ireland (Hansson, 2005).

These attitudes could be attributed to the absence of evocative cross-community contact, which somehow impacts the behaviour and integration of younger people (Devine and Schubotz, 2010). Social surveys, such as the Young Life and Times, also facilitate easy access to social and political data on Northern Ireland. The Access Research Knowledge (ARK: Northern Ireland Social Policy Hub) project, which has been running since 2003, conducts interviews with 16-year-olds living in Northern Ireland with regard to their experiences of integration/segregation, and it monitors attitudes to community relations and religious mixing (Stockinger, 2015). Young people have narrow prospects about extending their friendship cycles beyond school and their neighbourhood, while adults tend to often mix at workplaces (Ibid.). Other factors, such as religious and national identities, and living environment (rural or urban), also serve to increase their segregation, where religious people living in rural areas tend to be more segregated (Ibid.).

We aim have to address young people's relationship to territory in Northern Ireland. In a way, their dependent or independent status is still fragile, and in some cases, they cannot claim 'places of others', for example (Childress, 2004: p. 195). The result is that their experience of an association with the territory is often challenging and problematic compared to adults. These youngsters' status, growing up in segregated enclaves that perpetuate strong myths about the 'other side', provoked their fear and anxiety, while division, simultaneously, became part of their everyday life and ideology that could not be dismissed (Leonard and McKnight, 2011; Cummings et al., 2011). When relating or referencing past events, they have no memories of violence and must relate to history books and the *eyewitness* stories of their families to reflect on the national conflict. Indeed, recent violence and attacks mirror some of this past, so it has not entirely vanished. However, the undeniable fact is that young people are still growing up in a divided society where 'us'-and-'them' beliefs endure.

However, an embryonic form of negotiation is on the rise. Negotiation in this context articulates a framework of revolutionised spatial practices to bargain with the Others over the ownership of space. The question this chapter poses is whether the growing cultural and ethnic diversification of contemporary societies can lead to transformative social relations of integration and belonging beyond groups defined by their identity. We explain how territoriality and everyday encounters in Derry/Londonderry, Northern Ireland's second-largest city, are largely driven by the city's dense political history. We argue that even when communities engage on a daily basis, they have no choice but to employ *tactics* to challenge or resist these logistical realities by adopting alternative means of interaction in the city. In fact, they formulate their ways of contact or segregation strategies coloured by memories of the Troubles and bloody incidents (Cairns, 2008). People eventually generate closed, integrated groups limited to their members and distance themselves from the Others.

Understanding intertextual spaces in Derry/Londonderry

This chapter is informed by a multiple-dimensional discourse of analysis and theoretical encounters: the treatise of identity, memory, and social practices. We utilise the concept of *intertextuality*, developed by Fairclough (1992), which draws on the role of the past, as well as contemporary history. This paper provides accounts of how representations of place and territory have created 'manipulated geographies' interlocked with the place, history, and memory within the contested spheres of cultural identity and nation-building. These *texts* are concerned with 'mutual discourses of inclusion and exclusion', based on antagonism to the Other (Graham, 1997: p. 193). They are constructed to act as signifiers of particular discourses within the welter of contested identities that is modern Ireland. I explain how networks and narratives of historical events from their social environment inform young people's practices, thus treating these teenagers as competent social actors in their own right. It is recognised that they do not, or should not, reproduce adult assumptions about the world they live in but develop their methods of knowing. Therefore, we will shed light on some of these narratives and explore the ground-level dynamics and everyday struggles involved in the battle over space created by division.

This research was conducted through two phases of field interviews with young people aged 14 to 20 from the Fountain and the Bogside areas of Derry/Londonderry. Four community workers from each group were also included. The first phase covered semi-structured interviews with 20 young people (9 Protestants and 11 Catholics). The signification processes of their interpretation and reflected spatial practices in the form of hostile attitudes towards the other group were not always rationalised; but occasionally they contradicted views expressed by other interviewees, particularly when the boys were part of a bigger peer group. The second phase of interviews comprised three focus groups of 4 to 6 members each. The latter was structured around the topics and themes identified by participants. This qualitative research intends to provide reliable accounts and in-depth analysis of young people living within divided groups who share hostile attitudes towards each other.

Forming an identity of hurt and segregation

Division in Derry/Londonderry regulated how the city is experienced through collective memories of contestation grounded in its public sphere. Both communities, in fact, have lived and experienced disturbing pasts for several decades. A significant 'legacy of hurt' occurred from 1969 to 1973 following the Protestant exodus from the west bank of the Foyle to escape sectarian tensions. A dramatic rise in Irish Republican Army (IRA) recruitment and activity caused many Protestants to flee their homes for fear of intimidation. Clashes between the Royal Ulster Constabulary and Republican Nationalists erupted during the Battle of the Bogside in 1969, leading to civil unrest. Before 1969, around 16,000 Protestants lived in this area of Londonderry, but 20 years later, numbers had decreased by more than 80 percent. Also, in January 1972, the Bogside was turned into the site of a massacre of civilians known as 'Bloody Sunday', an event that hung like a dark cloud over the city for decades and which remains a pivotal event in the escalation of the Troubles throughout Northern Ireland (Ó Dochartaigh, 2010).

The incident occurred when a civil rights march against the policy of internment of Catholic residents of the Bogside was banned from entering the city centre. Angry young men then began to hurl stones at British soldiers; the upshot was that 13 Catholic men were shot dead close to Free Derry Corner. Ten years later, the bombing of the Droppin' Well bar in Ballykelly near Derry/Londonderry was described as 'one of the most horrific crimes in Ulster's tragic history': 11 soldiers and six civilians were killed when a bomb exploded during a disco in the pub (BBC, 2012). The Irish National Liberation Army (INLA), a Republican paramilitary group, carried out the attack targeting soldiers stationed at the nearby Shackleton barracks in Derry/Londonderry. Survivors of the attack still remember the pain and grieve until today. A 17-year-old boy, although not physically injured in the explosion, carried psychological damage in the years to follow. He said:

> It's just a nightmare that never goes away
> Everyone involved is going to be sore.
> They are going to remember the last time they spoke to the person that didn't come home.
>
> (Ibid.)

The youth and their relatives believe that events like the Bloody Sunday and many others have not been forgotten over time, the same way the 1972 exodus impacted the Protestant community too, heightening sectarian tensions within and without Derry's walls. Each community has very conflicting feelings: what one side considers a major abuse of human rights and inequality, the other side criticises as a matter of exaggeration and waste of resources (Melaugh, 2010). A campaign, led by the Bloody Sunday victims' relatives, to revive a full investigation into events ran for many years. For Catholics, Bloody Sunday brought outrage and grievance; for Protestants, it brought fame (Conway, 2003). Such beliefs mostly define clear-cut relationships and social behaviour between the communities and impact the lives of young people. These also have significant implications for shaping the identity of each one: Protestants were historically ranked above Catholics, a mind-set that determined the way the new state of Northern Ireland, created in 1921, acted towards and treated its Catholic population (Conway, 2003). This, in turn, influenced how Catholics defined their identity in opposition to that of Protestants, thereby constructing a social world of two opposing identity categories of 'us' and 'them' (Kirby et al., 2002).

The binary opposition, as is the case in Derry/Londonderry, normally generates a community that scrutinises the other, considering it a threat to its identity, and provides rational grounds for violence (White, 2001). In most cases, the only channels of mutual socialising materialise when each participates in violence or becomes victims of it. Disturbing incidents like Bloody Sunday become imprinted in memory and 'the lens through which people think about themselves; their past, goals, and ideals', so they subsequently position their contact with the Other accordingly (Murray, 2013; Conway, 2003: p. 17). These incidents led to the steady formation of 'in-groups' and 'out-groups' widely determined by the past with its mental representation (Woodward, 1997). People could be attached to events of the past in different ways (Hirsch, 1995). For example, communities living in Derry/Londonderry did not commemorate Bloody Sunday day for some time after they had rejected a state-approved form of remembrance, yet narrating stories of sorrow and grieving remained formatted and exhibited in other ways.

People's social relations and identities are represented by the synchronism of discourses, whereas 'people's lives, networks, and identities were patterned geographically and discursively . . . across different sites of activity, e.g. work, home, community' (Tajbakhsh, 2001: p. XIII). The broad interpretation and regulation of space establishes and reshapes social relationships and hierarchies, and constantly shifts subject positions. On the other hand, the social identity theory explains how people have a fundamental need to belong and possess a secure sense of self through participation in groups (Tajfel and Turner, 1979). Tajfel and Turner propose that groups to which people belong are an important source of pride and self-esteem because they provide their followers with a sense of social identity: a sense of belonging to the social world. Yet, to uplift our self-image, we tend to enhance the status of the group to which we belong – for example, saying, '[M]y community is the best in the city'. Groups can also increase their self-image by discriminating and holding prejudiced views against the *Other* group, to which they don't belong. They seek out negative stories of the *Other*, thereby enhancing their self-image (Tajfel and Turner, 1979). This explains why Nationalists in the Bogside and Unionists in the Fountain communicated their legendary battles through *lieux de memoire*, or sites of memory, which are parts of the built environment and places containing distilled reminiscences of the past objectified in the murals in housing estates, painted curbs, and flags (Nora, 1989; McBride, 2001).

In addressing the significance of emblematic place to understanding the contested nature and identity in Northern Ireland, Brian Graham (1997) notes that Unionism's adherents are largely defined by a 'shared negativity' expressed in 'adversarial otherness' (p. 192). He claims that 'Protestants react with a sense of inferiority and defensiveness, mostly stemming directly from ignorance of the Irish past, combined with a sense that history is being used against them in claims to the moral high ground' (Ibid.: 192). The symbolic representation of differences in Northern Ireland is forged through renegotiating the landscapes of memory to display reconstructed narratives of the past, and mostly their identity, which is less dependent on opposition to the *Other*. This, with no doubt, highlights a deviating path for Northern Ireland, where members of both religions continue to be 'locked into zero-sum thinking on the exclusivity of territoriality, parallel inflexible mindsets that are oblivious to any conception of the changes repositioning the contemporary Republic' (Ibid.). Although, for example, Protestants may self-identify themselves as 'Ulster' or 'Northern Irish' but not (Catholic Irish), they outwardly continue to refer to religion as an 'ethnic marker' in expressing identity more than their 'Britishness'.

Memory and intertextual spaces

Young people in Northern Ireland mostly learn about their history not only by hearing stories from their families and relatives but also by being exposed to elements, or what we call *objects of conflict*, which contextualise and spatialise conflict surrounding them everywhere. Successive generations in Northern Ireland in whom conflict is instilled predominantly communicate the memory of disturbing incidents through street and granite monuments displaying their sorrow and/or the bravery of 'their' people; these *objects* and monuments gradually become cultural expressions used to demarcate ownership and claim public spaces (Side, 2014; Selim, 2015). For decades, young people from the Fountain estate (a Protestant enclave on the overwhelmingly west bank or cityside of Derry) and the Bogside area (a predominantly Catholic area) have been exposed to these *objects* on daily basis, through their school journeys, trips to and from the town centre, accessing amenities, and visiting public parks.

The high number of murals in the Fountain and the Bogside enable people to reminisce and remember their past. Ingeniously, those that built them utilised their everyday living spaces in the service of remembrance by using original photographic materials and sharp colours to create a sensitive and sensible aesthetic appeal for passersby (Nic Craith, 2002) (Figure 9.2). When touring the Fountain, one cannot miss a famous Unionist mural stating 'Londonderry West Bank Loyalists Still Under Siege No Surrender'. This artwork profoundly conveys the sense of a wartime blockade and an attitude of defiance towards the invader (Selim, 2015). Another well-known mural records the Catholic bishop of Derry, known then as Fr Edward Daly, waving a bloodstained white handkerchief on Bloody Sunday as others carry a severely wounded young man through the streets of the Bogside. To this day, that mural remains an enduring image of the Troubles and perhaps stands out more than any other as a symbol of Bloody Sunday while also validating the identity of the Bogside community as a subjugated social group (Figure 9.1).

Here, we would like to draw additional attention to 'text' representing spaces shaped by mutual relations and boundaries. They normally presuppose discrete and structured delimitation, and, within their boundaries, a coherent internal structure. This could be described as spatial composition or, rather, as hypotactic structures of inter-spatial relationships. These spatial

Figure 9.1 Murals evoking the sense of a wartime blockade.

Figure 9.2 Top: the real image of Bloody Sunday confrontation in the Bogside; bottom: the mural that depicts the same scene in the Bogside.

compositions articulate and segment textually represented spaces and constitute their hierarchy, as well as dictating how people interact within the space. For example, people mobilise in the city in different ways and in different imaginaries which form the boundaries between one space and another or between different kinds of spaces, whether material or cognitive. As such, intertextuality is cognised as the practice of 'transposing, juxtaposing, and blending heterogeneous semiotic spaces, not only those represented in the textual world', through *objects* and *metaphors*, like murals and paintings, but also through those evoked by linguistic and genre forms on the textual surface (Juvan, 2004: p. 89). Intra-textual space also contributes to a significant part of the imaginary, since it is repeatedly attached to recurring elegiac memories that carry archetypical ideals to organise the subject's awareness of the past and future. Intertextuality, as interpreted in this discussion, is a central concept that explains ways in which people could interrogate new meanings in the production of space through the insertion of past 'texts' into the present (Fairclough, 1992: p. 84). This is of vital significance since memory and history are integral to people's everyday lives in Northern Ireland. These texts are materialised through powerful reminiscences, which allows people to construct and avail of the public realm in specific ways (Fairclough, 1992: p. 194).

Sites of memories in the Fountain and the Bogside epitomise history-related texts, whereby young people can express aspects of identity and contact. The Catholic memory of the Troubles and the Protestant memory of the Siege of Derry are manifested across both groups. Catholics living in the Bogside, for example, express their identity through commemoration revolving around the many deaths in their community since the recent conflict began in the late-1960s. The well-maintained Bloody Sunday Memorial is one. Free Derry Wall, erected in 1969 to separate the Bogside from the rest of the city, retains political and historical significance to the present day. It was also the venue of unpleasant celebrations following the death of former British prime minister Margaret Thatcher (McDonald, 2013). Sectarian attacks by Catholic youths on residents of the Fountain estate followed (Ibid.). These reminiscences and events, although different in type, maintain a refreshing image of stasis and ongoing memory, sometimes imagined and sometimes intimidating but still embedded in the minds and territories of the young; this is crucial to the group's ideological strength. When these symbols of the past play such as important role in the life of people today, disagreements and division within the city arise, as each display becomes a competition.

Protestants also experienced critical historical events, such as the 1641 Rebellion (when settlers were executed by Catholics rebelling against British rule), the Siege of Derry in 1689, the Battle of the Boyne in 1690, defiance to Home Rule between 1912–1914, and the signing of the Anglo–Irish Agreement in 1985. The symbols of Protestantism, displayed on murals and

Orange banners, indeed icon these events as chronicles of blood sacrifice and deception (Bryan, 2000). Nevertheless, these do not trigger an ongoing narrative or theme that connects them through a 'text' set by the representation of territory. For most adults, 'the mainstream cultural unionist identity remains highly reductionist in its version of the past, largely dependent on sectarian depictions of the Other to legitimate its discourse of exclusion' (Walker, 1992: p. 59).

In a way, we observe the reproduction of unique intertextual networks that manifest their feelings of prejudice and anger towards the other community (Bakhtin, 1986: p. 94, cited in Fairclough 1992: p. 102). The original texts are usually informed by adults' perceptions of the past or actual participation and involvement in one event or another related to violence or the struggle for freedom and civil rights and which eventually become masters of the narrative. Despite Derry/Londonderry now being relatively free from violence, young people still rely on their parents' accounts to better explain themselves and their hostile attitudes. For those that were involved in violence, the reproduction of histories constructs an opportunity not to feel regretful for what they may have done, as long as a senior member of the community did so in the past. This displays the vertical dimension of intertextuality in relations between actions and their original accounts in space (Kristeva, 1986: p. 36, cited in Fairclough, 1992: p. 103). Fathers' and sons' texts, for example, become interconnected and associated with each other to back their current practices, which become heavily informed by past formulas of bravery and pride, despite playing only a very marginal role in this narrative (Apter, 1997: p. 11).

As Raoul Vaneigem (1967: p. 231) argues, 'an ideology of history has one purpose only: to prevent people from making history . . . preventing them from coming to life, from rising from the dead and running once more through the streets of our daily lives'. For this, the Fountain and the Bogside youth interpret their social and spatial interaction practices according to their past imaginaries of the ingrained conflict. Apter (1997: p. 1) notes that 'in time, rooted and long-lasting violence tends to become a norm of the everyday reality, where individuals acquire defensive skills that live in them', although it must be conceded that it is now occurring on much lower levels than in the past. Residents gradually see the *objects* as *metaphors* to express their feelings and thoughts about inhabiting and living beyond their territories. Youngsters from the Fountain mostly incorporate these objects and metaphors into their everyday encounters (Interview 10). The *siege* conveys areas of attack and resistance in a battle and, therefore, suggests the militarisation of thought and practice as ways of protecting themselves, reacting, and progressing from day to day. Over time, the identity of places such as the Fountain and the Bogside become visualised and personalised by objects, which unknowingly inform mutual contact and practices of the people of that part of the city.

Indeed, Northern Ireland's young people are strongly seen as the nation's peace builders and its brightest hope to end over three decades of conflict (Magill and Hamber, 2010). Nevertheless, they face excessive forms of prejudice which can sometimes develop into serious violence. We still hear stories from both communities being reconciled with the current situation and basing their conclusions on what they have heard from history: 'Irish, and English don't like each other, and we will always have clashes, that's how we see it' (Interview 3). Statements like this explain why people's memories of the past are still shaping and legitimising their future relationships (Schmidt and Schröder, 2001: p. 8). In fact, *text* wreckages of the Troubles repeatedly arose in words used by the youth of the Bogside, even though, as teenagers, none of them has witnessed or remembers what the *Other* did in the past, as did the inevitability of a continuous struggle. They also interpreted violent events, although not those in which they have participated, into social and spatial texts of the present struggle and how it has shaped relations among them (Apter, 1997).

The broad current discourse concerning the Troubles seems to have largely shifted in favour of the Catholic community and provides a very powerful resource. In Derry/Londonderry, visitors and sightseers visit the Bogside to look at popular murals and visit the Museum of Free Derry which mostly provides a different restructuring of texts conditional to other relations of power. We also find that the social confines of young people from the Bogside are not very constrained, 'with the discourse of past suffering of their community providing a backing and considerable numerical superiority in comparison to the Fountain the position of power, at least for the first sight' (Conway, 2003: p. 21). Violence often starts as a minor altercation between young children but may easily escalate to a full-scale riot; therefore, the range of socio-spatial practices between groups linked to segregation becomes unpredictable. The questions here are, How could both segregated communities acknowledge sharing and using public spaces on an everyday basis without jeopardising their safety and emotional well-being? Do they share travel routes to schools, public transport, and access to basic services? The demographic decline of the Protestant population living on the west bank of the Foyle river in Derry/Londonderry, for example, paralleled a 'reduction in violence that led to re-engagement with the shopping areas in the Cityside' (Shirlow and Graham, 2005: p. 4). Protestants were willing to interact regularly and socialise with non-Protestants, but they remained *culturally* uncertain, leading to higher levels of marginalisation and a sense of inequality (Ibid.).

Young people performing territoriality

The Fountain estate presents a character similar to that of the Bogside, apart from having smaller houses and being trapped in behind 'peace walls'. The physical proximity of the Fountain and the Bogside regularly aggravates judgements when it comes to engagement and interaction in Derry's public spaces. The people of the Fountain are in relatively low-income or insecure forms of employment, and face housing and/or health concerns. They normally express community-based narratives of social disparity, injustice, and victimhood, acknowledging that these issues collectively are allowing minimal contact with Catholics living nearby. Their fear of contact is also controlling their mobility patterns. The fact that the estate is composed solely of housing units, with the exception of the school, the youth club, and the church, and lacks basic services has escalated the situation. The estate has 'no newsagents, cafés or restaurants, leaving its residents with a long trip outside the estate to reach basic amenities' (Interview 3). Some small shops were available in the past, but 'the migration of many people from the Fountain to the Waterside led to their closure' (Interview 5). The people then had no option but to travel to shops on Carlisle Road, which is a relatively long walk outside the estate.

Under stressful settings of communal anxiety, young people in Derry find it hard to have mutual respect for and integration with groups they perceive as a threat. Being prejudiced could become an asset for some individuals by presenting them as victims of their own failures. It also provides them with a conferred interest in favouring intolerance, even if a radical progression in individual encounters with the other side is seen. The community influence in the Fountain, for example, leads to a negative perception of the Bogside youth: 'If we are from the Fountain . . . we know that we would never become friends with them' (Interview 7). In some way, they refuted the opinions held by the Catholic community, scornfully expounding the matter of Bloody Sunday, the causes of riots in the late 1970s, and/or how the hunger strikers 'died for no reason' (Interview 8). Therefore, celebrating the achievements of the latter as evidently is the case in the Bogside, would not portray the speaker in a good light. In fact, a group of teenagers did not dismiss the Hunger Strikes of 1981 as intrinsically wrong, but being loyal to their community, and having the sense of *togetherness*, they interpreted the text from the past to be in favour of belonging to their own people – 'the British soldiers and the British citizens' (Interview 7). The boys believed that feeling themselves to be the victim of prejudice is not a problem: in fact, in their words, they are 'still making themselves victimised', with the government having 'spent a fortune on investigations, whereas Protestant civilian deaths were not investigated' (Interview 5).

Moreover, the local media, such as daily magazines, the *Derry Journal*, and TV programmes, usually condemn sectarian acts in accordance with the official public discourse of peace building and reconciliation. Many of the young people interviewed gradually started to draw up their views based on this discourse, and some even found themselves obliged to exert an explicit influence over others (Interview 10). However, in the discourse of political violence, the anti-state position is what stipulates that protests be held, its probable causes, and a 'discourse community' (Apter, 1997: p. 5). Yet, in Derry, the principle stays the same. While displaying hostile attitudes towards and rioting with the *Others*, in many cases, young people are encouraged to participate in confrontations and certainly do not face criticism from their community. One of the Bogside youths observed:

> We act like this because of what happened in the past . . . we were brought up with heartbreaking stories . . . we did not witness them . . . but my parents still have them live everyday . . . riots and violence are not bad and my community supports it. My family understands my actions and where it is coming from . . . there is no other way to make it work.

However, what is more, striking is how Derry's division manifests itself at the present day and how we observe expressions of violence, incivility, and discourtesy from both communities becoming naturalised acts of everyday encounters. In the past, celebrations of the siege were not only a frequent source of trouble but also a celebration of Protestant Unionist identity. That ceremony 'constitutes a dialogue, more or less a silent game of chess, enacted in the streets to remind people that despite the Catholic majority in Derry, the city continues to be Protestant territory' (Kockel, 2010: p. 27). The commanding position was taken up by Loyalists on the city walls during the parade often evokes intimidation and threat. Catholics in the Bogside also organise a small number of commemorative parades like the Easter Rising ceremony and Proclamation of the Irish Republic in 1916. These reinforce 'a rigid, unwritten law that Catholics could not march within the city walls', one enforced with violence by the police (Dawson, 2005: p. 158).

Still, much progress has been made in the last few years between the Bogside residents and the Apprentice Boys of Derry (organisers of the annual siege commemoration) regarding marching – and even the question of Nationalist marches on the walls has progressed successfully. This is evidenced by the recent Maiden City Accord protocol agreed and approved in 2014. This initiative from the local 'Loyal Orders' seeks to manage their parades in the city and 'promote a dignified, respectful parading culture'. The annual march was frequently a source of trouble, but this accord provides 'a real way forward, both for the Loyal Orders and for the entire community' (McCallister, 2014).

However, the Fountain's youth rarely bring up stories from the past and may have avoided talking about it (Interview 6). This is evident during the annual Orange Order parades on 12 July, for example. On that day, a carnival often moves from the Waterside, over the Craigavon Bridge and into the Fountain, passing by the Diamond area in the city centre. Teenage informants spoke of how they attend the annual parades: 'the same as others and so aren't restricted from celebrating their culture' (Interview 8). Yet, we still see that parades always require a heavy police presence to keep tensions between *the kids* at bay (Interview 7). Community workers also collaborate closely to ensure that young people from the other side are kept busy with activities organised during that time or are taken on field trips away from any possible trouble (Ibid.).

Even so, there are certain levels of imbalance caused by the physical location of both the Fountain and the Bogside communities and their relationships. The fact that essential amenities are located at some distance from the two estates highlights one form of instability and uncertainty. The result is that errands must be made at certain times of the day and, for some people, only in a group, which once again reveals a stronger version of the moral and political metaphor represented by *siege*. The closure of the gate in the Bishop Street wall at night also fuels a *siege* metaphor, whereby temporal and spatial dimensions of freedom are denied, and residents are 'hemmed in' and only allowed 'out' during the day (Interview 11). As one teenager explained, '[t]he physical presence of the gate is irreplaceable to alleviate tensions . . . as long as the walls are still there' (Interview 4).

To a certain degree, the present economic climate in Derry/Londonderry is preventing new facilities from being brought into the Fountain, leading people to be eager to increase free mobility without fear of attack from their Bogside neighbours, whereas fear and paranoia relating to 'the other side' would always remain. Despite this, a new play pitch was opened in the summer of 2012 for children of the Fountain community as part of the primary school and youth club landscape. Before then, the closest recreational area was the Riverview Play Park located in the Bogside and Brandywell areas, which the Fountain residents avoided for fear of violence despite efforts at integration having been put in place. This new venture was anticipated to improve facilities in the Fountain with the hope of establishing a better environment for engagement and contact.

The serpentine shape of the Peace Bridge erected in 2011 was designed as a structural handshake across the Foyle, creatively built to tackle the problem of separate communities by creating genuine and unique shared space. The new bridge across the river was a constructive materialisation of stimulating diversity in Derry/Londonderry. Although it was intended to improve connections on both sides of the river, patterns of movement available to both groups are yet to help in improving social interaction and experiences of a different culture. Using public transport is always preferable; as members of the youth club said, '[i]t is crucial not to walk in groups, but we prefer to take a bus to go anywhere, even on the shortest journeys' (Interviews 4 and 9). When a visit to the Peace Bridge was planned in 2013 for club members, some boys from the Bogside community were waiting at notorious interface areas, and violence broke out (Interview 5). In such cases, victims of this violence feel offended, disrespected, and powerless to

Figure 9.3 Young Nationalist children watch Loyalist bands through secured screens.

Figure 9.4 Police in riot gear guard the ancient Butcher's gate of Derry during the annual Orange Order parade.

the extent of being subject to administered and politicked mobility across the city.

For a couple of decades, cross-community organisations have been making progress, through great efforts, to *listen to communities* and promote contact (Murtagh, 1999). However, this initiative had had difficulties of its own: 'When both groups worked together, male youths from the Fountain were attacked after being recognised' (Interview 2). It is necessary to grasp discourses associated with the reproduction of social cultures, such as social relationships, identities, beliefs, and norms. By adhering to the discourse of feeling anxious and unsafe in the presence of members of the other community beyond the borders of the Fountain, although it might not be based on fact, informants build their sense of belonging with fellow residents and with their community. When the pitch was built in 2012, all community members gathered there with their children, instantaneously keeping intact both their boundaries with the other community and this potential new transformation.

Peace building and fostering intercultural dialogue

Since the peace process started, policy agendas in Derry have been determined by ideas of cultural diversity, which support the manifestation of the two traditions and fosters better intergroup relations (Nic Craith, 2002). Opponents claim that this approach has barely loosened ethnic boundaries and has not boosted reconciliation (Geoghegan, 2010). Nevertheless, recent years have seen intercultural initiatives and the Northern Ireland Executive's 'Building a United Community' scheme, both genuine responses to understanding 'the need to set the relationship between communities as the focal point of both official discourse and practice has been recognized more widely' (McDermott et al., 2016: p. 621). Besides, peace organisations, through financial support from the European Union, in particular, understand the significance of fostering dialogue between communities to produce events and programmes that address tensions subtly. They are also aware that 'neutralising the politics of identity is required to provide a better opportunity for inter-cultural exchange between Unionist and Nationalist communities' (Ibid.). Indeed, manifestations of peacebuilding in Northern Ireland are countless, but some particularly relevant local initiatives are noted in the following.

A number of initiatives have emerged from the context of intercultural and international communication using dialogic theory and practice in Northern Ireland (Caputo, 2016). Despite increasing efforts at resolving differences in that city, one could easily admit that 'there are two public spaces in Derry/Londonderry. The larger one is Catholic/Nationalist, and the smaller one is Protestant/Unionist' (McDermott et al., 2016: p. 611). Incidences of violence in Derry/Londonderry among the young demonstrate that proximity between the two communities has not brought about social transformation and, therefore, that there is a need for a building of new relationships and new generations of peacemakers in Northern Ireland. One remarkable venture that certainly brought the two communities closer together was Derry/Londonderry being designated the inaugural UK City of Culture (CoC) in 2013. Receipt of this distinction saw some tough questions being asked: Would this 'rebranding' gesture become 'life and place changing' (Boland et al., 2016), would it succeed in bringing 'new stories' as opposed to conflict (Doak, 2014), and would it lead to a rise in the 'profile of the City' (McDermott et al., 2016: p. 612)? Nonetheless, additional cross-community engagement was anticipated to have greater potential for stimulating peace and community benefits, and civic pride, and for healing wounds (Collins, 2016; Londonderry Sentinel, 2010b; Boland et al., 2016). For example, the Ebrington area was rebranded as a 'neutral and depoliticised space open for mutual cultural encounters with both communities, increasing levels of positive emotional impact and real cohesiveness and a sense of unity' (Collins, 2016: p. 67). For the first time, CoC empowered people in Derry/Londonderry to experience culture and arts away from their reference to past 'texts' and metaphors, thus progressively augmenting their fragmented community interactions.

Programmes delivered by the Youth Service in Derry/Londonderry vary; however, the city has undoubtedly witnessed progressive work on the youth working together, changing customs, and spatialised behaviours on the go. A promising venture inaugurated by the local education authority began in 2016. The 'Our Space' youth facility, located in Guildhall Square, was the first city-centre provision developed to engage young people who would not normally participate in youth service activities. Liam Curran, a senior figure in Youth Services, considered the venture 'a safe and neutral venue that acts as both a place where young people can meet and a place that promotes the ethos of participation, acceptance and understanding of others and the testing of values and beliefs' (Derry Journal, 2016). In addition, the Arts Council of Northern Ireland organised a sculpturing venture in 2011, 'Re-Imaging Communities'. Derry City Council supported this program to produce a number of artefacts designed by local schoolchildren and community groups (Derry City Council, 2011).

Indeed, endeavours like this is anticipated to bring communities together and to empower the 'recognition or acknowledgement of otherness in situational specificity', rather than, for example, to constantly develop robust bonds of friendship (Wise and Velayutham, 2009: p. 35). It is also a long-term strategy to learn for future developments by establishing social programmes set out to identify social niches through well-defined methods and processes of implementation. A similar scheme went ahead in July 2015, when Derry/Londonderry hosted 'Release the Pressure', a graffiti and mural art festival with renowned graffiti artists travelling to the city from all over the world. An 80-foot piece of graffiti art was created, in Ebrington Square, by Derry's youth from all communities and went on public display to mark the launch of the festival. The project aimed to build positive relationships among youth culture and address current issues, including hate crime, sectarianism, youth engagement, community cohesion, and urban regeneration. The groups had been working together for three weeks, participating in exciting graffiti- and street art–inspired workshops, creating art that was non-political but that promoted creative expression. During the festival, the young people had the opportunity to work with and meet international artists. Contributing artists from UV Arts stated,

> It will serve to change the perception of mural art and graffiti in Northern Ireland and celebrate the future of modern and contemporary non-political murals as a tool for social change.
>
> Releasing the Pressure is a great event for the young people in our city.
>
> After the festival, the young people will return to their areas where they will begin planning for a permanent mural, in consultation with their own community.

The apparent achievement for spatialising micro-publics of peace in Derry/Londonderry would be to pull down the dividing walls and for people to move freely and safely across the city (Blevins, 2013, Buckler, 2013). The Northern Ireland Executive set a target date of 2023 for the

Figure 9.5 Youth street art in Derry: 'Release the Pressure', 2015.

removal of all peace walls. There is an acknowledgement that such a strategy should include the consent and support of the residents that live beside these structures. To practically enforce this, long-term negotiations with Northern Ireland ministers and policymakers have been held during the past 10 years. A central obstacle in this plan is the absence of a central policy that reinforces all subdivisions represented within the Northern Ireland Executive, whereas 'peace walls continue to be viewed very much as a security issue, and therefore, one that requires a policy response underpinned by security values and processes' (Byrne and Gormley-Heenan, 2014: p. 453).

Stakeholders from both communities worked closely to make this initiative a reality, receiving tremendous support from the Peace Walls Programme, which has been embraced across the country to encourage both communities to oversee a transformation from the past and stop searching for differences. It also aimed to develop confidence and relationship-building interventions to help people reach a position where they feel it is safe and appropriate to move on with the removal of their local peace walls and to escape their violent and traumatic conflict for good. Up till today, limited actions towards peace wall, barrier, and fence removal are recorded, with one security gate removed in Derry/Londonderry and an 8-foot barrier long standing in an interface area in North Belfast (Selim, 2015). For young people living in Northern Ireland, the physical objects of segregation are not merely a symbol of the historical conflict, nor a reminder of the peace-building challenges that remain. In fact, the 'abnormal has become normal', and their acknowledgement of how peace is perceived and therefore represented and practised is momentously taking shape 'through a lens that is defined by physical division and permanent segregation' (Ibid.: p. 453).

10 Images of social memory and the construction of division in Belfast

The collective memory of spatial division and segregation

This chapter provides a critical synthesis of the peace walls in Belfast known locally as the Peaceline. It investigates how the walls have developed from relatively small coils of barbed wire into colossal barbaric enclosures and how communities on both sides of the interfaces perceive and culturally memorise causes of their existence. The goal is to exemplify the changes that have taken place in architecture and spatial planning thinking and practice in Northern Ireland since the Good Friday Agreement in 1989 using Belfast as a case study. We tend to look both at the planning ideology revealed in planning documents and manuals and in the conducting of planning processes by local architects and planners and methods in dealing with the divides.

We argue that divided cities, like Belfast, feature spatial memories of division that range from physical, clear-cut segregation to manifested actions of violence, and have become influential representations in the community's associative memory. The evidence is derived from interviews, maps and illustrations, to develop narratives that respond to the following questions: Do Belfast's peace walls serve a purpose in contemporary society? How has the associative architectural memory of the Peaceline walls impacted their importance in acting as a means of control in these spaces? Finally, what have been the strategies of architects and planners in the past, and they developed over time?

> My first memory was when my aunt got shot . . . It frightened me, so it did. She was only home from visiting my granny in England, and she was walking around the corner to my aunt's house. She got shot dead . . . I.R.A. [Irish Republican Army] crossfire . . . Well, you're afraid to go out, in case you get shot dead, so you are.
> (Dyer, *The Cost of the Troubles*, 1998)

Children and young people of Youth Group Survivors of Trauma and North Belfast Youth Group reported the preceding extracted testimony. Many children were conscious of the influence of unforgettable incidents they have witnessed an impact on shaping their future lives. The presence of such historical imprints is, however, inherently loaded with more than the mere picturesque value of the incident scene. For years that followed, the streets of Belfast represented traces of different societies that have not vanished until today but became part of everyday networks and relationships and subsequently infused by the presence of the past articulated in the city's architecture and the public sphere.

The architecture of conflict in Belfast had profound effects on the sensory engagement and historical memory of its society. It invariably conveyed hazy and insecure images of the present by reciting incidents from the past, even in the absence of first-hand events. Throughout Belfast's history its architecture has been a representation of painful memories that materialise stories of its troubling past. The aunt's house mentioned earlier, for example, serves as windows on the past to inform us of the magnitude of authority asserted on the populace and which may extend to the present. This 'living memory' is defined as the recollections of events that people were involved or witnessed first-hand. In preliterate societies throughout history, eyewitnesses were often relied on heavily to recount the events they had personally witnessed, transferring these 'living memories' to younger generations by word of mouth (Landsberg, 1997).

Various scholars have interrogated the integrity of architectural memory. Lewis Mumford, in *The Culture of Cities*, questions the legitimacy of architectural memory at a city scale, with the view that the city is a 'palimpsest of meaning' that could be revealed or concealed according to the changing views of an evolving culture (Bastea and Gorby, 2004: p. 26). Mumford claims another category of architectural memory, 'unchanging memory' – a history that preserves the identity of the city throughout time (Ibid.). The danger is of singling out particular memories, which, in turn, would result in losing the deeper sense of meaning and memory that the urban environment may possess for its people. Moreover, there was a danger of cities becoming 'packaged and imaged' for interpretation. The collective image of the city, therefore, could be that of ships coming into the docks or a grid view of a cityscape immersed in light and shadow.

Aspects of collective memory have been particularly prominent since the collapse of communism in 1989 and the iconic moment of the Berlin Wall being demolished. An 'episodic memory' has emerged, quite often allowing certain groups in positions of authority, who wish to taint this culture in their favour, to do so (Tulving, 1985: p. 59). In a way, 'the fault line between the mythic past and the real past is not always easy to draw' (Husseyn, 2003: p. 47). The relationship between memory and forgetting is constantly being transformed under cultural pressures; as a result, what we end up with is a set of 'imagined memories', characterised as 'prosthetic memories' – memories that have circulated publicly, are not organically based yet are still experienced by the individual (Landsberg, 2004: p. 19). By contrast, prosthetic memories often pose a threat to living memory, as they are quite often mass mediated and subject to revision and alteration, to promote one overall 'collective memory' (Abdelmonem and Selim, 2012: p. 164).

According to Nietzsche, collective memory manifests itself in the Darwinian principle of survival of the fittest, in that human beings adopt traits and transfer them to future generations, to ensure their survival (Richardson, 2004). It, therefore, marks a distinction between those 'who belong' and those 'who do not' (Ibid.). For buildings to have memory, an established link to time and history is crucial (Fig. 10.1). The visible link can be made through ageing or decay, or simply by being built in a particular style. As architecture witnesses events over time, it constructs a narrative of its age. Collective memories of events important to that sect of society are embedded into the individual, yet, when the individual is repositioned to a new environment, the idea of collective memory is often discarded and replaced with a new one (Mulholland et al., 2014).

In contrast to the idea of architecture instilling memory in people – what is viewed as a monument – there exist a reflection of our present sensibilities and a direct reflection to the original state, thus making it monumental; the memory we seek is what makes the monument (Reigl, 1903). Ruskin (2004), however, supports the view that architecture is society's primary harbour of memory, instilled in the people through built objects. Still, the danger is the influence that social and political control exerts over memory when one perceives such monuments. Whilst history significantly consolidates

Figure 10.1 Memories of conflict in Belfast, 1971.

perceptions of architectural memory, this could lead one to question the integrity of the memory bestowed on the built environment in many cases.

These spatial assignments are indications of the control of urban space occupied by older orders, in the way that the power and space relationship reinforces the existence of the new order. David Harvey (1989: p. 255) argues that 'reorganisation of spaces is always considered a reorganisation of the framework, through which political and social powers are expressed'. Individuals usually desire either to glorify their past conflict by comparing themselves with entirely different societies characterised as flawed or unhealthy, or when they desire to criticise their own society, they tend to glorify a society that appears to be different. Both approaches represent merely a projection of the other in one's mind, regardless of the other's actual state. However, even this view could be debated. What remains evident is that the urban structure of colonised cities has changed as a response to visualising this power.

Indeed, places connected to traumatic incidents are registered as a situated memory that is used to reinforce shared history and value systems. Places where of various recorded murders in Northern Ireland during the Troubles are still remembered for once losing a member of the family or a relative. Commemorating these instances by displaying murals or recalling those stories is a unique way to bring the past into the everyday practice of the present and a sharp declaration of the changing meaning of the place. When tragedies like this occur, places seem to gain mysterious connotations as sites of unprecedented events. Places of the past become merely spatial and physical containers that situate oral memories that are meaningful for the community and somewhat shapes its identity. In these events, perceptions of the past are preserved, although accidentally, through local strategies of active memory that create distinctive testimonials.

Belfast's embedded memory of division is evident in the complexities of its history when studied from the perspective of its representational elucidation: in its buildings, monuments, and artefacts. Though these clarifications all exist within the public domain, they are part of the history of multiple and overlapping claims to modernity. The artwork of the renowned Belfast-born wartime painter Colin Middleton, for example, shows how the perception of the city to the individual has changed over time. While the paintings reflect Middleton's own image of Belfast, it had a profound influence on collective memory, given that many people have viewed them over time. Middleton's paintings were primarily of Belfast during wartime, with each provoking a different memory to the observer. These certainly connote a sense of affiliation and affection towards a Belfast depicted as the industrial city it remains, in part, today, with its rows of Victorian housing and factory chimneys billowing smoke.

Religious segregation in Belfast is a topic of geography that is constantly evolving as a city with 'an invisible map' sometimes manifested in the non-physical (Gorby, 2004: p. 57). The social stigma and memory attached to the Peaceline walls enforce the local value in these segregated societies, and this notion is perhaps more significant than the walls fulfilling their function as 'divides' (Hyde, 2012). Their colossal nature and impact on communities living in Belfast increase clashes over religion, which is apparently the main cause of violence. In fact, the walls serve as a device to create a 'tenuous peace' (Ibid.). It is not a religion in the sacred, spiritual sense that is the cause of the divide, but it is the existence of religion in the cultural sense, as Christine Gorby claims (2007: p. 69). The majority of sectarian violence over the previous forty years occurred in working-class areas of the city – classed as 'high-intensity areas' (Fay et al., 1999). The result of this violence was that planners implemented a number of segregated enclaves as a means of separation, in the form of 'cul-de-sacs' (Ibid.). The need for dividing walls was questioned on the grounds that they serve no purpose because they are not 'enclosing' (Hyde, 2012). In fact, they exist as a symbol of segregation and do very little in terms of their purpose – keeping the two communities apart.

The gates are closed at night, creating a secure perimeter, but in principle, it's simply a deterrent to the flow of people rather than enclosure. There are no checkpoints. The boundaries are fluid and yet strictly obeyed, implicitly impermeable. To my foreign eyes, the seeming pointlessness of a massive wall that you can simply walk around highlights the utter arbitrariness of what these walls are separating (Hyde, 2012: p. 56).

Consequently, contemporary Belfast has shed its skin of concrete brutality in favour of lightweight, glass-clad steel structures reminiscent of other major UK cities, which, in turn, has contributed to a changing perception of the city, both from local and global perspectives. By turning its back on the past, Belfast has emerged as a city worthy of development. Nonetheless, within the contested areas of North and West Belfast, there are different attitudes amongst communities. Writers generally claim that the individual and collective memory in Northern Ireland has evolved to a stage of 'crisis', embedded in the displacement and erasure of conflict (Jameson, 1991). It is not, in fact, the Troubles that are the key cause of the problem in Belfast, but the attempted 'unifying' of these areas to the city centre, without taking into consideration issues of people's embedded memory of the clashes and its subsequent implications (Ibid.). It is the severity of segregation outside central Belfast, for example, that has corroded the local council's ambitions of mending the city's wounds the city through its re-imaging. Regardless of how the past has been perceived, the events of the Troubles led to severe losses on both sides of the conflict, and the council's attempts at erasing the memory associated with this dark past more often than not resulted in further violence and social disorder. Indeed, the Peaceline walls certainly does not evoke memories of peace.

It could be argued that recent planning interventions in Belfast's urban spaces followed immensely politicised ambitions. Here, the idea of politicised urbanism reflects the process of engineering visions to assure commitment in dismantling division and its associated memories while bringing communities together. Nevertheless, such approaches are not only shaped by the planners' aesthesis but also based on cultural and social concerns that act in shaping different objectives and outcomes. This urbanism determines an approach that structures new procedures and trends in planning and their course of implementation. It also forms the theoretical and physical trends, which accordingly are translated into projects that echo the city's urban fabric.

Drawing further on this type of innovative landscapes in Belfast, the chapter continues investigating the actual course of actions and planners' perceptions more deeply, in their attempts, to draw new maps of future development in conjunction with its active communities. In the following discussion, we argue that the Troubles in Belfast since the late 1960s mirrored various implications of the city's landscape. Belfast's urban fabric became fundamentally scarred with imposed and incompatible structures that corrupted its urban development for several decades. We also look at the association of the Peaceline walls with conflict in the people's embedded memories, a reality that is yet affecting the taking of positive steps towards their gradual elimination while, at the same time, implementing good design approaches that could temporally heal the situation.

Wounds in Belfast landscape

The societal division in Belfast is directly reproduced through its built fabric and territories that have been adopted by either side. Indeed, differences in political views demonstrate the divide in Belfast, but this is also visible through other barriers which range from flags, murals, and motifs to steel fences. They all have the dual aim of segregating the masses and instilling political ideals into the mindsets of residents, as a means of intimidating those who do not share the same political beliefs. The symbolic influence and memory that these artefacts provoke are significant in maintaining the collective identity of these areas of society. The most obvious of these divides are the Peaceline walls erected in various areas of conflict throughout Belfast (also known as interface areas). The first physical barriers in the city appeared in August 1969 when British troops erected temporary knife rests strung with concertina wire as a means of deterring boiling unrest between Republicans and Loyalists. The barriers were later made permanent, with the knife rests becoming spans of corrugated steel topped with coils of barbed wire, altering the physical landscape of the neighbourhoods by reinforcing boundaries of physical segregation.

While Belfast's contested spaces remain fascinating, they are not unique. Throughout history, there have been many instances where regimes have erected walls, such as the Berlin Wall in 1961, as a means of the divide – to protect different groups of societies. The wall, unlike the peace lines of Belfast, was largely impermeable. The circumstances surrounding its erection were not to divide opposing communities but to create a divide between a single community purely on geographical terms, with governments on either side imposing opposing ideologies on each populace. When the wall was removed, the people were united. Whether walls have been wanted or not by societies, they create lasting legacies on the people's daily lives that they have carved through. Today, there remains a cult of memory attached to the Berlin Wall. Many see its removal in 1989 as a relief from the oppression that was endured during the divide, and few have a positive memory of it. In instances, the memory associated with the walls was regarded as harmful and restricting.

There are a total of 99 different security barriers and forms of defensive architecture across the city, which remain in existence in predominantly urban, working-class Loyalist and Republican communities. They are predominantly in the north and west of the city, dissecting residential areas and in some cases, green areas. The responsibility for the construction and maintenance of these structures previously resided with the British government, until the devolution of policing and justice powers in 2010. After this point, the Northern Ireland Executive, through the Department of Justice, became responsible for all policymaking decisions around Peaceline walls. It is the case that none has ever been removed and that they continue to overshadow the landscapes of the working-class communities. Since the first paramilitary ceasefires in 1994, the Northern Ireland peace and political processes have addressed a series of sensitive and contentious issues relating to the conflict, including matters concerning policing, prisoner releases, the decommissioning of weapons, and power sharing. While the peace process has also, in part, begun to address challenging issues of segregation and the deep cultural division, it has not yet sufficiently progressed to address the most visible and highly physical evidence of this deep-rooted division – the Peaceline walls (OFMDFM, 2012: pp. 6–14).

The attitudes and indifference of those living on either side of the walls are mostly no different to those of a previous generation when the walls first appeared within the landscape. Their presence also attracts negative international attention and dilutes, to some degree, the devolved administration's response towards periods of annual communal tension and public disorder. They also have a financial impact on the delivery of public services and the opportunity to attract inward investment. The lifestyle and social potential for those communities living in the shadow of the walls have, for many years, been severely affected by the violence and disorder which the walls can attract. In the context of health and social well-being, each of the neighbourhoods within the walls is in the upper quartile of some of the most socially and economically deprived electoral wards in Northern Ireland. The devolved administration and local government have recently recognised this significance and have incorporated addressing physical division into some of their broader strategies and action plans that are designed to deal with segregation, community safety, and urban regeneration.

Many other visual symbols throughout Belfast assert identity and influence on its residents, most notably flags. They are displayed in excess throughout different areas of Belfast depending on their Unionist or Nationalist views (Unionists fly the Union Jack whilst Nationalists fly the Irish Tricolour). Kerbstones are emblazoned in the colours of these flags and prevalent in these areas are murals quite often of military iconography. Murals and monuments to fallen freedom fighters are highly prevalent in these areas and serve as a constant reminder to its communities of the struggles they endured throughout the Troubles. Dawson (2007: p. 35) argues for a 'dichotomy between the misconceptions of mythology and the scientific truths of history' and that the conception of the 'past' is not the same on both sides. The physical presence of murals and motifs only increases community pride in their respective causes, resulting in increased segregation and further polarisation. There are differing perceptions of the physical divides shared by 'outsiders' and 'insiders'. Insiders seem to perceive the walls as 'protectors' of their respective cultures and their formidable physical guardians.

In a more poetic sense, the walls 'create simultaneous conditions of porousness and impermeability in the city and that even though the Peaceline walls disconnect what was once a continuous urban fabric, the memory of the former gridded street patterns of West Belfast remains suspended in the minds of inhabitants – possibly to be later reclaimed' (Gorby, 2007: p. 240). The murals can be viewed as a means of control and security, signifying to the outsider that within the area there is a closed community of people with strong political beliefs, so much so that they are willing to wage war in order to stand by their political views. Quite often the murals express grievances held by the Other side; 'they evoke the sense of a wartime blockade and an attitude of defiance towards the invader' such as the infamous hunger strikers or murals depicting internment (Selim, 2015). Many murals were painted on the walls as *metaphors* to commemorate and celebrate martyrs who fought for their political cause and to reinforce remembrance in the populace that said martyrs died for the cause. It is also a purpose for educating and inspiring future generations of both community groups to hold similar extremist beliefs as it ultimately surrounds them everywhere (Ibid.).

(Re-)Imaging memories of contestation

The Orwellian-like term *re-imaging* is a word often used by the Northern Ireland government when working in contested areas. It is important to note that there are no memorial sites in Belfast city centre, despite the vast amount of fatalities that occurred around this place due to the Troubles. Indeed, a clear shift in architectural design trends in the centre of Belfast over the past three decades is evident. Up until relatively recently, Belfast was characterised by its forbidding concrete structures and its infamous ring of steel (the city centre itself was cordoned off, and its gates were closed at night during the height of the Troubles). With the lack of memorials at the sites of bombs or shootings, the councils 're-imaging' of Belfast demonstrated a total erasure of the Troubles and an attempt to wipe the local collective memory, but instead, we find that individual memory remains intact.

In fact, planning public spaces in Belfast is never a smooth mission, as a result of the divide and struggle with issues of memory. The zoning of new districts, such as the Titanic Quarter and Cathedral Quarter, is essentially an attempt to communicate a different tale of the city's socioeconomic past. Even in a choice of name, this is contested, however, bearing in mind that Titanic Quarter was originally called Queen's Island. This aligns to the government's process of 'erasing memory' or its re-imaging, given that the shipping industry, based in Queen's Island, was heavily discriminatory towards Nationalists. It is an endeavour in itself even to design for areas in the city that are considered largely neutral, and it is even a hot topic as to what colours can be used in graphical displays of projects – careful consideration needs to be given when using reds, blues, greens, and oranges, due to political connotations. Quite often, designers for projects in the city will stick to neutral palettes of greys and black to avoid offence. One could even consider this a metaphor for the design in these politically contested areas in themselves – neutral and non-appealing. As such, there needs to be 'reconciliation authenticity' about places and the memories associated with them, which can open a whole new set of narratives on previously marginalised stories and histories (Minty, 2006: p. 48).

A succession of devolved governments for planning policy in Northern Ireland has been largely ambivalent in strategies for interface areas. Throughout the 1990s, the government recognised and identified areas of contestation and acknowledged its impact on greater Belfast. This was evident in the resulting policy, which aimed to tie the emerging peace process to the correspondence between deprivation and the divide.[1] The policy aimed to address matters of division, in particular issues such as the allocation of housing and land in interface areas and the Peaceline walls, as well as the accessibility to employment for both sides in these areas. The result was manifested in a policy titled 'Shaping Our Future' in 1995, which involved cooperation with more than 500 local community representatives. The policy document posed the risk of further segregating the already polarised communities in Belfast, through its attempts to address numerous 'controversial and sensitive' points. Nonetheless, the policy went ahead but was later abandoned by the devolved government established in 1998 (McEldowney et al., 2001: p. 43).

Whilst the notion of alternative means of the divide is not entirely accurate when used in the context of Northern Ireland, considering that it is in a post-conflict state, the legacy of this conflict has continued through the memory associated with the built form of the city (Murtagh, 2002). Although the Peaceline walls manifest the conflict in a physical form, there are many more, perhaps less obvious, measures of the divide in physical forms throughout the city, mainly affecting its urban fabric patterns and future development.

If you examine Belfast in terms of the figure–ground relationship, pre-1960, you have this sort of grid layout developing in the form of interconnected streets. Then the peace lines are installed, and what develops is a total deviation from the grid, with a number of redevelopment areas appearing in the form of 'cul-de-sacs' (pp. 2–14).[2]

Although the walls provided a physical dimension to the already divided society, what developed from its existence was a further divide in these sub-societies. In housing estates off the Shankill Road, for example, planners followed a system whereby sets of houses were grouped around a housing square or shared space, following the ideals of renowned architect Oscar Newman and his notion of 'defensible space' (Newman, 1972: p. 106). This planning development allowed houses to form 'subcommunities' of 20 to 25 houses that took over ownership of their own shared space, yet it led to a weakening of the urban fabric by further separating this new unit from its neighbouring streets. It was pointed out, however, 'that this was not entirely a bad thing, as with ownership came responsibility, and in the areas where the shared space laid vacant and didn't hold claim by either side, violence and social disorder became more evident' (P1.14). The result, simply, was a wall that divided a planning system that further divided yet worked within itself, with the remaining space being occupied by social disorder. Essentially, this was about control and ownership. This system worked to a certain degree, but there was a danger in this approach being absorbed into the overall city plan, which is what happened in the late 1960s.

Unavoidably, planning in areas surrounding the Peaceline walls is extremely difficult, taking into consideration that the walls are there for a reason. 'Even if it is now only memory that is attached to the walls, memory itself is very powerful in instilling community pride and ties the current generation that has not necessarily experienced conflict first hand' (P1.14). By creating projects that straddle the peace line, architects must be very wary of implementing this approach. Strong links to clients and local people are vital. The recent Department of Social Development (DSD, 2013)–led project, the NIVCA building in the Duncairn area, straddles an interface zone and, as a result, acts almost as a buffer. This in itself demonstrates the impact that the Peaceline walls have on the emerging new architecture in Belfast's divided places. Even if the wall were removed, the very fact that this building has an entrance on either side will replace the memory of the wall and highlight the fact that the divide is still present.

From its inception in 2009, the Forum for Alternative Belfast (FAB) was dedicated to working directly with communities that had suffered from high levels of deprivation and were disadvantaged as a result of the environment they were living in. They have worked with the Belfast Conflict Resolution Consortium (BCRC; 2011) in producing a publication surrounding the needs and issues of locals in contested areas. The consortium is made up of ex-prisoners and political campaigners from both sides of the community, and one of the major points that was highlighted in the publication is that 'the one thing that unites the communities in the interface areas is their class and the one thing that divides them is their politics' (P4.14). They claim that communities in these areas of conflict all suffer from some form of degradation due to their social class. Through a process of consulting and working with the local communities, FAB created a publication about shared space that looked at a whole range of issues. Instead of directing attention on the apparent issues of Peaceline walls, FAB focused on the environment that the working-class communities were living and working in which was of poor quality, poorly designed, and not suitable for walking in. They also found that the issue of the infrastructure of roads secluding the areas prevented the communities living there from having a good connection to goods and the services in the city outside their area.

> We realised that from the beginning of the conflict, most single-identity communities looked in on themselves, becoming very insular and as a result, they tended to look for facilities within their community territory and boundaries that reinforced insularity – people wouldn't leave New Lodge/The Shankill/Tiger's Bay – they lived within it (P2.14).

Part of FAB's mission was to take on the Jane Jacob idea that neighbourhoods could be romanticised and that, in fact, this would mean that the whole city could become a single neighbourhood. The challenge was to open these communities and connect them to the city, thus undoing the cul-de-sac model that had been adopted by planners in the 1960s and 1970s. 'In a way, that was something that you could get agreement on; you could not get agreement on the peace walls because there would be great difficulty with that' (P. 2–14). While it is evident that removing the Peaceline walls would be no easy task, their presence in Belfast is largely viewed in a negative light. The very fact that these areas are economically deprived is only made worse in that the walls have a considerable impact on the delivery of goods and services. Investors see that there are signs of violence and disorder in the area, and all of a sudden, the potential for these communities to attract inward investment is reduced significantly. From a security perspective, the walls focus negative attention on the devolved government's response to communal violence and disorder.

Industrial buildings in Belfast are viewed as being highly effective in acting as largely neutral spaces in terms of ownership and in giving back both sides of the community jobs that had disappeared because of the Troubles. They increasingly appear as buffer zones along the interface areas in Belfast and seem to be relatively successful in terms of reducing social disorder. In fact, more 'guilty conscience' exists over how the government approached interface zones in the past. In addition, ownership is a controversial issue, should permanent alterations or removal of the walls come to fruition. In

North Belfast, there is a very high demand for housing on the Catholic side and little demand on the Protestant side – where there are vast areas of vacant space. These sites would typically be used to relieve this housing demand, yet for political reasons, this is difficult in Belfast due to significant concerns over territory and ownership, regardless of the use.

During the development process in the Ardoyne and New Lodge areas, as part of the Belfast Action Team in 1990, the task of the government's advisory team was to adopt new environmental approaches for addressing the interfaces. The results were a number of business parks situated in and around the interface zones. At the time, violence in the neighbouring Protestant area of Tiger's Bay, an area shielded from Duncairn by a massive wall, was high due to the political events surrounding the Anglo–Irish Agreement, and large numbers of houses were becoming derelict, with many people leaving their homes as a result. About 200 houses were demolished, one-tenth only having been built 15 years prior. Part of the deal with the Tiger's Bay community at the time was to consolidate the area and build some new houses towards the adjacent Limestone Road, as well as to insert a buffer zone, including a business park and buildings with other uses that would be neutral. It was evident that the government was directly responding to the residents' needs.

In terms of a divide being manifested through a physical wall, it is instead being created by the insertion of commercial property, quite often used as start-up incentives for local businesses. For example, an industrial centre in Duncairn, in particular, provoked debate between architects, planners and engineers, due to its site being an interface zone (Ibid.). When the design brief was issued, the planners insisted on there being a single entrance, located just off North Queen Street (P2.14). The engineers did not agree to the positioning of this entrance, due to the issue of the main road being too close and that it would affect sightlines. They proposed that a second entrance could be positioned at the rear of the building, that is, on the other side of the interface. Planners argued that in doing so, 'you would essentially end up with two entrances: a Protestant and a Catholic entrance to the building' (P6.14). After almost a year of debate, the engineers eventually agreed to have the single entrance positioned where it was initially proposed:

> It was a battle, but it was even difficult to make them even aware of the consequences of putting an entrance on either side of the interface. The project was another attempt to bring down levels of violence, and it was successful, as it put the communities too far apart. (Ibid.)

It is interesting to note the meticulous nature of the design of buildings in such contested spaces. In this instance, the planners (unlike the architects on NICVA) attempted to address the danger of the building becoming a buffer, by careful consideration of its entrance. The nature of the interfaces themselves determines the design and placing of buildings as buffers: at points such as Cupar Way, where the interface is at its most extreme, the task of designers is much more difficult.

> If you look at the interfaces, there is a distinct difference in the areas depending on where you go. The most iconic of the peace walls is the one on Cupar Way, the most prominent, longest, most permanent example of the wall. In North Belfast on the Glendore Gardens, you have the softest interface, which is equally fascinating. It divides a Protestant working-class area and a Catholic middle-class area. There is space between the two communities, there is no wall and space was formerly used as a bonfire site. Space is now used for a number of positive events, which is equally fascinating because here we have two communities that have worked together to find a solution. There is a shop, an old shipping container that is relatively famous in the area. It is positioned right in the centre of the contested space, and it has allowed interaction between the two communities; it is ugly, but most importantly, it works (P2.14).

Is it feasible to erase physical traces of the troubling past?

> Nonetheless, we made no effort at all to talk to people, but that was the government's approach at the time. It was a significant political breakthrough because it was about relieving community housing stresses and it was a heavily contested issue for the government, but no one asked the locals what they wanted
> – P3.14

From an architectural perspective, the Peaceline walls–associated memory serves as a catalyst and motivation for the design process in areas of division. Their physical existence gives considerable attention to Belfast and is a reliable indicator of the city's turbulent history as an actual manifestation of the cultural and religious differences that exist across the area. Studies have shown that more extremist views tend to be held in areas of social deprivation across the world (McDowell and Shirlow, 2011; Sterrett et al., 2012). Besides, the walls have generated considerable interest on international grounds over the years. In 2009, there was potential for economic investment on the part of Office of the First Minister and Deputy First Minister (OFMDFM; now named the Executive Office), to coincide with the 20th anniversary of the collapse of the Berlin Wall. A strategy was not devised on time, due to conflicting views from the areas, as the international investment was linked to a proposal to remove the walls. In 2008, Mayor Bloomberg of New York City also spoke of the economic potential in removing the walls in the form of investment. Nonetheless, the walls themselves have served as an artefact of the city's recent past.

A considerable change is manifested regarding methods that planners and architects employ over time. When Building Design Partnership, for example, was developing the cul-de-sac estates off the Falls and Shankill in the 1960s and 1970s, there was no community involvement, as the project was mostly to accommodate people relocated from elsewhere. Today, planning in contested areas is approached much differently compared to the way it was in the 1960s. A member from FAB noted,

> Our approach was very different in that we did not say we were going to negotiate with communities and take down the peace walls; we said that the first thing we were going to do was a proper and thorough analysis of the area surrounding the peace walls. Because if you look at somewhere like Cupar Way, an interface between the Shankill Road and Springfield Road, and you took the wall away now, you would still be left with two roads. The urban fabric has actually been designed within the context of the walls.
>
> (P1.14)

The overall goal of eradicating the walls is quite far-fetched, and the government's initiatives, as well as international pressure to eradicate them through financial incentives, are mostly ignorant of the communities in the contested space. Many communities see the walls as forms of security and protection, and proposals to remove them without thorough analysis and public cooperation are doomed to failure. Removal of the walls in a short period would likely raise territorial concerns and social disorder. A survey by OFMDFM in 2012 revealed that 69 percent of residents believe that political violence is still occurring today and that the walls help with protection on either side.

We have two conflicting ideologies here, but there is scope for conflict transformation and that means to transform what was formerly an arms' struggle to democratic debate and discussion. Older people suffered too much in the conflict to believe in the peace. Reconciliation may only come now with new generations. The peace will grow up with the kids, but in the meantime, it's the separation walls that grow (P3.14). In a way, the 'living memory' associated with the walls is still raw amongst communities, and it is mostly up to the government to pave the way for improving cross-community relationships in areas of conflict. Perhaps the most significant factor to address in the broader context of the situation is integrated schooling. As a member of the BCRC stated, segregated schooling on religious grounds is one of the core problems of the divide in these areas (P2.14).

There is a tremendous amount of segregation in daily lives, and this is most evident amongst working-class communities. The kids go to school in either Protestant schools or Catholic schools – there is nowhere in their daily lives where the two groups meet. This is not a consequence of the walls; the segregations and divisions were there long before the walls existed. Instead, the walls have fed into this and created further segregation. So now, we are in a situation whereby there is more segregation after 13 years of the peace process than there was during the actual conflict (Ibid.).

In the meantime, planning practice in Belfast is confronted with divisions and yet stranded by slow actions. Literature written by professionals on division and post-conflict solutions, which offers authoritative evidence of their sympathetic and nuanced understanding of conflicted territories, is valuable. However, it lacks practical frameworks and structures for the application. With professional practice drifting deeply into the city's political landscape, there is an urgent need to improve progressive policies and approaches for moving into contexts of realisation. The following are a number of strategies towards dealing with contested space surrounding the peace lines in post-conflict Belfast.

Planning practices being faced with re-imaging controversial contexts such as in Belfast is not unique; however, a trend has developed whereby planners are paralysing themselves through inability to act by trying to gain an understanding of the city's politics. The sociopolitical complexity of geography is often viewed as an overwhelming restriction on designers, but many within the field of design hold the view that it is their choice to be ambitious in proposals for contested areas. An 'unsolicited architecture' strategy has certainly been successful at a small scale, with the Sina's café being a prime example, but whether this success could be mirrored on a larger scale is debatable (Hyde, 2012). In a way, the Sina's café project owes much of its success to its temporary nature. The fact that it is a shipping container and not a permanent structure makes it impose much less on the communities on either side. Sina's owner pointed out that the local council opposes the container being there, arguing that it is 'unacceptable in its location and that it detracts from the character of the area' (P5.14). One could question the existence of 'character' in the area; nonetheless, to many, the café is a positive contribution to the area through its attempted neutralising of the contested space.

Diluting communities by bringing people from different faiths and religion to live and communicate in one place is one of the possible ways out. An architect from the Northern Ireland Housing Executive spoke of a new strategy for social housing whereby houses are delegated to people from different backgrounds, thus 'forcing them to live alongside one another' (P6.14). While this is still in its early stages, it appeared to be moderately successful. The problem that has manifested itself over recent decades is the approach of the cul-de-sac arrangement, which led to the further dividing of already insular communities. What now exists in the contested areas, and particularly in the Falls and Shankill areas, are communities of subcommunities, each with its subculture and religion.

By injecting vigour into housing schemes that will bring people of different views into a shared space, the divide will become less poignant (P1.14). The Metropolitan Arts Center (MAC) tower, by Hackett Hall McKnight, and the Lyric Theatre, by O'Donnell + Tuomey, for example, are a testament to the future of architecture in Belfast and have greatly improved the city centre and its southern reaches, partly through aesthetics but also by bringing more people into these places. Admittedly, such contexts are not contested spaces in any real way, but they are examples of how design can and should be executed. A landmark contextual project in the contested spaces could be the answer to unifying these communities. While designers have tried to unify these areas through industrial 'business park' schemes, they have largely failed, due in part to the economic recession and their lack of openness to the public. Yes, they address the needs of the workers by providing jobs, but overall, they serve little purpose other than accentuating the physical divide in an alternative manner (Figure 10.2).

Recent artistic interventions along the walls (particularly at Cupar Way) have proved to be welcomed by communities on either side; and in 2010, 98% of residents surrounding Alexandra Park in North Belfast welcomed the addition of a gate in the Peaceline wall within the park. Grounds for designing interventions to the wall as an attempt to readdress its identity – not as a barrier of the divide, but as something that both communities can take pride in and that will bring people into the area for its architectural integrity, not for its brutal nature as dividing a 'battlefield'. A group of graffiti artists working on the Cupar Way peace line spoke of how graffiti artists from all over the world come to paint on the wall and that it is widely recognised worldwide for its showcase of street art. (In fact, of the group I interviewed on the day, three were renowned street artists from New York and Australia who had come over to paint with the group.) The walls continue to be built, yet only one has been demolished. The wall is an immune response, a symptom of past generations; therefore, removing it without

Figure 10.2 Sina's café is a possible success that could be mirrored, Belfast.

treating the underlying condition could be making the same narrow-minded mistake as building it in the first place was.

From policy to practice: envisioning integration in a divided landscape

Throughout much of its history of civil unrest, Belfast has been a city torn apart and subsequently rebuilt. Northern Ireland has been portrayed as having politically 'moved on' from the Troubles era, and this is evident in the devolution of power to a local administration from 1998 to 2005. Nonetheless, there are many physical artefacts that remain throughout the city, which recaptures the ideals held by opposing sides during the conflict which are still maintained and actively pursued to the present day. While few people younger than 25 have a living memory of the Troubles, many strategies have been adopted by both sides to ensure the fighting spirit and memory of atrocities are instilled into the present-day youth, primarily through manipulation of collective memory. We have examined in this chapter the construction of collective memory in the city as being dependent on the predominant discourses of society. When these discourses are displaced and fragmented, the collective memory runs the risk of becoming split and almost schizophrenic. In a way, individual memories of division in Belfast will continue to be passed from generation to generation, becoming more fragmented and reliant on their experience of the city.

The role of the practical profession in post-conflict cities such as Belfast is both complex and challenging. Various strategies that have been explored and used in recent decades have had a chequered record of success and failure. Replanning and designing such places are in fact add a third dimension to the sociopolitical divide on the outskirts of the city centre. The modest planning in Belfast's contested areas has been the result of many detrimental factors, most significantly the poor understanding of the contextual complexity on the part of the designer or planner, whose overambitious vision proved a mismatch over and over. The areas explored in this study are highly political and sensitive, and the removal of something as significant as the walls is merely an overreaching goal. Architects cannot apply their broadly generic professional and design principles. History has proven that for any strategy to work, designers must incorporate the broader context of the walls themselves and include community groups in their decision-making, taking into consideration the influence such groups have. In fact, for any proposals to move forward, communities' interests must be taken on board.

On the other hand, the incorporation of industrial or commercial buildings at interface areas is crucial, mainly when executed incorrectly, as the so-called 'neutral' buildings are merely the manifestation of the divide in an alternative way. Many industrial sites lie vacant in poor condition, merely due to their location across the divide. Special care must be taken in order to prevent buildings being used as buffers: in particular, the positioning of the entrance is crucial. Proper planning and design approach must integrate housing schemes into the broader community while avoiding large, vacant spaces that are pluralist and open to people from different backgrounds. As such, this becomes an issue of diffusing and blurring territoriality. The government officials, as well as designers, are aware that they cannot merely gift vacant land on one side to alleviate a shortage of land on the other. Not only the liaison with cohesive community groups is vital in these situations, but also integrating mixed groups and religions into housing schemes through organisations such as the Housing Executive would be critical to respond to such problems and even dilute it. Nonetheless, weakening the divide between either side by creating subculture/religious societies is not something that can occur overnight.

Notes

1 See Making Belfast Work initiative (MBW). The initiative was launched in 1988 to address problems facing people living in the most disadvantaged areas of Belfast. www.dsdni.gov.uk/making_belfast_work.
2 Interviewees are coded based on the standard code used in this chapter (Px.yy), where (Px) refers the participant's code in list of interviews and (yy) is the year when the interview took place.

11 Derry/Londonderry's Siege monument and the new segregated urbanism

Introduction

Walled urban settlements have, over centuries, played a significant role in shaping the characteristics of the communities they embrace. Cities such as San Gimignano in Italy, Carcassonne in France and Nicosia in North Cyprus display a long-lasting fabric of civil defence, articulating inherent geographies of heritage, displaying considerable potential as cultural resources and exhibiting substantial challenges, practical and theoretical (Doratli et al., 2004). Walls in towns are intellectualised as a 'dissonant' form of heritage whose value is commonly contested among different interest groups and whose meaning is not static but can be interpreted in various ways. During periods of insecurity and past endeavours, walls portrayed cities as achieving order from chaos and providing protection for citizens, at the expense of putting up barriers to their free movement (Creighton, 2007).

The identities and heritage of walled cities are multilayered and fluid, what renders them vulnerable to reinvention. By their very existence as defensive fortresses, walled cities witnessed violent histories that changed their political and national allegiance over time (Mulholland et al., 2014; Selim, 2015). These cities, while superficially embracing citizenship and collective sense of spatial belongings, are also inescapably performing other forms of exclusion and marginalisation of other social groups. The urban impact of walled cities on infusing segregation has been well documented. Andreas Huyssen (2003) interrogated the Berlin Wall through narratives of people's collective memory and past experience of spatial division that continue to exist as an invisible barrier in the psyche of many residents until today. Eyal Weizman (2007) examined the Jerusalem/Palestine Wall through a keen understanding of the critical political and social motivations of its construction. Others employed visual analysis to understand the forced urbanism of interface areas in Belfast and Northern Ireland by documenting shifts in religion, mobility, and settlements (Abdelmonem and McWhinney, 2015; Selim and Abraham, 2016). Tracing physical attributes of segregated landscapes such as frontiers, watchtowers, and housing decay offer an insight of how spatial geography shifts in post-conflict cities for a long time after peace has been achieved (Misselwitz and Rieniets, 2006).

The walled city, Derry/Londonderry in Northern Ireland, has been branded as a city that exhibits long-rooted clashes of religious identities between Catholics/Nationalists and Protestants/Unionists. It was named the UK City of Culture (CoC) in 2013, building on the successful experience of Liverpool as the EU Capital of Culture in 2008. This unique status has offered local authorities the advent prospect of refashioning the city as a model of unity and healing while being distanced from its troubled past. In part, this included redefining multiple readings of the city's character, history and heritage. The complete 17th-century circuit wall surrounding the post-conflict renaissance city had stood intact as a symbol of civilisation for hundreds of years (Murtagh et al., 2017). The uninterrupted and continuous city wall is one of the oldest historical defensive walls to survive in Europe (Hume, 2002). The transformation of the wall during the 20th century eroded an architectural dialogue with the heritage of the city and shaped the urbanism of defences and segregated settlements (see figure 11.1).

This chapter aims to interrogate how the military blockades, peace lines, and watchtowers have influenced the segregated urban planning of Derry/Londonderry being imposed on the city's historic walls during the roubles in the second half of the 20th century. Tracing two pivotal moments of transformation prior to the 'Great Siege' of 1689 and the 'Battle of the Bogside' of 1968 illuminates the shifting residential settlements in the Bogside/Fountain areas and the migration of Protestant settlements towards the waterside on the east bank of the Foyle river. Each era of transformation resulted in significant shifts in the settlement, segregating communities using natural as well as physical boundaries as domains of division. The chapter also uncovers narratives of the 'no-man's land' developments at the peripheries of the monument, including the disintegration of public space within the city walls and negative space at the external peripheries of the monument due to the evolution of military transformation.

The approach adopted for tracing the transformation of Derry/Londonderry's city walls over time is based on a significant monograph written by Nobel laureate John Hume (Hume, 2002). His descriptive approach enabled analytical mapping to be conducted and the main events of conflict and statistical data to be cross-referenced. This research documents void spaces and disused sites at the peripheries of the city walls over several site visits and investigative fieldwork. To understand the physical presence of military transformation in the Bogside settlement, site sections were sketched to document the change to the Bogside interface from 1968. The sections illustrated the physical prominence of Walker's Pillar (a Unionist monument) before it was blown up by the Irish Republican Army (IRA) in 1973 and the subsequent erection of a 60-metre Masonic watchtower outpost by the British Army to survey the Bogside area. Finally, analysis of current dwellings within each residential settlement was conducted using mapping and

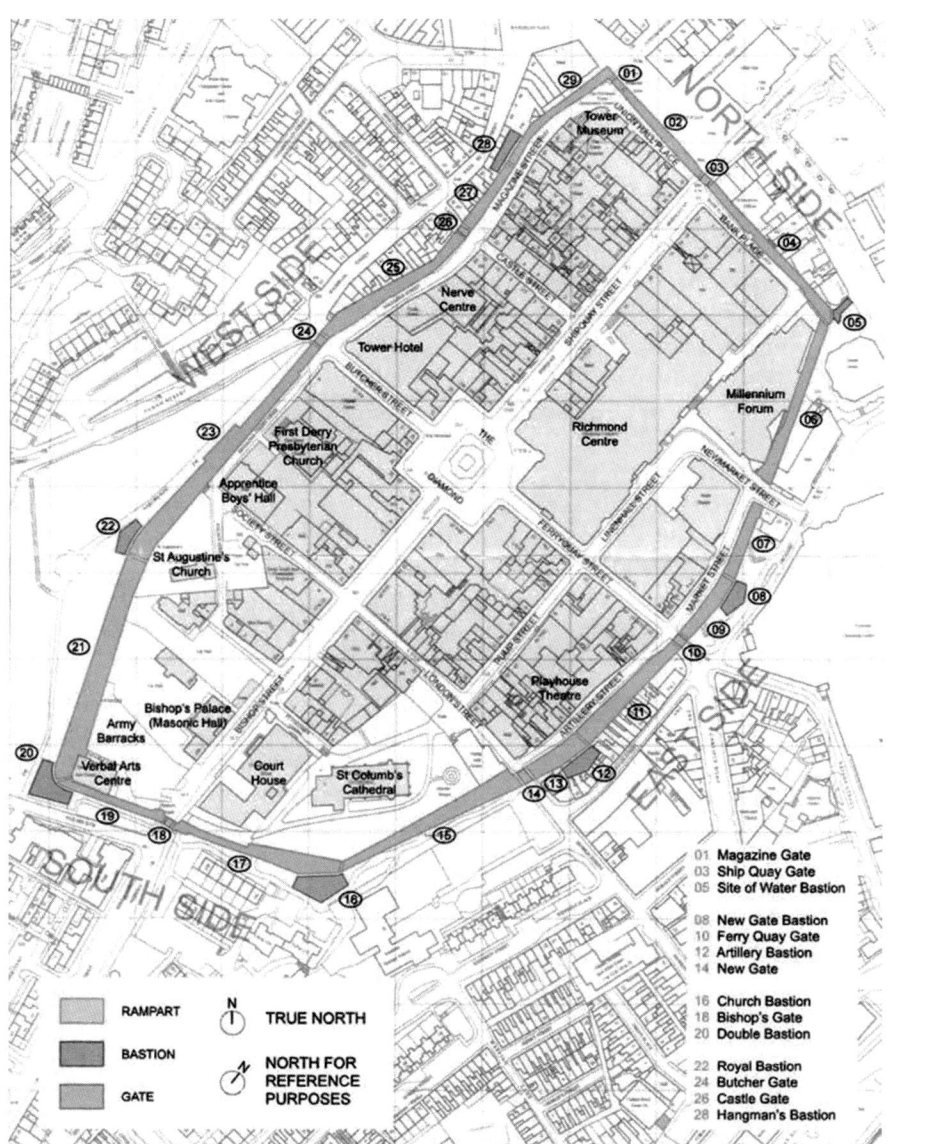

Figure 11.1 Walls of Derry/Londonderry.

Source: NI Government (2011, 2017).

first-hand census data to obtain a clear depiction of segregated settlements at the periphery of the city walls.

History and transformation of Derry/Londonderry

Derry/Londonderry's fortifications have followed a simple pattern: 'their walls consist of large mounds of earth and sods dug out of the ground leaving a deep trench'; these mounds were transformed into necessary defensive ramparts, sometimes reinforced with timber with parapets of earth, stone or wood fashioned on top (Hippsley, 2012). In its early foundation, the city of Doire Colmcille was established as a monastic settlement in early Christian Ireland, where the monastery was founded near an oak grove by Colmcille (Columba) in 546 AD (Hamilton, 1999), around which Flathbert O'Brolchain built a stone 'Cashel' fortification in 1156. It became the monastic site of Long Tower Church, Bogside, and served as a base point for early English settlers to build the first defensive fortifications in 1566. Initially, the fortifications were undermined by the continuous movement of settlers who were prepared to flee to the countryside. Sir Henry Docwra arrived in Londonderry in 1600, at a time of rising religious tension in Europe and Ireland, that were to erupt later in Derry/Londonderry (Ibid.).

Two additional fortifications were built using locally sourced earth materials in preparation for the impending conflict; transforming simpler structures into a significant defensive complex, signalling the beginning of a strong military presence in Derry/Londonderry (Docwra and Kelly, 2008). This was approximately a quarter of the area later constructed by the Irish Society of London between 1614 and 1619 that resisted the attacks of Catholic King James II during the Great Siege, 1688–1689. A small settlement of Protestants was founded just outside the Walls only to move inside when in face of the influx of Catholic settlers from Donegal. Bogside settlers had taken refuge within the walled city temporarily before returning to rebuild outside Butcher's gate following the Royalist siege of 1649 (Free Derry Museum, 2012). The fluid, elastic moves of settlements continued throughout the Middle Ages on the back of continuous religious wars.

Flourishing linen industry of the 19th century had brought about new patterns of spatial demographics with the growing use of the city's port for migration, especially in the years following the potato famine of 1845. The growing trade with the Western Hemisphere saw the population of Derry rise from around 11,000 in 1800 to 40,000 by the end of the century (McSheffrey, 2000). In August 1803, the Irish Society made an unsuccessful attempt to remove all housing within 40 feet of the monument to prevent encroachment on the walls. However, a decision was made to preserve the city walls while it continues to accommodate local inhabitants (Milligan,

1948). More than a century later, In October 1943, town planning officer Major A. T. Marshall unsuccessfully articulated the desirability of a green belt around the exterior of the walls. A similarity in void space between the monument and the Bogside interface is present to this day.

The second era of transformation occurred during the latter half of the 20th century. These transitions coincided with the 1968 Urban Area Plan and key events of the conflict, such as Bloody Sunday (30 January 1972), which linked together to form new segregated urbanism. During this era, the monument was largely 'constructed from random rubble shale with dressed brown sandstone used on the outer walls for copings to parapets, dressings to embrasures and loops and quoins to bastion angles' (NIEA, 2011: p. 29). Throughout 1968, Derry Housing Action Committee staged several protests, most notably the Civil Rights March of 5 October (which culminated in violence at Duke Street, Waterside) to highlight deteriorating conditions in dwellings huddled beneath the walls. In the same year, the '*Derry Area Plan stated the need for 9,600 houses in the city between the periods of 1968–81*' (Murtagh, 1996: p. 45), leading to a complete rebuilding of the Bogside. This decision signalled the commencement of an era in which the monument would play a key role in violence and forced segregation that persists to the present day.

Throughout the Troubles, the entire wall walkway was resurfaced in exposed-aggregate concrete circa 1985 and subdivided into sets of palisade fences and gates erected for security purposes. The attractive promenade became somewhat diminished by the spontaneous evolution of its military transformation. In summary, the following timeline was produced to indicate major shifts in the spatial structure of division:

British Army Checkpoints at City Gates (1969–1980): Each gate in the city walls had restricted mobility, and civilian and vehicle searches were required for entry into them. This attests to the deterioration of mobility through the walls from 1969 to the early 1980s, as security force checkpoints at all city gates were constructed to prevent potential IRA movement from the Bogside throughout the city centre.

Closure of Walls as Public Space (1969–2005): The beginning of the Troubles signalled the end of the city walls as a public space within Londonderry. Due to the walls bordering several contested spaces, and in view of rising tensions between settlements, the British Army barricaded the walkways to maintain peace, thereby using the monument as a buffer between settlements.

Watchtowers and British Compound on the City Walls (1973–2005): At the north-western corner of the walls of Derry, as seen from the Bogside, the watchtower remained a prominent feature from the early 1970s until the end of 2005. This surveillance point was known as the Masonic Observation Post, as it was built next to the Masons' Hall, currently the Verbal Arts Centre. It was a facility for watching and listening to the Nationalist Bogside below.

City Walls and Political Graffiti (1973 onwards): '*It is one of the ironies of Londonderry that long stretches of its walls are now more visible than they have been at any stage in the past 150 years, and so they make a much clearer, and so to many people a more unacceptable, statement that they used to*' (Cornforth, 1985c: p. 1060). Presently, the walls are often used to display both Unionist and Nationalist political graffiti.

Peace Line Constructed: Bishop's Street (1975): The Bogside/Fountain peace line served two functions: it provided 'peace of mind' for residents and protection against repeated attacks on either estate. These functions are crucial to the stability and long-term sustainability of communities.

Peace Line Constructed: City Walls (1975 onwards): Several steel posts and wire mesh secondary defences were placed upon the existing medieval walls. The peace line overlooked the Bogside area and prevented missiles from being thrown from within the city walls at two buildings of heritage – the Apprentice Boys Hall and First Presbyterian Church, the latter constructed in 1702.

Figure 11.2 British Army checkpoints at city gates.

Source: Courtesy of University of Ulster.

Impact of 1968 Derry area plan on social segregation

During the 1960s, apart from the Provisional IRA bombings in Northern Ireland, the violence in Derry/Londonderry was often the result of clashes with security forces but not between communities. The 1968 physical plan for the city aimed to retain and expand the city centre to avoid an emerging dual city with twin centres based on ethnic groupings. Planners anticipated that social goals could be achieved through physical means. Thus, the plan showed high ambitions for better housing conditions, the attraction of new industries, and a developed and enhanced commercial centre. Despite the high hopes for the Derry/Londonderry's future, we witness today overwhelming segregation between Catholics mostly living in the west bank and the Waterside on the east bank dominated by Protestants (McSheffrey, 2000: p. 112).

Until 1947, when the first plans were made to alleviate overcrowding around the periphery of the city walls, much of Derry's housing stock dated from the 19th century, and most of the dwellings in the inner city were completely unfit for human habitation by the late 1940s (Ó Dochartaigh, 1999). At that time, Unionist mayors of Derry were allocating houses on a sectarian basis, leaving the Northern Ireland Housing Trust (NIHT) with a housing waiting list that was almost exclusively Catholic (Ó Dochartaigh, 1999). By 1962, no interventions were made to halt the deterioration in housing following the Bogside demolition (Cornforth, 1985a). The Rossville Flats were constructed then and were completely alien to the city, as 'a horrifying view' (Cornforth, 1985a: p. 1090). The flats were built as 10-storey deck-access blocks based on the ideals of Swiss-born architect Le Corbusier.

In 1967, NIHT approved the new 537-dwelling Creggan estate, overlooking the Bogside, on a hill in the southward of the city: 'The estate was expanded haphazardly, and Creggan estate was eventually to have 1,800 houses and by the late 1960s a population of at least 15,000 people . . . it was overwhelmingly Catholic in population' (Ó Dochartaigh, 1999: p. 5). The latter recalls comparison being made between the Bogside and Creggan settlements as 'Catholic ghettos' and that these settlements created tension with nearby Protestant settlements like the Fountain. Ó Dochartaigh (1999) further recollects that in September 1963, the NIHT began its first slum-clearance scheme in the city by taking ownership of all properties in the Rossville Street 'redevelopment' area and overseeing the complete demolition and rebuilding of the settlement. This shifted the spatial arrangement of the Bogside/City Wall interface, pushing the settlement back farther from the monument.

The Victorian commercial and residential buildings fronting the walls were in an advanced state of disrepair, with many on the verge of collapse. McSheffrey (2000) states: 'Today, the walls have been exposed and the talus landscaped; they form attractive glimpses of how the walls might have appeared when first built in the seventeenth century' (p. 122). In fact, the

Figure 11.3 British troops post on the walls, 1969.

Source: Courtesy of i.pinimg.com.

1968 area plan had a crucial role in transitioning the urbanism surrounding the city Walls. While development of some kind was inevitable, even in the absence of a plan, it is doubtful whether much-needed large-scale housing developments on the west bank of the Foyle would have taken place (McSheffrey, 2000: p. 116). Demolition has opened up new views of the Walls but resulted in the loss of some streets and buildings which reflect the pattern of historic settlements outside the walls (Planning NI, 2011).

The 1905 Londonderry property valuation map produced by the Royal Irish Academy (2005) shows that more than 50 percent of property valued lowest (from £5.00 to £14.19) is situated in the Bogside, particularly in the streets near the walls. This housing was left untouched until 1947; therefore, low-income housing became a major factor in spatial segregation (Ó Dochartaigh, 1999). By 1990, equilibrium had been reached through the improved housing in segregated settlements. A report prepared by John

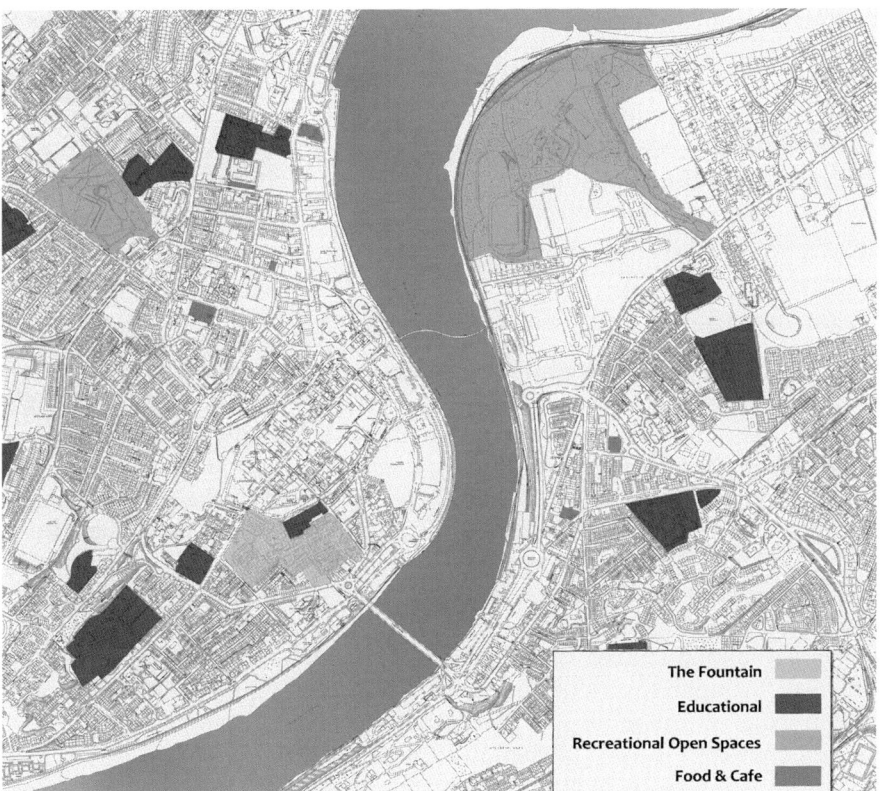

Figure 11.4 Derry/Londonderry 1968 plan.

Source: Courtesy of http://cain.ulst.ac.uk/.

Hume contained ample evidence of the horror of some of the housing conditions encountered:

> The Association had carried out their own survey and had found, for example, that 336 families, or 25% of those surveyed, lived in tenements and 160 completely in one room. Altogether, about 1,300 shared toilet facilities . . . 181 had to carry water from outside . . . In 140 cases, the principal worry is rats. In a flat in Bishop's Street, a mother discovered a rat feeding on the baby's bottle in the cot.
>
> (McSheffrey, 2000: p. 64)

In identifying the housing shortage as a key factor in the migration of Bogside residents, McDowell and Switzer (2011) suggest that due to impoverished housing in the Bogside, about 15,000 people had left that area by 1974, 'halving its population density but breaking up extended families, religious, social and community ties' (p. 84). The Bogside disaster, as it is described by McDowell and Switzer (2011), arose in the sense that 'disasters are moments when the social fabric is torn . . . violence and legacy have had a profound effect on the streetscape of the Bogside' (p. 100). The urban renewal, that is, the removal of entries, the layout of cul-de-sacs, large open spaces, and positioning of public buildings, all functioned to maintain order in the settlement and offered the military access streamlines to defuse hostile situations. This suggests that the basis for new segregated urban planning in the Bogside was the prevention or uncomplicated easing of conflict with neighbouring Protestant communities.

Transformations of city walls

The rituals associated with the walls' martial past were a major factor in the creation of various contested spaces in the city (Creighton, 2007). Both the Unionist celebration of annual marches around the walls and contested spaces exemplify the walls as a symbol of division. For decades, the walls, looking down on the Bogside, represented a symbolic partition. In an account of life on the interface of the Bogside throughout the 1950s, Deane (1992, 1997) observes that the Protestant cathedral was girded by the city walls, while Governor Walker's monument towered over the small huddled houses of the Bogside. In fact, Derry's town planning was a key factor in developing unused negative space at the peripheries of the city walls, whereas 'the open spaces of earlier years have been replaced by bleak apartment blocks . . . the shape of the neighbourhood has been changed . . . a city besieged within the siege' (Deane, 1992: p. 18).

Listing the reasons behind the fragmentation of the Bogside settlement from the walls, in particular those imposed on the monument overlooking the Bogside, Cornforth (1985b: p. 1091) explains that the walls' military transformation over the course of 1969 to 1985 played a key role in continuing segregation. The Apprentice Boys of Derry's hall just behind the wall served as a 'convenient point for lobbing missiles over . . . hence, the mesh screen was constructed upon the city walls' (ibid.: p. 1060). In 1969, a ballot was held amongst Bogside residents in response to the 'Bogside Peace Ring' barricades and police actions. It is notable that 3,613 residents voted 'no' when asked whether the barricades should be taken down immediately and unconditionally, a figure over three times higher than had said 'yes'. Furthermore, a very similar vote in favour of a dedicated police force for the Bogside, one unconnected to the Royal Ulster Constabulary, implies that many Bogside residents were satisfied with imposed segregation and would have chosen to set up services organised within the Bogside itself independently of the city authorities.

In order to develop a vehicular buffer zone between the city walls and the Bogside, only two possibilities existed: one that would have cut through the Bogside (the 'Lecky Road Flyover') or the quayside route. Either 'would assist in the early clearance of obsolete and unsightly buildings' (McSheffrey, 2000: p. 77). The former, constructed in June 1974, effectively cut off the Bogside and associated Nationalist murals from the embankment, over which the walls loom. McSheffrey (2000) notes that people were worried about MacKinder's insensitivity to the importance of the existing city fabric, regarding him as a Baron Hausmann, 'the most famous exponent of massive urban surgery' in the 19th century who had destroyed the medieval areas of Paris to create his splendid boulevards (p. 77).

A significant shift in population density at the periphery of the city walls took place over the course of the 20th century. This shift is mainly attributed to the change in housing density from 1948 to 2012, following the 1968 area plan and replacement of the Bogside's terraced housing with accommodation blocks rising as high as the medieval walls on the hill above. The terrain above the walls served to accelerate segregation afterwards. The oblique drop from the walls to the Bogside below gave the British Army a panoramic view of the ground below to monitor signs of imminent conflict. Due to this surveillance, the Fountain was permitted to become a protected enclave on higher terrain:

> As the role of the British Army expanded, Protestants in the Fountain had less and less contact with and knowledge of the conflict in the city due to the peace line. While this ensured that the conflict did not have as strong a sectarian component as Belfast, it also served to distance the Protestant community further from the Catholic community.
>
> (Ó Dochartaigh, 1997: p. 31)

As the 1948 site section depicts, the progression of the Bogside city Wall interface, the density of pre-existing terrace housing and the dominance of Walker's Monument antagonised the Nationalist community below. Figures 11.5 and 11.6 also show the movement of the Bogside

Table 11.1 Analysis of void space within 400-metre radius of monument following transformations

	Area (m²)	%
Total Void Space	141,679	
Fountain settlement	25,448	18
Bogside settlement	88,694	63
Other	27,537	19
Void Space within Monument	10,696	8
Void space at interfaces	9,619	90
Other	1,077	10
Void Space at exterior of Monument	130,983	92
Exterior void space at military interfaces	39,117	93
Void Space in Direct Contact with Lecky Road Flyover	20,882	15
Void space Incorporated within flyover	4,181	20
Void Space as a result of Transformations	71,596	51
Bogside Peace Ring, 1968–1970	17,764	25
Dismountable peace lines on city walls, 1968–2013	28,197	39
Bishop Street peace line, 1975–2013	12,783	18
Masonic Watchtower/British Army Compound, 1975–2005	37,008	52
Political graffiti	25,960	36

away from the Walls, creating an area of no man's land between the walls, the Free Derry Monument, Nationalist murals, and the sparse cul-de-sac housing beyond.

By that time, settlements were manipulated and moulded around the contours set out by military transformation. The Unionist Fountain estate has become an enclosed enclave due to the brick-and-wire Peaceline wall separating it from the Bogside. With a majority of people moving to the east bank of the River Foyle, the Fountain exists as a Protestant minority on the city side. The Nationalist Bogside has also been pushed back from the Walls, and its pre-existing density of terraced housing has been lost, with cul-de-sac micro-settlements sprawling back from the monument. The line the Bogside Peace Ring took in 1968 contains the Bogside settlement to this day, despite the fortifications now being long deconstructed. This is evident in the undulating shape of the settlement's edge, following the line of pre-existing defences. Perhaps most striking about the results is the apparent area of no-man's land fronting the walls' peace lines. A clear break in the settlement has occurred, aided by the Lecky Flyover.

The transformation of the walls reduced mobility in the years following the Battle of the Bogside (1969) was regulated, with restricted access at both Butcher's Gate and Bishop's Street Gate bordering the Fountain. Residents

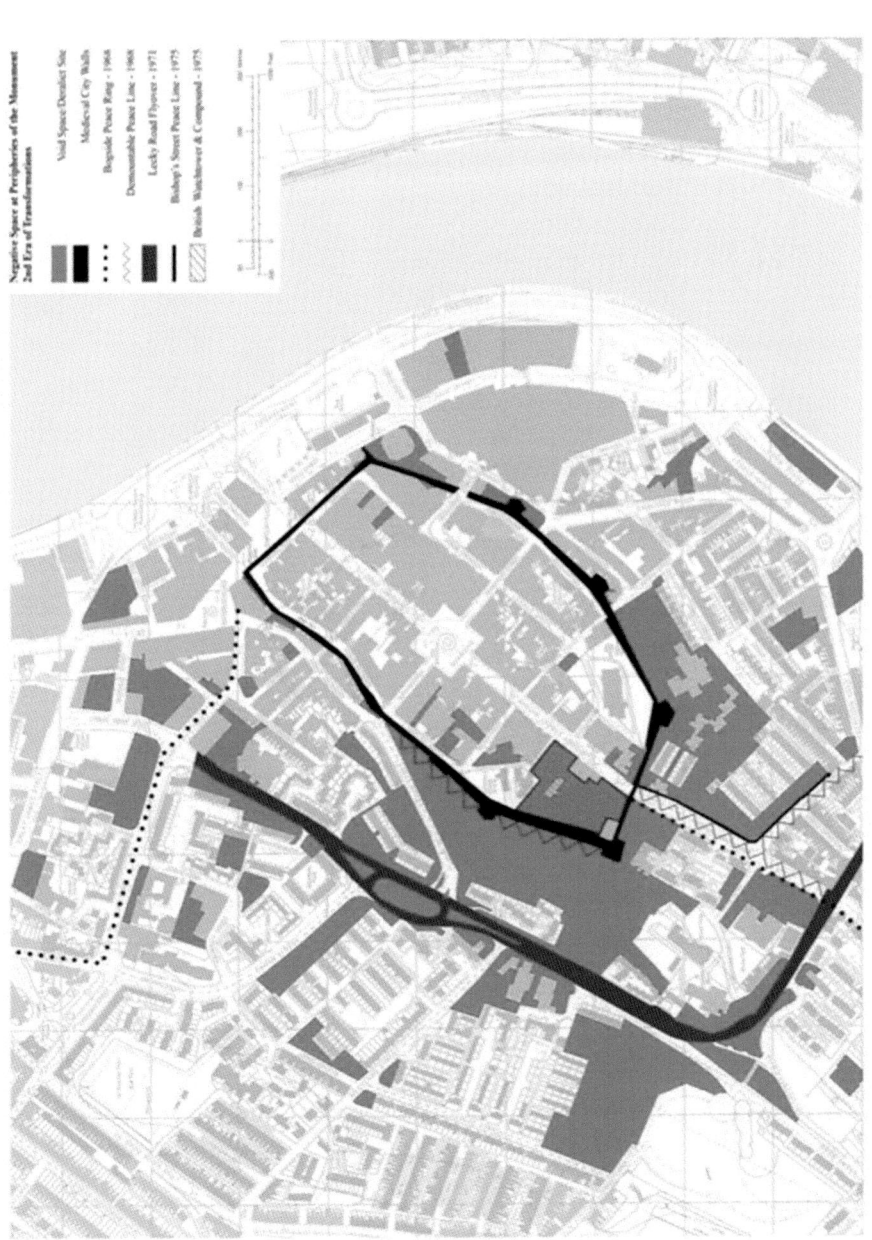

Figure 11.5 2013 settlement migration and social segregation based on 1951 OSNI historical base map – second era of transformations.

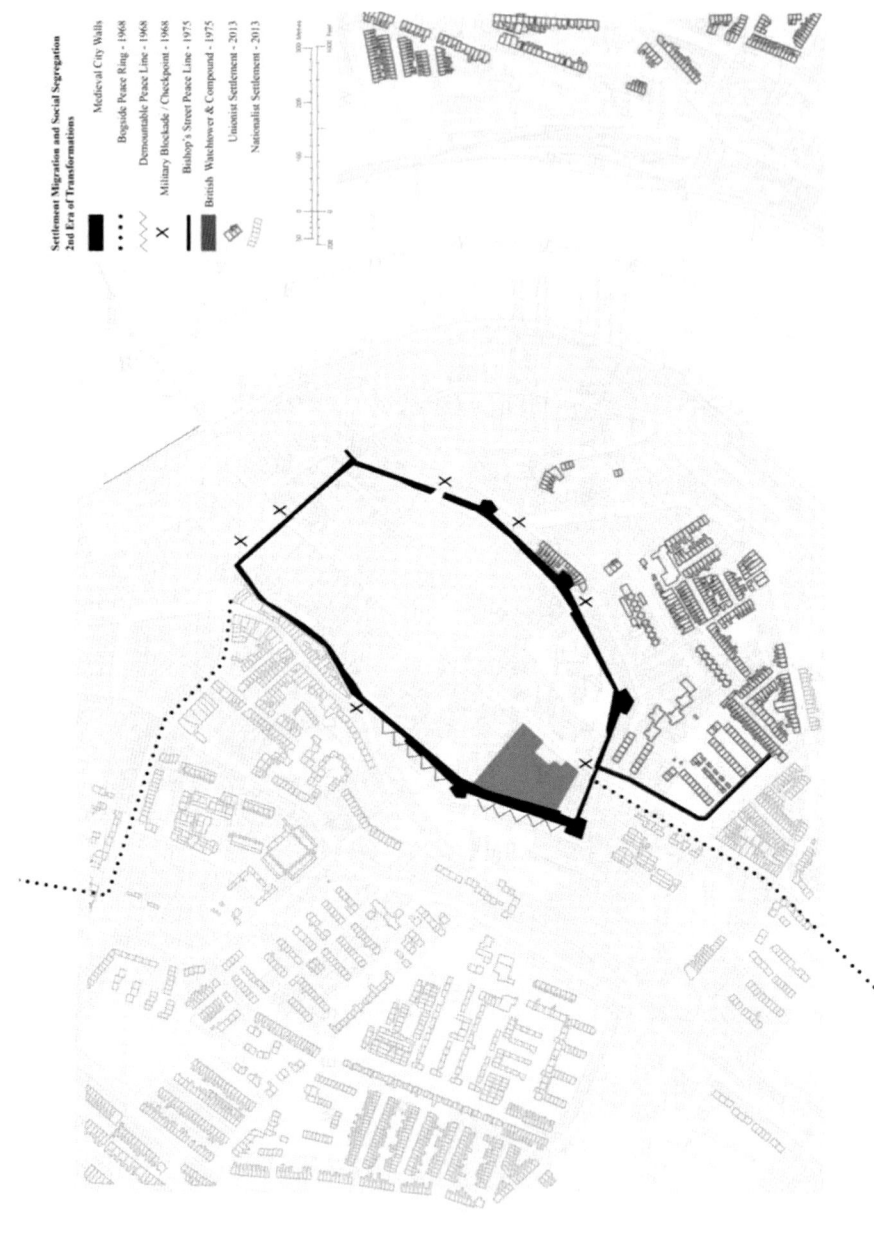

Figure 11.6 Negative space at peripheries of the monument, based on 2012 OSNI base map – second era of transformations.

of the latter estate also have restricted access to the city centre, with the settlement becoming increasingly enclosed within its surrounding fortifications, both historical and modern. Evidence supports an influx of Protestant settlers into the east bank of the city over time. As the 20th century progressed, Catholic settlements began to expand into the western quarter of the city, while Protestant communities migrated across the River Foyle. Hence, due to the physical transformation and fortification of the Walls, only the Fountain enclave remains on the city side.

The vast areas of no man's land at the peripheries of the Bogside and Fountain interface illustrate that 63 percent of void space within a 400-metre radius of the monument lies within the Bogside. Figures show that military intervention in the Bogside has resulted in the area migrating from its original proximity to the Walls. The void space (18 percent) contained within the Fountain enclave accounts for 40 percent of the total area of the settlement, with the majority of negative space occurring at the peripheries of the monument or Bishop Street peace line. The formation of cul-de-sac housing to replace terraced housing has also contributed towards this situation. Only 8 percent of total void space is found within the walls; however, 90 percent of this occurs at areas of direct military transformation. The Masonic Observation Watchtower and British Compound account for 6,555 square metres or 68 percent of void space within the walls.

This area, once belonging to the bishop of Derry, was transformed into a compound for the British Army in 1975 and functioned as such until 2005 when the base was decommissioned. The area now serves as a car park, due to the proximity to the Bogside/city walls interface lined with dismountable peace lines. Of the 30 percent of void space at the exterior peripheries of the monument, 93 percent was in direct contact with a physical transformation or military interface point. The Lecky Road Flyover, which cuts off the Bogside from the hill on which the monument sits, accounts for 15 percent of the total void space in the 400-metre radius. Of that amount, 20 percent is due to physical 'islands' or other buffers built as an infrastructure requirement.

In fact, the formation of void space following military transformation accounts for 51 percent of the total negative space within the designated radius. This is evidence of the shifting of settlements due to military intervention, with negative space being left behind. Of this total, the Masonic Observation Watchtower accounts for the highest amount of negative space (52 percent) due to the combination of derelict space within and without the walls. The progression of Walker's Pillar to an even more dominant vertical presence has led to an area of no-man's land beneath the walls, where rows of terraced houses previously stood. Bishop Street peace line accounts for 18 percent of this total due to a combination of void space within the settlement and at the Bogside/Fountain interface. Peace lines established on the monument following the British Army's closure of the city walls as public space impacted not only on the surrounding Bogside area but also on the streets within it. Missiles thrown at the Presbyterian Church and Apprentice Boys' hall were a threat both to architectural heritage and human life. This area fell into decline throughout the Troubles, with many sites remaining vacant today.

Coda
What lies ahead?

The geographies of the political and economic environment of division allow groups to justify their encounters and antagonistic behaviours as instituting prejudice. The perception of public spaces in a divided city is fundamentally territorial, resulting in a non-visual, non-physical fortification and ownership as a defensive strategy. These are more evident in interface areas, which were subsequently divided into territories attached to adjacent insular communities. While interface border areas are overloaded with negative experiences and perceptions as territorialised fabric, new spaces offer new possibilities for experimentation with spatial relationships of integration. Isolating divisions within its current territories and expanding into a new land with glimpses of the pluralist space is emerging as an attractive strategy that is yet to be socially integrative as well as being physically designed.

Contact Theory scholars stress that when few individuals of one group display negative behaviour towards the other, a generalised animosity will likely develop towards the entire group. This was one of the main reasons behind the increased number of Peaceline walls after the Good Friday Agreement. Negative encounters tend to be generalised while positives only represent individual endeavours. The judgements from both sides are usually based on their intertextual accounts of the Troubles. The inheritance of fear, insecurity, and painful memories of the Troubles have primarily impacted the way people perceive and engage with public spaces in Northern Ireland. The evidence indicates that the demand over territory is driven by a sense of insecurity within unsettled society. Taking advantage of their geographic dominance, communities expand beyond their perceived territory and assume some control over broad areas of public services, integrated parks, and urban squares.

Instead of looking at the spatial geographies of division as a commonplace in Northern Irish politics, this book embarked on a more in-depth analysis of the implicit and underlying condition of shareness. Reading between the lines of antagonism and rival identities, we were interested in finding instances of similarities and shared perceptions between members and groups of both communities. We wished to explore whether such rival identities and contestation over territories may conceal other patterns of engagement or mutual agreements on the level of ordinary people. Through our conversations with colleagues, students, and friends, it was clear that many members within both communities showed frequent instances of displeasure of the current conditions of segregation and division. The grand narratives of coherent communities and loyalty may be a political stance rather than satisfaction with the spatial geographies of the city. Centred on the encounters and narratives of everyday life; hence, this book sought to examine the notion of *shareness* in the divided landscapes of post-conflict Northern Ireland.

In cities that are divided by ethnonational rivalry, public space, and its architecture become the crucible of contestation related to ethnicity, territoriality, and national identity. Physical barriers, such as the Peaceline walls, integrated zones materialise this paradoxical relationship of the edge as a line of separation and attachment, which is the inevitable reality of coexistence in a 'landscape of risk'. Our investigation of the spatial practices and patterns of activities in different public spaces, buildings, or rural landscape has revealed the extent to which an atmosphere of prejudice is dictated by political tension over issues of identity, territorial gains and a contest over 'who controls the space' rather than by 'who uses the space'. When this position is reversed, one can see clear instances of shared displeasure with the current condition of segregation and insular enclaves that dissect the city into a set of binaries: go/no-go areas, safe/unsafe, ours/theirs.

Through the investigation of different case studies and different contexts: urban/rural, present/past, architecture/urban space, we argued that a deep understanding of modes and tools of spatial division is needed for professionals and policymakers to develop socio-spatial experiences that blur territorial boundaries and encourage integration. The ability of planners and designers to capture the dynamics of sociocultural and cognitive encounters in these conditions are particularly essential for what should be investigative design processes. The conventional design principles, in such contexts, do not work as the dynamics of rival politics turn spatial configurations into territorial gains. Under the pressure of coexistence, shared spaces are prone to becoming partitioned into non-physical territories where members of the other community feel intimidated. Yet, the condition of division should not be taken for face value without looking deeper into the communal and behavioural patterns in everyday life. We have established that such condition of rival identities, in fact, conceal common and inherent perceptions towards shared experiences, displeasure and collective interest in a shared future.

In this context of division, it is legitimate for space makers, architects, urban planners, and policymakers, to strive for a utopian image of inclusive socio-spatial cohesion and integration. To counter a long history of violence and painful memory, it is inevitable to have an intelligible and imaginative vision towards resurrecting memories of shared past through facilitating the perception of coexistence as an everyday reality where equal rights to the city and its spaces are warranted. For this to happen, such strategies need to face a few challenges. The spatial reconciliation in the city has first to confront authority and leadership structures, a mind-set of self-sufficient living within communities that are centred on the agency of the group. The cognitive trust in the group as an agent of protection, accessibility, and social support deprive the city and its public spaces of fulfilling their role as spheres of interdependent social engagement. Instead, such agency of the group needs to turn into an agency for coexistence in a shared city.

Such vision is far from straightforward, however. Handling urban design and architecture in divided landscapes invokes responsibility towards the social design of its integrated venues as pluralist public spheres, which are much more complicated than their physical and spatial characteristics. The strategic aim of those spheres is to offer equal access to services, events, and interaction that may not be a magic solution to eradicate the cognitive psychology of division instantly. Instead, they offer a sophisticated and multilayered approach to design to focus on interweaved pathways, passages, or shared routes where spatial and social conciliation is possible and could be practised on a daily basis.

The judgement of the success or failure of those spaces is multifaceted. Indeed, the planning and design of public space including its building facades have a direct influence on the pedestrian activity and subsequent occupancy of the space, in general. Buildings frame the edges of public and urban spaces and by a consequence affect the sense of integration, accessibility, and safe occupancy. For a public space to be lively, be it a public square or a pedestrian street, it must be lined with lively edges; people attract people. However, antisocial behaviour or hostile attitudes within public spaces combined with the lack of accessibility would drive peaceful and ordinary users away.

The encouraging sign in the spatial politics of Northern Ireland is the increasing awareness of the architects, and urban planners' role is enablers for positive change. Several practices, social enterprises, and community-led groups continue to contest a top-down approach to design, planning and urban development that disregard the community needs or the social-cultural context of the local groups. They are also aware that neutralising the politics of identity is required to provide a better opportunity for inter-cultural exchange between communities. Indeed, manifestations of peace-building in Northern Ireland are countless, but the practical implementation and outcome remain unpredictable and the main challenge.

While history showed us that the linen industry was key to several economic activities and shared ethnic-free living in both urban and rural communities, contemporary projects are resurrecting the notion that intermixed and integrated communities that were the norm during post-war era could be the way forward. From the Forum for Alternative Belfast proposed regeneration development for Divis Street to Translink's Weavers Cross transportation hub in Belfast, among others, architects and urban planners started to act as agents of change through schemes that look beyond division and more into everyday integration and shared living. New schemes rely on principles of populating public spaces with ordinary users and commercial units to maintain active and smooth users and pedestrian flow. However, the concern with new projects would rest on a few questions about how young generations would engage with these new modelled environments and how antisocial behaviour and antagonistic practices would impact the actual use of the space. Planners and architects must also take steps to ensure that communities on either side of the divide do not represent particular sectors of dominance.

Problems of integration and shared living in Northern Ireland have continued for several decades, if not centuries, and it is unlikely that individual actions of short-term strategies will provide an overnight remedy. In fact, time is the primary factor in bringing about change to the communities in Northern Ireland. We should not forget that current generations that experienced the full nature of violence and tension during the Troubles find it challenging to change their views and attitudes towards the political rivalry, whereas the next generation of young people could be the key to providing permanent change and eventual integration between communities. Attitudes are evidently changing, with many people eager to move on with their lives; however, this is a slow process to show significant shifts. As we saw in the first demolition of a Peace Line Walls, the most contentious of sites could be the catalyst for positive change. The slow process or negative experiences should not distract from the general upturn of the resurrection of shared living in Northern Ireland. If *shareness* in such a divided nation is an ultimate goal to be achieved, it will require architecture, space, and memory of shared history to work in tandem to resurrect the practice of shared living as a matter of normality in Northern Ireland.

References

Abdelmonem, M. G. (ed.) (2013). *Portrush: Architecture for the North Irish coast*. Belfast: Ulster Tatler.

Abdelmonem, M. G. (2016). *The architecture of home in Cairo: Socio-spatial practice of the Hawari's everyday life*. London: Routledge.

Abdelmonem, M. G. and McWhinney, R. (2015). In search of common grounds: Stitching the divided landscape of urban parks in Belfast. *Cities*, 44, pp. 40–49.

Abdelmonem, M. G. and Selim, G. (2012). Architecture, memory and historical continuity in old Cairo. *The Journal of Architecture*, 17(2), pp. 167–192.

Adams, T. and White, W. B. (1945). *Agency: Working with uncertain architectures*. Bessbrook, Belfast: Routledge.

Allport, G. W. (1954). *The nature of prejudice*. Cambridge, MA: Perseus Books.

Amin, A. (2002). Ethnicity and the multicultural city: Living with diversity. *Environment and Planning A*, 34, pp. 959–980.

Amin, A. (2013). Land of strangers. *Identities*, 20(1), pp. 1–8.

Anderson, J. (2004). *Political demography in Northern Ireland: Making a bad situation worse, political and social significance of the 2001 census of population*. Belfast: Centre for Spatial Territorial Analysis and Research.

Anderson, J. (2008). *From empires to ethno-national conflicts: A framework for studying 'Divided Cities' in 'Contested States Part 1'*. Thesis, Divided Cities/Contested States: Working Paper No. 1.

Anderson, J. (2013). *From empires to ethno-national conflicts: A framework for studying 'Divided Cities', in 'Contested States'*. Available at: www.conflictincities.org/PDFs/WorkingPaper1_5.8.08.pdf: Conflict in Cities and the Contested State.

Antonsich, M. (2010). Searching for belonging – an analytical framework. *Geography Compass*, 4, pp. 644–659.

Apter, D. (1997). *The legitimization of violence*. New York: New York University Press.

Arendt, H. (1958). *The human condition*. Chicago: University of Chicago Press.

Askins, K. (2008). Renegotiations: Towards a transformative geopolitics of fear and otherness. In: Pain, R. and Smith, S. J. (eds.), *Fear: Critical geopolitics and everyday life*. Aldershot: Ashgate, pp. 149–172.

Awan, N. (2008). Words and objects in transposing desire and making space. *Architectural Research Quarterly*, 12(3–4), pp. 263–268.

Awan, N., Schneider, T. and Till, J. (2011). *Spatial agency*. London: Routledge.

Baird, G. (2011). *Public space: Cultural/political theory: Street photography*. Amsterdam: SUN Architecture.

Bairner, A. and Shirlow, P. (2003). When leisure turns to fear: Fear, mobility, and ethno-sectarianism in Belfast. *Leisure Studies*, 22(3), pp. 203–221.

Bakhtin, M. (1986). *Speech genres and other late essays* (McGee, V. W., trans.). Austin: University of Texas Press.

Banxia. (2011). *Banxia software*. Available at: www.banxia.com/dexplore/ [Last Updated 2011].

Barakat, S. (1993). *Civil unrest shaping the built environment in Northern Ireland: The case of Belfast*. York: University of York.

Bassett, G. H. (1886). *County down guide and directory*. Dublin: Bassett.

Bastea, E. and Gorby, C. (2004). *Memory and architecture*. Albuquerque, N.M University of New Mexico Press.

Bauman, Z. (2000). *Liquid modernity*. Cambridge: Polity Press.

BBC News. (2012a). *Droppin' well bombing: Atrocity remembered 30 years on* [online]. Available at: www.bbc.co.uk/news/uk-northern-ireland-foyle-west-20623070 [Accessed April 1, 2017].

BBC News. (2012b). *Last update. 15 Police officers injured during Belfast city hall violence*. Available at: www.bbc.co.uk/news/uk-northern-ireland-20589957.

BBC News. (2016). *North Belfast: Work begins on removing interface wall*. Available at: www.bbc.co.uk/news/uk-northern-ireland-35658665.

BCRC. (2011). *Shared space report*. Belfast: The Belfast Conflict Resolution Consortium.

Bell, A. (2013). Spatial agents of change: Redefining the role of an architect within community regeneration in the twenty-first century. Unpublished Master's Dissertation, Belfast: Queen's University Belfast.

Bell, D. (1990). *Acts of union: Youth culture and sectarianism in Northern Ireland*. London: Palgrave Macmillan.

Bell, J., Jarman, N. and Harvey, B. (2010). *Beyond Belfast: Contested spaces in urban rural and cross boarder settings, community relations council*. Available at: www.community-relations.org.uk/fs/doc/master-beyond-report-web1.pdf.

Bell, A. (2013). Spatial Agents of Change: Redefining the role of an architect within community regeneration in the twenty-first century. Unpublished Master Dissertation. Belfast: Queen's University Belfast

Bevan, R. (2006). *The destruction of memory: Architecture at war*. London: Reaktion Books.

Birrell, D. (1994). Social policy responses to urban violence in Northern Ireland. In: Keele, S. D. (ed.), *Managing divided cities*. Staffordshire: Ryburn Publishing.

Black, R. (2016). One peace wall down, 109 across Northern Ireland still to go. *Belfast Telegraph* (February 26, 2016) [online]. Available at: https://www.belfast telegraph.co.uk/news/northern-ireland/one-peace-wall-down-109-across-northern-ireland-still-to-go-34486822.html.

Blackman, T. (1991). *Planning Belfast: A case study of public policy and community action*. Aldershot: Avebury.

Blevins, D. (2013). Northern Ireland: Deal to demolish 'peace' walls. *Sky News* (June 14, 2013). Available at: http://news.sky.com/story/1103497/northern-ireland-deal-to-demolish-peace-walls.

Boal, F. W. (1969). Territoriality on the Shankill-Falls divide, Belfast. *Irish Geography*, 6(1), pp. 30–50.

Boal, F. W. (1995). Belfast: Hindsight or foresight – planning in an unstable environment. In: Doherty, P. (ed.), *Geographical perspectives on the Belfast region.* Newtownabbey: Geographical Society of Ireland.

Boal, F. W. (2002). Belfast: Walls within. *Political Geography*, 21(5), pp. 687–694.

Boal, FW.(2008). Territoriality on the Shankill-Falls Divide, Belfast. *Irish Geography*, 41 (3), pp. 30–50

Boal, F. W. and Douglas, J. N. H. (1982). *Integration and division: Geographical perspectives on the Northern Ireland problem.* Belfast: Queen's University Press.

Boland, P., Murtagh, B. and Shirlow, P. (2016). Fashioning a city of culture: Life and place changing or 12 month party? *International Journal of Cultural Policy*, 25(2); pp.246–265

Bollens, S. A. (1998). *Urban peace building in divided societies.* Boulder: Westview Press.

Bollens, S. A. (1999a). *Role of public policy in deeply divided cities: Belfast, Jerusalem, Johannesburg.* Boulder: Westview Press.

Bollens, S. A. (1999b). *Urban peace building in divided societies.* Belfast, Johannesburg, Boulder: Westview Press.

Bollens, S. A. (2000). *On narrow ground: Urban policy and ethnic conflict in Jerusalem.* Belfast: Sunny Press.

Bollens, S. A. (2007). *Cities, nationalisation and democratization.* New York: Routledge.

Brand, R. (2009a). Urban artifacts and social practices in a contested city [Belfast]. *Journal of Urban Technology*, 16(2–3), pp. 35–60.

Brand, R. (2009b). Written and unwritten building conventions in a contested city: The case of Belfast. *Urban Studies*, 46(12), pp. 2669–2689.

Brand, R. and Ferognese, S. (2013). *The Radical's City: Urban environment, polarisation, cohesion.* London: Ashgate.

Brand, R., et al. (2008). *Changing the contested city: Understanding the contested city.* Belfast: Queen's University Belfast.

Bridge, G. and Watson, S. (2002). Lest power be forgotten: Networks, division and difference in the city. *The Sociological Review*, (50), pp. 507–524.

Bryan, D. (2000). *Orange parades: The politics of ritual, tradition and control.* London: Pluto Press.

Bryan, D. (2009). *Negotiating civic space in Belfast or the tricolour: Here today, gone tomorrow* Online paper, available at: https://pure.qub.ac.uk/portal/files/700510/WorkingPaper13_7.1.10.pdf.

Bryan, D. (2015). Parades, flags, carnivals and riots: Public space, contestation and transformation in Northern Ireland. *Peace and Conflict: Journal of Peace Psychology*, 21(4), pp. 565–573.

Bryan, D., Stevenson, C., Gillespie, G. and Bell, J. (2010). *Public displays of flags and emblems in Northern Ireland.* Belfast: Institute of Irish Studies, Queen's University Belfast.

Buckler, C. (2013). N Ireland: Calls to remove 'peace walls' in Belfast. *BBC News* (April 10, 2013). Available at: www.bbc.co.uk/news/uk-northern-ireland-22088273.

Buckley, V. (1985). *Memory Ireland: insights into the contemporary Irish condition.* New York: Penguin Books, p. 251.

Buonfino, A. and Hilder, P. (2006). *Neighbouring in contemporary Britain.* York: Joseph Rowntree Foundation.

Butlin, R. A. (ed.) (1977). *The development of the Irish town*. London: Croom Helm.

Byrne, J. and Gormley-Heenan, C. (2014). Beyond the walls: Dismantling Belfast's conflict architecture. *City*, 18(4–5), pp. 447–454.

Byrne, J. and Jarman, N. (2011). Ten years after pattern: Young people and policing in Northern Ireland. *Youth and Society*, 43(2), pp. 433–452.

Caballero, C., Edwards, R. and Smith, D. (2008). Cultures of mixing: Understanding partnerships across ethnicity. *Twenty-First Century Society: Journal of the Academy of Social Sciences*, 3(1), pp. 49–63 [online]. Available at: http://dx.doi.org/10.1080/17450140701749171 [Accessed April 1, 2017].

CAIN. (n.d.). *Watchtower and British compound overlooking the Bogside, 1975*. Available at: http://cain.ulst.ac.uk/images/photos/derry/citywalls/watchtower1.htm.

Cairns, A. (2002). *The church and community of St. John the Evangelist Gilford*. Belfast: Inglewood Press.

Cairns, D. (2008). Moving in transition: Northern Ireland youth and geographical mobility. *Young*, 16(3), pp. 227–249.

Calame, J. and Charlesworth, E. (2009). *Divided cities: Belfast, Beirut, Jerusalem, Mostar and Nicosia*. Philadelphia, PA: University of Pennsylvania Press.

Calley, D. (2013). *City of Derry: A historical gazetteer of the buildings of Londonderry*. Belfast: Ulster Architectural Heritage Society, p. 189.

Caputo, J. (2016). Peacebuilding through dialogue in Northern Ireland. In: Roy, S. and Shaw, I. S. (eds.), *Communicating differences culture, media, peace and conflict negotiation*. London: Palgrave Macmillan, pp. 54–67.

Carmona, M., et al. (2003). *Public places, urban spaces: The dimensions of urban design*. Boston: Architectural Press.

Childress, H. (2004). Teenagers, territory and the appropriate of space. *Childhood*, 11(2), pp. 195–205.

CinC – Conflict in cities and the contested state. (2012). *Sharing space in divided cities: Why everyday activities and mixing in urban spaces matter, conflict in cities and the contested state – Briefing Paper Launch*, p. 1.

Collins, T. (2016). Urban civic pride and the new localism. *Transactions of the Institute of British Geographers*, 41(2), pp. 175–186.

Connerton, P. (1989). *How societies remember*. Cambridge: Cambridge University Press.

Conway, B. (2003). Active remembering, selective forgetting, and collective identity: The case of bloody Sunday. *Identity: An International Journal of Theory and Research*, 3(4), pp. 305–323.

Cornforth, J. (1985a). Survival of a city: Londonderry I. *Country Life*, 178(4596), pp. 784–787.

Cornforth, J. (1985b). The grid within the Walls: Londonderry II. *Country Life*, 178(4598), pp. 974–976.

Cornforth, J. (1985c). Views of a city: Londonderry III. *Country Life*, 178(4599), pp. 1060–1062.

Coulter, C. (1999). *Contemporary Northern Irish Society: An introduction*. London: Pluto Press.

Coulter, C. and Murray, M. (2008). *Northern Ireland after the troubles: A society in transition*. Manchester: Manchester University Press.

Crawford, M. (1991). *Out of site: A social criticism of architecture*. Seattle: Bay Press.

Crawford, W. H. (1972). *Domestic industry in Ireland*. Lithographic Universal Ltd.

Crawford, W. H. (1987). *The Irish Linen industry.* Belfast: Ulster Folk and Transport Museum.

Creighton, O. (2007). Contested townscapes: The walled city as world heritage. *World Archaeology*, 39(3), pp. 339–354.Cummings, E. M., Merrilees, C. E., Schermerhorn, A. C., Goeke-Morey, M. C., Shirlow, P. and Cairns, E. (2011). Longitudinal pathways between political violence and child adjustment: The role of emotional security about the community in Northern Ireland. *Journal of Abnormal Child Psychology*, 39, pp. 213–224.

Cummings, E. M., Shirlow, P., Browne, B., Dwyer, C., Merrilees, C. and Taylor, L. (2016). *Growing up on an interface: Findings and implications for the social needs, mental health and lifetime opportunities of Belfast youth* [online]. Available at: www.executiveoffice-ni.gov.uk/sites/default/files/publications/ofmdfm/growing-up-on-an-interface.pdf.

Cunningham, W. (2001). *Violent conflict in Northern Ireland: Complex life at the edge of chaos, complexity, and conflict resolution theories, 2001 national conference on peacemaking and conflict resolution.*

Cunninghama, N. and Gregory, I. (2014). Hard to miss, easy to blame? Peacelines, interfaces and political deaths in Belfast during the troubles. *Political Geography*, 40, pp. 64–78.

Darby, J. (1974). *Intimidation in housing: Chapter 6, community case studies.* Available at: http://cain.ulst.ac.uk/issues/housing/docs/nicrc6.htm [Last Updated March 14, 2011].

Darby, J. (2003). *Northern Ireland: The background to the peace process.* Available at: http://cain.ulst.ac.uk/events/peace/darby03.htm [Last Updated March 2011].

Dawson, G. (1984). *Planning in the shadow of urban civil conflict.* Liverpool: University of Liverpool.

Dawson, G. (2005). Trauma, place and the politics of memory: Bloody Sunday, Derry, 1972–2004. *History Workshop Journal*, 59.

Dawson, G. (2007). *Making peace with the past? Memories, Trauma and the Irish troubles.* Manchester: Manchester University Press.

Day, A. (1990). *Ordnance survey memoirs of Ireland; parishes of co. Down 1.* Belfast: Institute of Irish Studies.

Deane, S. (1992). Derry: City besieged within the siege. *Fortnight*, 198, pp. 18–19.

Deane, S. (1997). *Reading in the dark.* London: Vintage Books.

De Certeau, Michel. (1984). *The practice of everyday life.* Berkeley, CA, London: University of California Press.

Deloitte. (2007). *Research into the financial cost of the Northern Ireland divide.* Belfast: Deloitte.

Department of the Environment. (1977). *Sion mills: Conservation area.* Belfast: DOE.

Department of the Environment. (2011). *Building on tradition—A sustainable design guide for the Northern Ireland countryside.* Available at: www.planningni.gov.uk/index/policy/ supplementary_guidance/guides/ [Accessed January 24, 2012].

Department of the Environment. (2012a). *Buildings at risk in Northern Ireland.* Available at: www.doeni.gov.uk/niea/content--databases--barni.htm?

Department of the Environment. (2012b). *The Northern Ireland buildings database* (January 12, 2012). Available at: www.doeni.gov.uk/niea/content--databases--buildlist.htm? [Accessed December 18, 2011].

Derry City Council. (2010). *Temporary closure of play park* (October 11, 2011). Available at: www.derrycity.gov.uk/News/Temporary-closure-of-play-park.

Derry City Council. (2011). *Temporary closure of play park* [online]. Available at: www.derrycity.gov.uk/News/Temporary-closure-of-play-park [Accessed April 1, 2017].

Derry Journal. (2016). 'Our Space' youth facility opens in city centre to better engage young people. *Derry Journal* (June 7, 2016) [online]. Available at: www.derryjournal.com/news/our-space-youth-facility-opens-in-city-centre-to-better-engage-young-people-1–7418745 [Accessed April 1, 2017].

Devine, P. and Schubotz, D. (2010). Caught up in the past? The views of 16-year olds on community relations in Northern Ireland. *Shared Space*, 10, pp. 5–22.

Dixon, H. (1973). *Ulster architecture 1800–1900, Brough*. Belfast: Cox and Dunn Ltd.

Doak, P. (2014). Beyond Derry or Londonderry: Towards a framework for understanding the emerging spatial contradictions of Derry – Londonderry – UK city of culture 2013. *City*, 18(4–5), pp. 488–496.

Docwra, H. and Kelly, W. (2008). *Docwra's Derry: A narration of events in North-West Ulster 1600–1604*. Belfast: Ulster Historical Foundation.

Doratli, N., Hoskara, S. O. and Fasli, M. (2004). An analytical methodology for revitalization strategies in historic urban quarters: A case study of the walled city of Nicosia, North Cyprus. *Cities*, 21(4), pp. 329–348.

DSD. (2003a). Department for social development. In: *People and place: A strategy fort neighbourhood renewal in Northern Ireland*. Belfast: DSD. Available at: www.dsdni.gov.uk/nr_belfast_imp_plan_final.pdf.

DSD. (2003b). *The department of social development's Belfast city centre regeneration policy statement*. Available at: www.communities-ni.gov.uk/.

Dunne, T. (1998). Wexford's Comoradh '98: Politics, heritage and history. *History Ireland*, 6(2), p. 51.

Dunne, T. (2004). *Rebellions: Memoir, memory and 1798*. Dublin: Lilliput Press.

Dutton, T. (1989). Cities, cultures, and resistance: Beyond Leon Krier and the post-modern condition. *Journal of Architectural Education*, 42(2), pp. 3–8.

Dyer, J. (1998). *Do you see what I see? Young people's experience of the troubles in their own words and photographs: The Cost of the Troubles Study, International Conflict Research Institute (INCORE)*. Belfast, Northern Ireland. Available at: http://cain.ulst.ac.uk/issues/violence/cts/dyer.htm.

Elliott, M. (2017). *Hearthlands: A memoir of the white city housing estates in Belfast*. Newtownards: Black Staff Press.

English, Richard. (2008). *Armed struggle: The history of the IRA* London: Pan.

Evans, D. and Patton, M. (1987). *The diamond as big as a square: A guide to Ulster's towns and buildings*. Belfast: UAHS.

Fainstein, S. S. (1994). *The city builders: Property, politics, and planning in London and New York*. Cambridge: Blackwell.

Fairclough, N. (1992). *Discourse and social change*. Cambridge: Polity Press.

Farrell, M. (1980). *Northern Ireland: The Orange State*. London: Pluto Press.

Fay, M. T., Morrissey, M. and Smyth, M. (1999). *Northern Ireland's troubles: The human costs*. London: Pluto Press.

Ferguson, C. (2005). *The Herdsman's and Sion Mills: 1835-2005*. Sion Mills: Sion Mills Buildings Preservative Trust.

Fletcher, M. (2000). *Silver linings, travels around Northern Ireland, little*. London: Brown and Co.

Forbes, D. H. (2004). Ethnic conflict and the contact hypothesis. In: Lee, Y. T., McCauley, C., Moghaadam, F. and Worchel, S. (eds.), *The psychology of ethnic and cultural conflict*. Greenwood, Westport, CT, pp. 69–88.

Forty, A. (2000). *Word and buildings: A vocabulary of modern architecture, part two: character*. London: Thames & Hudson.

Forum for Alternative Belfast (FAB) (2015). *Website*. Available at: https://www.forumbelfast.org/.

Free Derry Museum. (2012). *Website*. Available at: www.museumoffreederry.org/history-bogside01.html.

Gaffikin, F. (2010). M. McEldowney, and K. Sterret, creating shared public space in the contested city: The role of urban design. *Journal of Urban Design*, pp. 493–513.

Gaffikin, F. and Morrissey, M. (2011). *Planning in divided cities: Collaborative shaping of contested space*. Oxford: Wiley-Blackwell.

Gaffikin, F., Mceldowney, M., Rafferty, G. and Sterrett, K. (2008). *Public space for a shared Belfast: Belfast city council funded research report*. Belfast: Belfast City Council.

Gaffikin, F., Mceldowney, M. and Sterrett, K. (2010). Creating shared public space in the contested city: The role of urban design. *Journal of Urban Design*, 15(4), pp. 493–513.

Gaffikin, F., Sterrett, K., McEldowney, M., Morrissey, M. and Hardy, M. (2009). Planning shared space for a shared future. In: Doak, N. (ed.), *The challenges of peace*. Belfast: Community Relations Commission, pp. 163–187.

Gehl, J. (2006). *Life between buildings: Using public space*. Copenhagen: Danish Architectural Press.

Gehl, J. (2010). *Cities for people*. Washington, DC: Island Press.

Gehl, J. (2011). *Life between buildings: Using public space*, 6th edition. Washington, DC: Island Press.

Gehl, J. and Gemzoe, L. (2000). *New city spaces*. Copenhagen: Danish Architectural Press.

Gehl, J. and Gemzoe, L. (2004). *Public spaces – public life*. Copenhagen: Danish Architectural Press.

Gehl, J., Johansen-Kaefer, L. and Reigstad, S. (2005). Close encounters with buildings. *Town Planning and Architecture*, 2, pp. 70–80.

Geoghegan, P. (2015). Will Belfast ever have a Berlin Wall moment and tear down its 'peace walls'? *The Guardian* (September 29, 2015) [online]. Available at: https://www.theguardian.com/cities/2015/sep/29/belfast-berlin-wall-moment-permanent-peace-walls [Accessed April 1, 2018].

Geoghegan, P. (2010). The search for equality: Race, religion and public policy in Northern Ireland. *Shared Space*, 9, pp. 35–51.

Giddens, A. (1991). *Modernity and self-identity self and society in the late modern age*. Stanford, CA: Stanford University Press.

Gill, C. (1964). *The rise of the Irish Linen industry*. Oxford: Oxford University Press.

Gilligan, C. (2006). Traumatised by peace? A critique of five assumptions in the theory of conflict-related trauma. *Policy and Politics*, 34(2), pp. 325–345.

Goldie, R. and Ruddy, B. (2010). *Crossing the line: Key features of effective practice in the development of shared space in areas close to an interface*. Belfast: Belfast Interface Project.

Gorby, C. (2004). Diffused spaces: A sacred study of West Belfast, North Ireland. In: Bastéa, E. (ed.), *Memory and Architecture*. New Mexico: UNM Press.

Gordon, I. and Monastiriotis, V. (2006). Urban size, spatial segregation and inequality in educational outcomes. *Urban Studies*, 43(1), pp. 213–236.

Graham, B. J. (1997). The imagining of place: Representation and identity in contemporary Ireland. In: Graham, B. J. (ed.), *In search of Ireland: A cultural geography*. London: Routledge, pp. 192–212.

Graham, B. J. and Nash, C. (2006). A shared future: Territoriality, pluralism and public policy in Northern Ireland. *Political Geography*, 25(2), pp. 253–278.

Gregory, D. and Urry, J. (eds.) (1985). *Social relations and spatial structures*. Basingstoke: Macmillan.

Griffith, P. (2013). Interview with Paul Griffith by Ashlee Bell, as documented. In: Bell, A. (ed.), *Spatial agents of change: Redefining the role of an architect within community regeneration in the twenty-first century*. Belfast: Queen's University Belfast, Unpublished Masters Dissertation.

Hamilton, R. (1999). *100 years of Derry*. Belfast: Blackstaff Press.

Hansson, U. (2005). *Troubled youth? Young people, violence and disorder in Northern Ireland*. Belfast: Institute for Conflict Research.

Harbottle, M. (1970). *The impartial soldier*. London: Oxford University Press.

Harland, K. (2011). Violent youth culture in Northern Ireland: Young men, violence and the challenges of peacebuilding. *Youth and Society*, 43(2), pp. 422–430.

Harland, K. and McCready, S. (2012). *Taking boys seriously*. Research Report No. 59. Coleraine: University of Ulster.

Harrison, R. S. (2008). *The Richardson's of Bessbrook*. Dublin: Original Writing Ltd.

Harvey, D. (1989). *The condition of postmodernity: An enquiry into the origins of cultural change*. Oxford: Basil Blackwell.

Harvey, D. (2000). *Spaces of hope*. Berkeley: University of California Press.

Harvey, D. (2005). *A brief history of neoliberalism*. Oxford: Oxford University Press.Hepburn, A. (2004). *Contested cities in the modern West*. Basingstoke: Palgrave Macmillan.

Hickey, J. (1984). *Religion and the Northern Ireland problem*. Dublin: Gill and MacMillan.

Higgins, B. (2006). *Gilford during the second world war*. Gilford: Gilford Together.

Hippsley, P. (2012). *The walls of Derry, Londonderry*. Available at: www.derryswalls.com.

Hirsch, H. (1995). *Genocide and the politics of memory: Studying death to preserve life*. Chapel Hill, NC: The University of North Carolina Press.

Hirst, P. Q. (2005). *Space and power: Politics, war and architecture*. Cambridge: Polity Press.

Ho, C. (2011). Respecting the presence of others: School micropublics and everyday multiculturalism. *Journal of Intercultural Studies*, 32(6), 603–619.

Hocking, B. T. (2015). *The great reimagining: Public art, urban space and the symbolic landscapes of a 'new' Northern Ireland*. New York: Berghahn Books.

Howe, S. (2011). Memory and history in Northern Ireland. *History Workshop Journal*, 71(1), pp. 219–231.

Hume, J. (2002). *Derry beyond the walls: Social and economic aspects of the growth of Derry: 1825–1850*. Belfast: Ulster Historical Foundation.

Huse, T. (2014). *Everyday life in the gentrifying city: On displacement, ethnic privileging and the right to stay put.* Farnham: Ashgate.

Hutcheon, L. (2003). *The politics of postmodernism.* London: Routledge.

Huyssen, A. (2003). *Present pasts: Urban palimpsests and the politics of memory.* Stanford, CA: Stanford University Press.

Hyde, R. (2012). *Future practice: Conversations from the edge of architecture.* London: Routledge.

Irish Times. (2010). Available at: www.irishtimes.com/newspaper/magazine/; The shop around the corner [Last Updated December 2010].

Iveson, K. (2007). *Publics and the City.* Oxford: Wiley-Blackwell, p. 6.

Jacob, J. (1962). *The Death and Life of Great American Cities.* London: Jonathan Cape

Jameson, F. (1991). *Postmodernism, or the ill-logic of late capitalism.* Durham: Duke University Press.

Jarman, N. (1998). Painting landscapes: The place of murals in the symbolic construction of urban space. In: Buckley, A. D. (ed.), *Symbols in Northern Ireland.* Belfast: The Institute of Irish Studies.

Jarman, N. (1999). Drawing back from the edge: Community based response to violence in North Belfast. In: *Community development centre.* Belfast: Special Edition.

Jarman, N. (2003). Managing disorder: Responses to interface violence in North Belfast. In: Hargie, O. and Dickson, D. (eds.), *Researching the troubles.* Edinburgh: Mainstream Press, pp. 227–244.

Jarman, N. (2004). *Demography, development and disorder: Changing patterns of interface areas report.* Belfast: Institute for Conflict Research.

Jarman, N. (2005). Changing places, moving boundaries: The development of new interface areas. *Shared Space*, 1.

Jarman, N. (2012). *Belfast interfaces: Security barriers and defensive use of space.* Belfast: Belfast Interface Project.

Jarman, N. and Bell, J. (2009). *Routine divisions segregation and daily life in Northern Ireland.* IBIS Working Papers, 87. Dublin: University College Dublin. Institute for British-Irish Studies.

Jarman, N. and Bryan, D. (1998). From riots to rights: Nationalist parades in the North of Ireland. In: *Centre for the study of conflict.* Belfast: University of Ulster, Special Edition.

Jenks, C. (2005). *The iconic building.* New York: Rizzoli.

Jones, P. and Boujenko, N. (2011). Rethinking transport and connectivity for a shared city. *Shared Space: A Research Journal on Peace, Conflict and Community Relations in Northern Ireland.* Available at: www.community-relations.org.uk/fs/doc/chapter-one1.pdf.

Jordan, G. (2011). Building space: Regeneration and reconciliation. In: Spenser, G. (ed.), *Forgiving and remembering in Northern Ireland: Approaches to conflict resolution.* London: Continuum Publishing.

Juvan, M. (2004). Spaces of intertextuality/The intertextuality of space. Scientific research centre of the Slovenian academy of sciences and arts. *Primerjalna književnost*, 82(27), pp. 85–96 [online]. Available at: www.dlib.si/stream/URN:NBN:SI:DOC-5LYFXYF7/3db07bc6-3939 . . . /TEXT [Accessed April 1, 2017].

Kearney, R. (1997). *Postnationalist Ireland: Politics, culture, philosophy.* New York: Routledge.

Keen, J. (1989). Interiors: Architecture in the lives of people with dementia. *International Journal of Geriatric Psychiatry*, 4, 255–272.

Keirsey, D. and Gatrell, J. D. (2001). *Ideology on the walls: Contested space in planned urban areas of Northern Ireland*. A working paper, People's Art & Conflict in Everyday Spaces: Loyalist & Nationalist Murals in Northern Ireland. On-line publication. Available at: http://scholar.googleusercontent.com/scholar?q=cache:FMWPpm2_fUUJ:scholar.google.com/&hl=en&as_sdt=0,5.

Kelly, B. (2012). Neoliberal Belfast: Disaster ahead? *Irish Marxist Review*, p. 44.

Kempen, R. and Ozueren, S. A. (1998). Ethnic segregation in cities: New forms and explanations in a dynamic world. *Urban Studies*, 35(10), pp. 1631–1656.

Kilkelly, U., Kilpatrick, R., Lundy, L., Moore, L., Scraton, P., Davey, C., Dwyer, C. and McAlister, S. (2004). *Children's rights in Northern Ireland*. Belfast: Northern Ireland Commissioner for Children and Young People.

Kirby, P., Gibbons, L. and Cronin, M. (2002). *Reinventing Ireland: Culture, society, and the global economy*. London: Pluto Press.

Kirkland, R. (1996). *Literature and culture in Northern Ireland since 1965: Moment of danger*. New York: Addison Wesley Longman.

Kockel, U. (2010). *Re-visioning Europe: Frontiers, place identities and journeys in debatable lands*. Basingstoke: Palgrave Macmillan.

Komarova, M. (2010). *Shared space in Belfast and the limits of a shared future, conflict in cities and the contested state*. Available at: www.conflictincities.org/workingpapers.html.

Komarova, M. (2011). Imagining 'a shared future': Post-conflict discourses on peace building. In: Hayward, K. and O'Donnell, C. (eds.), *Political discourse and conflict resolution: Debating peace in Northern Ireland*. Oxon: Routledge.

Kostof, S. (2000). *The architect*. Berkeley: University of California Press.

Kristeva, J. (1986). Word, dialogue and novel. In: Moi, T. (ed.), *The Kristeva reader*. Oxford: Basil Blackwell, pp. 34–61.

Kuusisto-Arponen, A. K. (2003). *Our places – their spaces: Urban territoriality in the Northern Irish conflict*. Tampere: Tampere University Press.

Kwan, M. P. (2000). Gender difference in space-time constrains. *Area*, 32(2), pp. 145–156.

Kwan, M. P. (2009). From place based to people based exposure measures. *Social Science and Medicine*, 69, pp. 1311–1313.

Landsberg, A. (1997). *America: The Holocaust and the mass culture of memory: Toward the radical politics of empathy*. New German Critique: Duke University Press.

Landsberg, A. (2004). *Prosthetic memory: The transformation of American remembrance in the age of mass culture*. New York: Columbia University Press.

Larmour, J. (2013). Portrush through water and architecture: The story of the Public Baths. In: Abdelmonem, M. G. (ed.), *Portrush: Architecture for the North Irish Coast*. Belfast: Ulster Tatler, pp. 29–39.

Laurier, E. and Philo, C. (2006). Cold shoulders and napkins handed: Gestures of responsibility. *Transactions of the Institute of British Geographers*, 31, pp. 193–207.

Le Corbusier Sketchbook, Vol 4, 1957–1964; Foundation Le Corbusier; MIT Press, 1982.

Lee, A. (2013). Introduction: Post-conflict Belfast. *City: Analysis of Urban Trends, Culture, Theory, Policy, Action*, pp. 523–525.

Lefebvre, H. (1974). *The production of space*. Trans. Donald Nicholson-Smith. Cambridge, MA: Blackwell.

Lefebvre, H. (1996). *Writings on cities*. Cambridge, MA: Wiley-Blackwell.

Leonard, M. (2006). Teens and territory in contested spaces: Negotiating sectarian interfaces in Northern Ireland. *Children's Geographies*, 4(2), pp. 225–238.

Leonard, M. and McKnight, M. (2011). Bringing down the walls: Young people's perspectives on peace-walls in Belfast. *International Journal of Sociology and Social Policy*, 31(9/10), pp. 569–582.

Lincoln, B. (1999). *Theorizing myth: Narrative, ideology and scholarship*. Chicago: University of Chicago Press.

Logan, R. A. (1999). A window on the past: A history of Gilford, Co. Down. *Banbridge Chronicle*.

Londonderry Sentinel. (2010a). Tension mounts over attacks on Fountain Estate (March 4, 2010).

Londonderry Sentinel. (2010b). The 'Troubles' swayed city of culture judges (November 28, 2010) [online]. Available at: www.londonderrysentinel.co.uk/news/local/the-troubles-swayed-city-of-culture-judges-1-2104255 [Accessed April 1, 2017].

Longley, E. (1991). The rising, the Somme and Irish memory. In: Dhonnchadha, M. and Dorgan, T. (eds.), *Revising the rising*. Derry: Field Day.

Low, S. M. (1997). Urban fear: Building the fortress city. *City and Society*, pp. 53–71.

Low, S. M., Taplin, D. and Scheld, S. (2009). *Rethinking urban parks: Public space and cultural diversity*. Texas: University of Texas Press.

Lownsbrough, H. and Beunderman, J. (2007). *Equally spaced? Public space and interaction between diverse communities*. London: Commission for Racial Equality.

Lynch, K. (1981). *A theory of good city form*. Cambridge: MIT Press.

Lynch, K. (1990). *City sense and city design*. Cambridge: MIT Press.

MacGabhann, T. and McAllister, K. (2013). Ulster coastal architecture: A standpoint. In: Abdelmonem, M. G. (ed.), *Portrush: Architecture for the North Irish Coast*. Belfast: Ulster Tatler, pp. 49–59.

Mackel, C. (2011). *Impact of the conflict on public space and architecture: A troubles archive essay*. Belfast: Arts Council of Northern Ireland.

Macneice, D. S. (1981). *Industrial villages of Ulster, 1800–1900*. Belfast: Blackstaff.

Madanipour, A. (1996). *Design of urban space: An inquiry into a socio-spatial process*. Chichester: John Wiley.

Madanipour, A. (2010). Marginal public spaces in European cities. *Journal of Urban Design*, pp. 267–286.

Magill, C. and Hamber, B. (2010). If they don't start listening to us, the future is going to look the same as the past: Young people and reconciliation in Northern Ireland and Bosnia and Herzegovina. *Youth and Society*, 43, pp. 509–527.

Marcus, C. C., et al. (1997). Neighbourhood parks. In: Marcus, C. C. and Francis, C. (eds.), *People places: Design guidelines for urban open space*, 2nd edition. Canada: John Wiley.

Matejskova, T. and Leitner, H. (2011). Urban encounters with difference: The contact hypothesis and immigrant integration projects in Eastern Berlin. *Social and Cultural Geography*, 12(7), pp. 717–741.

McAlister, S., Haydon, D. and Scraton, P. (2013). Violence in the lives of children and youth in 'Post-Conflict' Northern Ireland. *Children, Youth and Environments*, 23(1), pp. 1–22.

McAtackney, L. (2011). Peace maintenance and political messages: The significance of walls during and after the *'troubles'* in Northern Ireland. *Journal of Social Archaeology*, 11(1), pp. 77–98.

McBride, I. (2001). *History and memory in modern Ireland*. Cambridge: Cambridge University Press.

McCallister, J. (2014). Derry, Londonderry, the Maiden City, the Walled City: Both a story of pain and of hope. *Belfast Telegraph* (August 12, 2014) [online]. Available at: https://www.belfasttelegraph.co.uk/opinion/columnists/archive/john-mccallister/derry-londonderry-the-maiden-city-the-walled-city-both-a-story-of-pain-and-of-hope-30503000.html.

McCann, E. (1993). *War and an Irish town*. London: Pluto Press, CAIN. Available at: http://cain.ulst.ac.uk/events/crights/mccann93.htm.

McCann, E. (1999). Race, protest, and public space: Contextualizing Lefebvre in the US city. *Antipode*, 31, pp. 163–184.

McClelland, A. (2009). Sinton's Mill, Tandragee, county Armagh. *Perspectives*, 18(6).

McDermott, M. J. (1975). *Ireland's architectural heritage: An outline of the history of Irish architecture*. Dublin: Folens and Co. Ltd.

McDermott, P., Nic Craith, M. and Strani, K. (2016). Public space, collective memory and intercultural dialogue in a (UK) city of culture. *Identities*, 23(5), pp. 610–627.

McDonald, H. (2013). Thatcher death celebrations in Derry and Belfast condemned. *The Guardian* (April 9, 2013) [online]. Available at: www.theguardian.com/politics/2013/apr/09/thatcher-death-celebrations-derry-belfast [Accessed April 1, 2017].

McDonald, M. (1986). *Children of wrath: Political violence in Northern Ireland*. London: Polity Press.McDowell, S. and Shirlow, P. (2011). Geographies of conflict and post-conflict Northern Ireland. *Geography Compass*, 5(9), pp. 700–709.

McDowell, S. and Switzer, C. (2011). Violence and the vernacular: Conflict, commemoration & rebuilding in the urban context. *Journal of the Vernacular Architecture Forum*, 18(2), pp. 82–104.

McEldowney, M., Sterrett, K. and Gaffakin, F. (2001). Architectural ambivalence: The built environment and cultural identity in Belfast. In: Neill, W. J. and Schwedler, H. U. (eds.), *Urban planning and cultural inclusion*. Basingstoke: Palgrave Macmillan, pp. 100–109.

McGrellis, S. (2010). In transition: Young people in Northern Ireland growing up in, and out of, divided communities. *Ethnic and Racial Studies*, 33(5), pp. 761–778.

McKeown, S., Cairns, E. D. and Stringer, M. (2012). *Is shared space really shared? Shared space: A research journal on peace, conflict and community relations in Northern Ireland*. Available at: www.community-relations.org.uk/fs/doc/mckeonstringer.pdf.

McKittrick, D. and McVea, D. (2002). *Making sense of the Troubles: The story of the conflict in Northern Ireland*. Amsterdam: New Amsterdam Books.

McSheffrey, G. (2000). *Planning Derry: Planning and politics in Northern Ireland*. Liverpool: Liverpool University Press.

Melaugh, M. (2010). *Political party support in Northern Ireland, 1969 to the present* [online]. Available at: http://cain.ulst.ac.uk/othelem/glossary.htm [Accessed April 1, 2017].

Meredith, F. (2011). Don't let policy despots bankrupt our creativity. *Belfast Telegraph* [Last Updated March 2011].

Miller, G. and Dingwall, R. (1997). *Context and method in qualitative research.* London: Sage.

Milligan, C. D. (1948). *The walls of Derry: Their building, defending and preserving.* Londonderry: The Londonderry Sentinel Printing Works.

Minty, Z. (2006). Post-apartheid public art in cape town: Symbolic reparations and public space. *Urban Studies*, 43(2), pp. 421–440.

Misselwitz, P. and Rieniets, T. (2006). *City of collision: Jerusalem and the principles of conflict urbanism.* Walter de Gruyter: Switzerland.

Misselwitz, P. and Reiniets, T. (2009). Jerusalem and the principles of conflict urbanism. *Journal of Urban Technology*, 16(2–3), pp. 61–78.

Morrissey, M. and Gaffikin, F. (2006). Planning for peace in contested space. *International Journal of Urban and Regional Research*, 30(4), pp. 873–893.

Mulholland, C., Abdelmonem, M. G. and Selim, G. (2014). Narratives of spatial division: The role of social memory in shaping urban space in Belfast. *Journal of Civil Engineering and Architecture*, 8(6), pp. 746–760.

Murray, D. (2013). *Everyday life in the Northern Ireland troubles (1968–1988)* [online]. Available at: www.bbc.co.uk/history/topics/troubles_everyday_life [Accessed April 1, 2017].

Murray, M. (1991). *The politics and pragmatism of urban containment: Belfast since 1940.* Aldershot: Avebury, p. 268.

Murtagh, B. (1996). On Derry's Walls, segregation and space in Northern Ireland. *Administration*, 44(1), pp. 30–47.

Murtagh, B. (1999). Listening to communities: Locality research and planning. *Urban Studies*, 36(7), pp. 1181–1193.

Murtagh, B. (2001). *The politics of territory.* London: Palgrave Macmillan.

Murtagh, B. (2002). *The politics of territory: Policy and segregation in Northern Ireland.* London: Palgrave-Macmillan, p. 224.

Murtagh, B. (2010). Desegregation and place restructuring in the new Belfast. *Urban Studies*, pp. 1119–1135.

Murtagh, B. (2011). Ethno-religious segregation in post-conflict Belfast. *Built Environment*, pp. 213–225.

Murtagh, B., Boland, P. and Shirlow, P. (2017). Contested heritages and cultural tourism. *International Journal of Heritage Studies*, 23(6), pp. 506–520. http://dx.doi.org/10.1080/13527258.2017.1287118.

Nagle, J. (2009). Sites of social centrality and segregation: Lefebvre in Belfast, a 'divided city'. *Antipode*, 41(2), pp. 326–347.

Newman, O. (1972). *Defensible space.* London: Architectural Press.

Nic Craith, M. (2002). *Plural identities – singular narratives: The case of Northern Ireland.* New York: Berghahn.

NISRA. (2001a). *Census reports for population of Gilford, data obtained from email.*

NISRA. (2001b). *Census reports for population of Sion Mills, data obtained from email.*

NISRA. (2008a). *Census mid-year reports for population of Gilford, data obtained from email.*

NISRA. (2008b). *Census mid-year reports for population of Sion Mills, data obtained from email.*

Nolan, P. (2014). *Northern Ireland peace monitoring report, Vol.3.* Belfast: Community Relations Council, pp. 21–22.

Nora, P. (1989). Between memory and history: Les lieux de mémoire. *Representations,* 26(special issue), pp. 7–24.

Northern Ireland Environment Agency (NIEA). (2011). *Derry city walls Gazetteer October 2011.* Available at: www.communities-ni.gov.uk/publications/derry-city-walls-gazetteer-october-2011.

Northern Ireland Government. (2017). *The Derry walls.* Available at: www.communities-ni.gov.uk/articles/conservation-case-studies.

Northern Ireland Planning Advisory Board. (1947). *The Ulster countryside: A report by the planning advisory board on amenities in Northern Ireland.* Belfast: H. M. Stationery Off.

O'Brien, G. and Nolan, W. (1999). *Derry and Londonderry: History and society: Interdisciplinary essays on the history of an Irish county.* Dublin: Geography Publications.

Ó Dochartaigh, N. (1997). *From civil rights to Armalites: Derry and the birth of the Irish Troubles,* 2nd edition. London: Palgrave Macmillan.

Ó Dochartaigh, N. (1999). *Housing and conflict: Social change and collective action in Derry in the 1960s.* Derry and Londonderry: History and Society.

Ó Dochartaigh, N. (2010). Bloody Sunday: Error or design? *Contemporary British History,* 24(1), pp. 89–108.

O'Dowd, L. and Komarova, M. (2013). Three narratives in search of a city: Researching Belfast's 'post-conflict' transitions. *City,* pp. 526–546.

OFMDFM. (2012). *Attitudes to peace walls: Government report.* Belfast: Office of First Minister and Deputy First Minister. Available at: www.ofmdfmni.gov.uk/attitudes-to-peace-walls-june-2012.pdf.

O'Neill, N. (2013). *Interview with Nial O'Neil architects by Ashlee Bell, as documented in*: Bell, A. (2013). Spatial Agents of Change: Redefining the role of an architect within community regeneration in the twenty-first century. Unpublished Master's Dissertation. Belfast: Queen's University Belfast.

Orr, Russell. (2012). *Pioneering the measurement of the micro-ecology of segregation in a non-racial setting: Northern Ireland.* PhD Thesis, University of Ulster.

Paddison, R. and McCann, E. (2014). *Cities and social change: Encounters with contemporary urbanism.* Los Angeles and London: Sage. Parekh, B. C. (2000). *Rethinking multiculturalism: Cultural diversity and political theory.* London: Palgrave Macmillan.

Peach, C., Robinson, V. and Smith, S. (1981). *Ethnic segregation in cities.* London: Croom Helm.

Pettigrew, T. F. and Tropp, L. R. (2006). A meta-analytic test of intergroup contact theory. *Journal of Personality and Social Psychology,* 90, pp. 751–783.

Pickering, J., Kintrea, K. and Bannister, J. (2012). Invisible walls and visible youth: Territoriality among young people in British cities. *Urban Studies,* 49(5), pp. 945–960.

Pike, B. (1981). *The image of the city in modern literature.* Princeton, NJ: Princeton University Press.

Pinimg. (n.d.). *Bogside demolition and construction of Rossville flats in 1963*. Available at: https://s-media-cache ak0.pinimg.com/736x/4a/0f/97/4a0f97bd9a9a2b81 ab974921f6be5090 – irish-flats.jpg.

Planning Northern Ireland. (2011). *Derry area plan*. Available at: www.planningni. gov.uk/index/policy/development_plans/devplans_az/derry_2011/derry_benviron-ment/derry_benv_policies/derry_benv_policies2.htm.

Porter, J. E. (1986). Intertextuality and the discourse community. *Rhetoric Review*, 5(1), pp. 34–47.

Pratt, M. L. (1992). *Imperial eyes: Travel writing and transculturation*. London, New York: Routledge.

PressForty, A. (2001). Introduction. In: Forty, A. and Kuchler, S. (eds.), *The art of forgetting*. Oxford: Berg.

Questions of perception, phenomenology of architecture, Steven Holl, Juhani Pallasmaa & Alberto Perez-Gomez; A+U architecture & urbanism (June 1994) Special Issue. Specify, December 2012, pp. 36–40.

Reigl, A. (1903). *The modern cult of monuments*. Vienna: Braumuller.

Richardson, J. (1989). *The Local Historian's Encyclopaedia*. New Barnet: Historical Publications.

Ritchie, J. E. (1876). *Bessbrook and its Linen Mills: A short narrative of a model temperance town*. London: William Tweedie & Co. Ltd.

Rolston, B. (2010). Trying to reach the future through the past: Murals and memory in Northern Ireland. *Crime, Media, Culture*, 6, pp. 285–307.

Rosenfeld, G. D. (2000). *Munich and memory: Architecture, monuments and the legacy of the Third Reich*. London: University of California Press.

Rothery, S. (1997). *A field guide to the buildings of Ireland: Illustrating the smaller buildings of town and countryside*. Dublin: Lillipet Pet Press.

Rowan, M. (2012). *Why we build*. London: Picador.

Ruskin, J. (1849). The Seven Lamps of Architecture. London: Smith, Elder & Co.

Sadiki, L. (2013). The void of power and the power of void: Arab societies negotiation of democratic faragh. In: Sadiki, L., et al. (eds.), *Democratic transition in the middle east*. London: Routledge, p. 8.

Sandercock, L. (1998). *Towards cosmopolis: Planning for multicultural cities*. Chichester: John Wiley.

Schiller, N. G. and Irving, A. (2014). *Whose cosmopolitanism? Critical perspectives, relationalities and discontents*. New York: Berghahn Books.

Schmidt, E. and Schröder, I. (2001). *Anthropology of violence and conflict*. London: Routledge.

Schneider, T. and Till, J. (2009). Beyond discourse: Notes on spatial agency. *Footprint*, January, pp. 97–111.

Schnell, I. and Yoav, B. (2001). The sociospatial isolation of agents in everyday life spaces as an aspect of segregation. *Annals of the Association of American Geographers*, 91(4), pp. 622–636.

Scott, R. (2000). *A breath of fresh air: The story of Belfast's parks*. Belfast: Belfast City Council.

Selim, G. (2015). The landscape of differences: Contact and segregation in the everyday encounters. *Cities*, 46, pp. 16–25.

Selim, G. and Abraham, A. (2016). Peace by piece: (Re) imagining division in Belfast's contested spaces through memory. *Athens Journal of Architecture*, 2(3), pp. 197–221.

Sennett, R. (1977). *The fall of public man*. Cambridge: Cambridge University Press.

Sennett, R. (2005). Capitalism and the city: Globalization, flexibility, and indifference. In: Kazepov, Y. (ed.). *Cities of Europe: Changing contexts, local arrangements, and challenge to urban cohesion*. Oxford: Wiley-Blackwell, pp. 109–122.

Sheller, M. and Urry, J. (2003). Mobile transformations of 'Public' and 'Private' life. *Theory Culture Society*, pp. 107–125.

Shirlow, P. (1997). Class materialism and the fracturing of traditional alignments. In: Graham, B. (ed.), *In search of Ireland*. London: Routledge, pp. 87–107.

Shirlow, P. (2003). Who fears to speak? Fear, mobility and ethno-sectarianism in the two 'Ardoynes'. *The Global Review of Ethnopolitics*, 3(1), pp. 76–91.

Shirlow, P. and Graham, B., et al. (2005). *Population change and social inclusion study: Derry/Londonderry*. Available at: www.ofmdfmni.gov.uk/derryreport.pdf.

Shirlow, P. and Murtagh, B. (2006). *Belfast: Segregation, violence and the city*. London: Pluto Press, p. 216.

Shirlow, P., Tonge, J., McAuley, J. and McGlynn, C. (2012). *Abandoning historical conflict? Former political prisoners and reconciliation in Northern Ireland*. Manchester: Manchester University Press.

Shuttleworth, I. G. and Lloyd, C. D. (2007). *Mapping segregation in Belfast NIHE housing estates*. Belfast: Northern Ireland Housing Executive. Available at: www.nihe.gov.uk/mapping_segregation_final_report.pdf.

Sibley, D. (1995). *Geographies of exclusion: Society and difference in the west*. London: Routledge.

Side, K. (2014). Visual and textual narratives of conflict-related displacement in Northern Ireland. *Identities*, 21(6), pp. 1–22.

Slevin, J. (2000). *The Internet and society*. Cambridge: Polity Press.

SLIG. (2008). *Suffolk lenadoon interface group: Stewardstown road regeneration project*. Available at: www.srrp.net/ [Last Updated 2013].

Smailes, A. E. (1953). *The geography of towns*. William Brendon and Son, Ltd.

Smith, M. E. (2005). *Reckoning with the past: Teaching history in Northern Ireland*. Oxford, Lanham, MD: Lexington Books.

Smith, N. (2002). New globalism, new urbanism: Gentrification as global urban strategy. *Antipode*, 34(3), pp. 427–450.

Soja, E. (2000). *Postmetropolis: Critical studies of cities and regions*. Oxford: Blackwell.

Sore, B. (2011). *Planning Bill Northern Ireland: A response by the royal town planning institute Northern Ireland*. Craigavon: Royal Town Planning Institute Northern Ireland.

Speech to the House of Commons. (1943). *On plans for the rebuilding of the chamber* (destroyed by an enemy bomb May 10, 1941), in Never Give In!: The best of Winston Churchill's Speeches (2003), Hyperion (October 28, 2003).

Sterrett, K., Hackett, M. and Hill, D. (2011). Agitating for a design regeneration agenda in a post-conflict city: The case of Belfast. *The Journal of Architecture*, 16(1), pp. 99–119.

Sterrett, K., Hackett, M. and Hill, D. (2012). The social consequences of broken urban structures: A case study of Belfast. *Journal of Transport Geography*, 21, pp. 49–61.

Stevenson, C. (2010). *Beyond divided territories: How changing popular understandings of public space in Northern Ireland can facilitate new identity dynamics.* Dublin: Institute for British-Irish Studies, University College Dublin.

Stewart, P. J. and Strathern, A. (2002). *Violence: Theory and Ethnography.* London: Continuum.

Stockinger, H. (2015). Young people's experiences of integration and segregation in Northern Ireland. *ARK Research Update*, 99 [online]. Available at: www.ark. ac.uk/publications/updates/update99.pdf [Accessed April 1, 2017].

Stollard, P. (1984). The architecture of No-Man's land. *Architect's Journal*, 180(31), pp. 24–39.

Tajbakhsh, K. (2001). *The promise of the city: Space, identity and politics in contemporary social thought.* Berkeley, CA: University of California Press.

Tajfel, H. and Turner, J. C. (1979). An integrative theory of intergroup conflict. *The Social Psychology of Intergroup Relations*, pp. 33–47.

Thompson, K. (2012). *The effects of Linen industry on the rural ulster landscape.* Unpublished Masters Dissertation, Belfast: Queen's University Belfast.

Tonkiss, F. (2005). *Space the city and social theory.* Cambridge: Polity Press, p. 69.

Translink. (2017). Weavers Cross project. Available at: http://www.translink.co.uk/ Translink-Footer/the-hub/ [Accessed April 2017].

Tulving, E. (1985). *Elements of episodic memory.* Oxford: Oxford University Press.

Urban, E. (2011). *Community politics and the peace process in contemporary Northern Irish drama.* Bern: Peter Lang AG.

Valentine, G. (2008). Living with difference: Reflections on geographies of encounter. *Progress in Human Geography*, 32(3), pp. 323–337.

Valentine, G. and McDonald, I. (2004). *Understanding prejudice: Attitudes towards minorities.* London: Stonewall.

Valentine, G. and Skelton, T. (2003). Living on the edge: The marginalization and resistance of deaf youth. *Environment and Planning A*, 35, pp. 301–321.

Vanderbeck, R. (2007). Intergenerational geographies: Age relations, segregation and re-engagements. *Geography Compass*, 1(2), pp. 200–221.

Vaneigem, R. (1967). *The revolution of everyday life.* New York: Rebel Press.

Vertovec, S. (2007a). *New complexities of cohesion in Britain: Super-diversity, transnationalism and civil-integration.* Oxford: ERCR Centre on Migration Policy and Society.

Vertovec, S. (2007b). Super-diversity and its implications. *Ethnic and Racial Studies*, 30(6), pp. 1024–1054.

Walker, B. (1992). 1641, 1689, 1690 and all that: The Unionist sense of history. *Irish Review*, 12, pp. 56–64.

Watson, S. (2013). *City publics: The (Dis)enchantments of urban encounters.* London: Routledge.

Watt, P. and Stenson, K. (1998). It's a bit dodgy round here: Safety, danger, ethnicity and young people's use of public space. In: Skelton, T. and Valentine, G. (eds.), *Cool places: Geographies of youth cultures.* London: Routledge.

Weizman, E. (2007). *Hollow land: Israel's architecture of occupation.* London: Verso Books.

White, R. (2001). Social and role identities and political violence: Identity as a window on violence in Northern Ireland. In: Ashmore, R. D., Jussim, L. and Wilder, D. (eds.), *Social identity, intergroup conflict, and conflict resolution*. New York: Oxford University Press, pp. 159–183.

Whyte, W. H. (1980). *The social life of small urban spaces*. Washington, DC: Conservation Foundation.

Wiedenhoeft, R. (1981). *Cities for people: Practical measures for improving urban environments*. New York, London: Van Nostrand Reinhold.

Wilson, J. and Stapleton, K. (eds.) (2016a). *Devolution and identity*. London: Routledge.

Wilson, J. and Stapleton, K. (eds.) (2016b). Identity categories in use: Britishness, devolution and the ulster scots identity in northern Ireland. In: Wilson, J. and Stapleton, K. (eds.), *Devolution and identity*. London: Routledge.

Wise, A. (2009). Everyday multiculturalism: Transversal crossings and working class cosmopolitanisms. In: Wise, A. and Velayutham, S. (eds.), *Everyday multiculturalism*. London: Palgrave Macmillan, pp. 21–45.

Wise, A. and Velayutham, S. (2009). *Everyday multiculturalism*. London: Palgrave Macmillan.

Woodward, K. (1997). *Identity and difference*. London: Sage, Open University Press.

Yaari, M. (2008). *Rethinking the French city: Architecture, dwelling, and display after 1968*. Amsterdam: Rodopi.

Yacobi, H. (2009). *The Jewish-Arab city: Spatio-politics in a mixed community*. London: Routledge.

Yarwood, J. (ed.) (2006). *The Dublin-Belfast development corridor: Ireland's megacity region?* Farnham: Ashgate.

Index

Note: page numbers in *italics* indicate figures and page numbers in **bold** indicate tables.